DEV

DEVELOPING KEY PRIVACY RIGHTS

Edited by

MADELEINE COLVIN

·HART·
PUBLISHING
OXFORD AND PORTLAND, OREGON
2002

Hart Publishing
Oxford and Portland, Oregon

Published in North America (US and Canada) by
Hart Publishing c/o
International Specialized Book Services
5804 NE Hassalo Street
Portland, Oregon
97213-3644
USA

Distributed in the Netherlands, Belgium and Luxembourg by
Intersentia, Churchillaan 108
B2900 Schoten
Antwerpen
Belgium

Hart Publishing is a specialist legal publisher based in Oxford,
England.
To order further copies of this book or to request a list of other
publications please write to:

Hart Publishing, Salter's Boatyard, Folly Bridge,
Abingdon Road, Oxford OX1 4LB
Telephone: +44 (0)1865 245533 or Fax: +44 (0)1865 794882
e-mail: mail@hartpub.co.uk
WEBSITE: http//www.hartpub.co.uk

British Library Cataloguing in Publication Data
Data Available
ISBN 1–84113–168–7 (paperback)

Typeset by Hope Services (Abingdon) Ltd.
Printed and bound in Great Britain by
Bell and Bain, Ltd, Glasgow

Foreword

This is an excellent book which should be read by all media lawyers as we continue to wrestle with developing privacy rights in this jurisdiction and balancing them with the equally, if not more, important right to free speech. Given the speed of modern communications, it is necessary for practitioners not only to know the English legal position but also to appreciate the laws of other jurisdictions. Furthermore, in other jurisdictions, privacy law concepts are better developed than in the UK. By analysing what has happened abroad, we may get a better understanding of what should happen here in the future.

This book describes how privacy laws versus free speech laws have historically developed in France, Germany, Canada, New Zealand and Australia. All the pieces are written by expert practitioners in their fields. In addition, there is an excellent piece by Jemima Stratford commenting on the position taken by the European Court of Human Rights in Strasbourg, which of course is very important as it overarches UK and other European domestic laws.

It is fascinating to read how privacy laws have developed in such different ways in the compared jurisdictions. Although privacy is not protected by the Canadian Charter or Rights and Freedoms, the Supreme Court still decided that it was a fundamental right for Canadians. In New Zealand the decisions of the media regulators have been very important in developing their privacy laws. France has well-developed privacy laws, which protect celebrities and politicians as well as private individuals, but it may not be as easy as one might have thought to get injunctive relief. An "unbearable" breach of privacy usually has to be shown. In Germany the courts take the view that the more public the persona, the greater the need to protect privacy. Whilst the data protection laws seem to be relatively homogenous, it should still be noted that much greater protection is given to the media in this respect in New Zealand and Australia than in this country.

I certainly learned a great deal by reading this book and I am sure that other media lawyers will do so as well.

Jennifer McDermott
Media Partner
Lovells

Contents

Contributors

Madeleine Colvin is a qualified barrister who practised for ten years before becoming a founding member of the Children's Legal Centre in 1980. She has also been a legal officer at the civil rights organisation, Liberty and more recently was the Director of Legal Policy at JUSTICE. She has written a number of reports, including *Under Surveillance: covert policing and human rights standards* (1998) and *The Schengen Information System: compliance with human rights standards* (2000). She is currently a human rights consultant and part-time Immigration Adjudicator.

Catherine Dupré is a Jean Monnet Research Fellow in Law at the European University Institute in Florence, Italy. Her main area of research is post-communist transitions in Eastern Europe on which she is currently finishing a monograph. She has also published on comparative human rights and has taught French Law, British Public Law and Comparative Constitutional Law.

Rosalind English is a former college lecturer at Merton College Oxford and currently works as Academic Consultant at One Crown Office Row, providing comparative law research for their human rights cases. She also writes weekly commentaries on human rights cases from Strasbourg and the domestic courts. She is joint author with Andrew Le Sueur and Javan Herbers of *Principles of Public Law* (Cavendish Publishing, 1999) and editor with Philip Havers of *Human Rights and the Common Law* (Hart Publishing, 2000).

David Lindsay is a Research Fellow at the Law School at the University of Melbourne. He specialises in Internet and media law, and has published widely in a range of related areas, including recent monographs on digital copyright and on-line defamation. He is currently completing research relating to Internet privacy and the regulation of domain names. Mr Lindsay is the co-author of *Media Law in Australia* (Oxford University Press, Melbourne, 1995).

Marguerite Russell was called to the UK Bar in 1972 and has specialised in high profile criminal defence work in the UK. She has a

LLM from Queens University in Canada and is a member of the Law Society of Upper Canada. She has both written and lectured on the human rights of women and on human rights issues for lesbians and gays.

Jemima Stratford is a barrister practising from Brick Court Chambers. She specialises in human rights, EU law, public law and general commercial law. Jemima has acted for both applicants and the UK Government in a number of cases raising issues under the European Convention on Human Rights, and is currently instructed in several cases pending before the European Court of Human Rights in Strasbourg. These cases concern issues ranging from the right of access to medical records by an ex-serviceman (Articles 6, 8, 10 and 13), through the right to an independent and impartial disciplinary tribunal (Article 6), to the right not to have property expropriated by retrospective legislation (Article 1 of Protocol No 1).

Rosemary Tobin is a Senior Lecturer at the Faculty of Law at the University of Auckland, and a barrister and Solicitor of the High Court of New Zealand. She teaches papers in the Law of Torts and Media Law, and has a particular interest in privacy law.

1

Introduction

Madeleine Colvin

With the introduction of the Human Rights Act 1998 (HRA), the UK courts are increasingly being called upon to strike the balance between two potentially conflicting fundamental rights: one person's right to private life with another's right to freedom of expression. This tension between Articles 8 and 10 of the European Convention on Human Rights (ECHR) is most obvious in cases concerning the media. Since the HRA came into force in October 2000, several cases—particularly *Douglas, Zeta-Jones and Northern and Shell plc v Hello!*[1] and, more recently, the *A v B and C* case[2]—have highlighted this, leading to much comment and speculation as to how the conflict will be resolved.

This development under the HRA has to be seen against a background where such rights have previously either not been recognised or not been provided the status of a fundamental right under English law. For example, as is well known, there has been no general remedy for an infringement of privacy under English law as emphasised in the notorious case of *Kaye v Robertson*.[3] Apart from certain statutory exceptions—principally data protection legislation[4]—the notion of privacy has been partially protected within several common law doctrines, including trespass, nuisance, breach of confidence and defamation. Such actions are limited however. For instance, the law of confidentiality is of little assistance unless private information is misused in some way and the law of defamation offers little protection when true but private facts are published.

---

[1] [2001] 2 WLR 992, CA.

[2] [2001] EWCA Civ 337, 11 March 2002. See also *Venables and Thompson v News Group Newspapers Ltd* [2001] 2 WLR 1038 and *Naomi Campbell v Mirror Group Newspapers Ltd*, QBD, Morland J, 27 March 2002.

[3] [1991] FSR 62.

[4] Data Protection Act 1998. And, for example, the Harassment Act 1997 as it has been applied by the courts including in the recent case of *Esther Thomas v (1) News Group Newspapers Ltd (2) Simon Hughes* (2001) 98 (34) LSG 43.

Even though the courts have referred to Articles 8 and 10 of the ECHR and to the jurisprudence of the European Court of Human Rights (ECtHR) on a number of occasions,[5] privacy and freedom of expression have nevertheless been seen as residual rights. The effects of the lack of development of either have been keenest in relation to the media. Although there have been proposals to introduce statutory controls to protect individual privacy rights in relation to the press,[6] these have not been pursued, for largely political reasons, and the press therefore continues to be regulated by the Press Complaints Commission's voluntary code.

Under the HRA the position of these rights in English law is now set to change. The present position is that these rights have been introduced under a statutory formula where only the state and its emanations through public authorities are directly bound to comply. As most of the media organisations are not public authorities, one of the key questions is the extent to which the rights are actionable horizontally against private parties as well as vertically against public authorities. While recent decisions[7] show that the HRA has given the courts the opportunity to develop ECHR rights between private persons, it remains to be seen whether and to what extent the courts are willing to create a new horizontal right of privacy, particularly following remarks in the recent case of *A v B and C* (see further below).

By examining the jurisprudence of several other countries, this book is intended to provide comparative material that may be helpful to UK courts when faced with this issue. Each chapter therefore describes the legal and constitutional development of privacy and freedom of expression rights and the relationship between them when a conflict has arisen. The intention is not to suggest that our courts should copy from others but rather to offer ideas. The countries have been chosen for several reasons: Canada and New Zealand because they have both recently introduced Bills of Rights—even

---

[5] *Derbyshire County Council v Times Newspapers Ltd* [1993] AC 534; *Attorney-Gerneral v Guardian Newspapers Ltd (No 2)* [1990] 1 AC 109; *Reynolds v Times Newspapers Ltd* [1999] 3 WLR 1010.

[6] See, for example, the Calcutt Report, *Review of Press Self-Regulation*, Cm 2135 (1993).

[7] See n 2 above. Also, for example, *W (children)* [2001] EWCA Civ 757; *Payne v Payne* [2001] 2 WLR 1826; *Wilson v First County Trust Ltd* [2001] 3 WLR 42.

though these laws have significantly different legal status in each; France and Germany are included because they already have separate and well-developed privacy laws, and Australia because it is a jurisdiction that remains without a constitutional framework of rights and which therefore continues to rely on a doctrine of residual rights as did the UK prior to the HRA.

As it is also important to place the issue firmly within the context of the ECHR and the decisions of the Strasbourg court, a separate chapter looks in detail at the development of both Articles 8 and 10. This ECHR jurisprudence has already had an important impact on developments in UK law and, with the courts being obliged to take this case law into account under the HRA,[8] it is likely to continue to do so.

DEVELOPMENT OF A PRIVACY RIGHT

As Jemima Stratford notes in chapter one, Article 8 has been subject to a relatively dynamic interpretation by the Strasbourg court so as to bring a range of interests and areas within its ambit. Whilst the right is split into four main categories—private life, family life, home and correspondence—there is no exhaustive definition of the concept of "private life" which clearly incorporates notions of personal autonomy and development as well.[9] It is clear from the areas where Article 8 has been successfully invoked that it is significantly broader than any or all of the common law actions that have been used under UK law to plug the gap.

The ECHR is mainly concerned with interference by state authorities. However, the Strasbourg court has also placed states under a positive obligation to protect rights in some circumstances. And even though criticised for a somewhat incoherent approach to this, the cases of *Young, James and Webster v United Kingdom*,[10] *A v United*

---

[8] HRA, s 2(1).

[9] Added to this, there is additional privacy protection arising from Article 10(2) which allows an interference with freedom of expression where this is necessary "for the protection of the rights of others".

[10] (1981) 4 EHRR 38; (1982) 5 EHRR 201.

Kingdom[11] and *X and Y v the Netherlands*[12] are cited as examples of Strasbourg decisions that apply ECHR rights to private parties where the state has a positive obligation to do so.

This issue of positive obligation is at the core of the debate on how far Article 8 of the ECHR might develop into a true privacy right under UK domestic law.[13] That is whether it will also have "horizontal effect" and confer rights as between private individuals, as mentioned above.[14] On a strict reading of the HRA, section 6 only places a duty on public authorities (including the courts) to ensure compliance. However, a number of legal commentators have suggested that this is unlikely to remain the case. They argue that the courts acting as public authorities are bound under section 6 of the HRA to ensure that ECHR rights are protected, whether the case is between private persons or against a public authority.[15] On the other hand, in opposing this view, others point to the fact that the ECHR and its rights are of a public law nature and inherently inapplicable between private persons.[16]

The ingrained tendency of UK courts to work incrementally has also led to a middle-way view referred to as "indirect horizontal effect".[17] This is that, whilst the ECHR will significantly influence private law, it will not of itself create a new "right of privacy" tort. It is supported by pointing to UK court decisions over the past ten years or

[11] (1998) 2 FLR 959.

[12] (1985) 8 EHRR 235.

[13] See the case of *W and B (Children)* n 7 above for the application and development of this doctrine under the HRA.

[14] On one level, there is no doubt that the HRA does have a horizontal effect. This is because the duty on courts under s 3 to interpret legislation so as to be compatible with the ECHR "so far as it is possible to do so" also applies to legislation governing a private claim.

[15] See, for example, Sir William Wade QC, "The Horizons of Horizontality", (2000) 116 LQR 217. HRA, s 6 is also relied upon to argue that where a public body is given powers that could be used to protect a person's privacy, failure to do so might be an unlawful act. This would mean, for instance, that the Information Commissioner might be in breach of Article 8 for failing to take effective enforcement action where the privacy of a data subject is infringed and so might the media watchdogs of the Broadcasting Standards Commission and the Press Complaints Commission: I Leigh, "Horizontal Rights, the Human Rights Act and Privacy: Lessons from the Commonwealth?" (1999) 48 ICLQ 57, 75–85.

[16] See, for example, Sir Richard Buxton "The Human Rights Act and Private Law" (2000) 116 LQR 48.

[17] For a recent article on this issue, see I Hare "Vertically Challenged: Private Parties, Privacy and the Human Rights Act" [2001] EHRLR Issue 5.

so where the ECHR requirements have been used either to interpret the common law or to exercise a judicial discretion in both public and private law cases. For example, in the case of *Hellewell v Chief Constable of Derbyshire*,[18] Laws J (as he then was) discusses the position of using a telephoto lens, from a distance and without consent, to gain a photograph of persons engaged in a private act. He said that:

> In such a case, the law would protect what might reasonably be called a right of privacy, although the name accorded to the cause of action would be breach of confidence.

The Court of Appeal essentially took the same approach in their recent case of *A v B and C* (see further below).

The question whether the HRA has horizontal effect is particularly relevant to the media. This is in part due to uncertainty as to where the line is drawn between those media bodies that are public authorities, falling within the duties of section 6 of the HRA, and those that are not: although the Press Complaints Commission (PCC) is a self-regulatory body without any statutory powers, the Government, during debates on the HRA took the view that it is a public authority as it undertakes public functions.[19] Similarly, because of the way that they have been established, the BBC and Channel 4 are said to be public authorities or bodies exercising a public function whereas other commercial television channels and newspapers are not. This question of which body or organisation is deemed to be a public authority would, however, be far less significant if the courts develop the horizontal effect of the rights guaranteed under the HRA into private law.[20]

Whilst the chapters in this book show that the statutory regulation of informational privacy through data protection laws has followed a largely similar path in each of the jurisdictions covered, the development of an action for breach of privacy has taken different and varied courses. In New Zealand a common law tort of invasion of privacy had already emerged in case law prior to the introduction of the 1990 Bill of Rights which, in fact, does not specifically provide for

---

[18] [1995] 1 WLR 804.

[19] *Hansard* HC Debs, 6th ser Col 414.

[20] It is also pointed out that, in the absence of some horizontality, the HRA will create a new hierarchy of rights in this and other areas of the law—particularly employment and health—where there are both public and private operators.

a privacy right. As Rosemary Tobin emphasises in chapter five, the tort of privacy (and the influential privacy principles developed by the Broadcasting Standards Authority (BSA)) in New Zealand evolved directly from the privacy jurisprudence in the American courts. The rationale for the tort was clearly stated in the 1986 case of *Tucker v News Media Ownership Ltd* when Jeffries J said:

> a person who lives an ordinary private life has a right to be left alone and to live the private aspects of his life without being subjected to unwarranted or undesired publicity or public disclosure.[21]

This has essentially resulted in two forms of action developing in New Zealand: one for public disclosure of private facts and another for intentional intrusion into a person's seclusion. Whilst the boundaries of the privacy tort remain uncertain, Rosemary Tobin believes that the several hundred case decisions involving privacy made by the BSA are an important jurisprudence for the future development of the common law tort.

Like New Zealand, the Charter of Rights and Freedoms enacted in Canada in 1982 does not include a right to privacy provision. It was excluded because legislators considered it dangerous to leave it to the courts to determine the exact application of such a right. However, as Marguerite Russell points out in chapter four, the exclusion of "privacy" from the literal text of the Charter has not prevented privacy rights from being argued and recognised in Charter cases. In the very first Charter case to reach the Supreme Court of Canada, the Court took the opportunity to say that the "right to privacy" was among the fundamental rights and freedoms protected by the Charter.[22]

Perhaps most interesting for the UK is the way that the Canadian Charter has affected private litigation. Like the HRA, there is provision that the Charter applies only to state action. However, in a line of decisions including the *Dolphin Delivery* case,[23] *Hill v Church of Scientology*[24] and most recently *Aubry v Editions Vice-Versa*,[25] the Supreme Court has concluded that the common law must evolve

---

[21] [1986] 2 NZLR 716, 731.
[22] *Hunter v Southam* [1984] 2 SCR 145.
[23] *Retail, Wholesale and Department Store Union v Dolphin Delivery* [1996] 2 SCR 573.
[24] [1995] 2 SCR 1130.
[25] [1998] 1 SCR 591.

consistently with "Charter values". So, although the Charter does not apply directly to private litigants, it will apply indirectly as the common law is brought into line with its values. At the same time, several lower court decisions in Ontario show that "invasion of privacy" is now developing as a tort in its own right in some provinces.

In Australia, which still has no Bill of Rights, there is a patchwork of laws and legal principles covering both privacy and freedom of expression. As David Lindsay says in chapter six, these only provide partial legal protection. A person seeking redress for privacy in the Australian courts has to try to fit the complaint within established forms of action not designed to protect privacy. And, in David Lindsay's opinion, this has resulted in the distortion of common law principles in areas such as defamation and breach of confidence as the courts have strained to protect individual privacy. In fact, self-regulatory media codes are currently seen as the most significant feature of media regulation in Australia.

The protection of privacy rights in Germany and France has long been a serious matter. Both countries now have highly developed privacy laws both as between private persons and with the state. In France, for example, the right to private life is based on legislation introduced as long ago as 1970 and incorporated into the Civil Code. As this does not contain a precise definition, the notion of private life has been developed case by case to encompass such matters as personal identity, health, emotional and family life, correspondence and disclosure of wealth. However, as Catherine Dupre points out in chapter two, the exact full nature and scope of the right is still the subject of much speculation.

In Germany, privacy rights have essentially been developed case by case on the basis of the inclusion of personality rights in Articles 1 and 2 of the German Basic Law. According to Rosalind English in chapter three, its evolution should provide a fascinating model for the UK. By examining landmark rulings of the German Federal Constitutional and Supreme Courts, including the recent cases of *Caroline I* and *Soraya* which deal with the publication of fabricated interviews, she shows how certain constitutional values have produced a sophisticated system for the horizontal application of such rights to private persons. This has been either through the direct effect ("Drittwirkung") or the radiating effect ("Ausstrahlungswirkung") of constitutional norms.

FREEDOM OF EXPRESSION

Under the HRA the UK courts are now obliged to ensure respect for the right of freedom of expression as guaranted by Article 10 of the ECHR. The recent case *of R v Secretary of State for the Home Department, ex parte Simms*[26] concerning the right of prisoners to communicate with journalists underlines this; as does the case of *Redmond-Bate v DPP.*[27] The latter concerned Christian fundamentalist preachers who were arrested for breach of the peace after refusing to comply with instructions to stop preaching on the steps of Wakefield Cathedral. The Court of Appeal particularly emphasised the importance of protecting unpopular or offensive speech in the context of expression rights.

In one of its earliest rulings on Article 10, the European Court of Human Rights (ECtHR) in *Handyside v UK*[28] stressed the central role of freedom of expression in any democratic society: "one of the basic conditions for the progress of democratic societies and for the development of each individual". However, as Jemima Stratford points out in chapter one, despite taking a broad approach to the content of expression and the forms it may take, the Court can be criticised for its erratic and sometimes inconsistent case law in this area. In her view, it is also to be regretted that the Court has deliberately steered away from developing a right to seek information as a facet of Article 10, thereby leaving a lacuna which can only partly been filled by resort to Article 8 in cases such as *Gaskin v UK.*[29]

Whilst the ECtHR has not expressly adopted the US "public figure" doctrine advanced in *New York Times v Sullivan*,[30] it has said that the limits of acceptable speech about politicians is wider that ordinary citizens. In *Castells v Spain*[31] this was even wider when it came to criticism of government rather than individual politicians.

It has also made it clear that prior restraints on freedom of expression are to be carefully scrutinised. As it said in *The Observer and the*

[26] [2000] AC 115.
[27] (1999) 7 BHRC 375.
[28] (1976) 1 EHRR 737.
[29] (1989) 12 EHRR 36
[30] 376 US 254 (1964)
[31] (1992) 14 EHRR 445

Guardian v UK,[32] news is a "perishable commodity and to delay its publication, even for a short period, may well deprive it of all its value and interest".

The European Court's acknowledgement of the special position of the media in relation to freedom of expression—particularly in terms of political speech—is acknowledged in each of the countries examined in this book. This includes exemptions from data protection laws and special codes of practice.

The different treatment is also reflected in the provisions of the HRA. Under section 12, the courts are to have "particular regard to the importance of the Convention right to freedom of expression" and sets out matters in favour of the media. For example, the section restricts the granting of relief on an *ex parte* basis, has new provisions for pre-trial injunctions to make the likelihood of success at trial the decisive element[33] and provides the media with a public interest defence.[34] The courts must also have particular regard to whether it is in the public interest for the material to be published and to any relevant privacy code. These special arrangements for the media in relation to freedom of expression are also reflected in the exemptions to comply with the data protection principles of the Data Protection Act 1998.[35]

BALANCING THE RIGHTS

It is not inevitable that privacy and free speech rights conflict, but where a conflict exists, how to resolve the competing values encompassed in these rights becomes an essential and unavoidable question. With UK case law developing, there is a need for workable and consistent criteria to assist the courts in undertaking this task. For instance, should the UK courts adopt a hierarchical approach to rights with freedom of expression weighing the heavier as it does in the United States or should the starting point be that these two rights

---

[32] (1991) 14 EHRR 153

[33] Thereby rejecting the *American Cyanamid Co v Ethicon Ltd* test of arguable case and balance of convenience.

[34] See Court of Appeal in *Douglas v Hello!* [2001] 2 WLR 992, and *A v B and C* [2002] EWCA Civ 337.

[35] See s 32.

are of equal status? Is it in fact a balancing exercise for the courts or does it perhaps involve a more complex process? This is where the experience of other jurisdictions may be especially important.

Starting with the ECtHR itself, chapter one makes detailed reference to a relatively small but important body of cases where the tension between Articles 8 and 10 has been expressly acknowledged. And for those involving the UK, the Court additionally had to consider whether the absence of a right to privacy in English law breached Article 8.[36] Whilst the European Convention provides no obligatory point at which the balance must be struck, the Court has said that any interference with either right must be justified by reference to the principles of legality, pressing social need and proportionality. In cases such as *Bladet Tromso and Stensaas v Norway*[37] it has particularly emphasised the "duties and responsibilities" attaching to the exercise of freedom of expression under Article 10(2)—in other words that there is a concept of responsible reporting which shows due respect to another's conflicting rights.

The approach in Germany is to treat the rights as equal and apply a proportionality test to each individual case: the damage to privacy resulting from public representation must not be out of proportion to the importance of the publication upholding the freedom of speech. As the Federal Constitutional Court has observed:

> it must be remembered that according to the intention of the Constitution both constitutional concerns are essential aspects of the liberal democratic order . . . with the result that neither can claim precedence in principle over the other.

Some of the matters brought into this process include the motives of the publisher, the importance of the speech, the way in which the information was obtained, the extent of its dissemination, the accuracy of the statement and the breadth of the restriction to be put on the speech rights. And, as Rosalind English points out in chapter three, the German courts have taken a starkly different approach to the usual "public figure" doctrine: far from being accorded less protection, the courts have held that a person with public status is

---

[36] It found that it did not in the 1986 case of *Winer v UK* (1986) 48 D & R 154 but that it might in the 1998 case of *Spencer v UK* (1998) 25 EHRR CD 105.

[37] (1997) 23 EHRR CD 40.

entitled to greater protection of privacy. This is because a publication may have a more damaging effect than it would have on a less public person.

Although, like Germany, France places the two rights on the same level in formal legal terms, the courts have ruled that freedom of expression should be the rule to which private life is an exception. This means that in order to succeed with a privacy complaint in France it is necessary to show that the interference would be an "unbearable breach" of private life or a breach of "intimate private life" before a limitation may be placed on free expression.

There are varying considerations coming out of the case decisions in each of the common law jurisdictions. In New Zealand the courts have specifically referred to a balancing exercise of the various competing interests. The factors to be weighed include the significance in the particular case of the values underlying the Bill of Rights, the importance of the intrusion on a protected right in public interest terms, the limits that will be placed on the common law in the particular case and the effectiveness of the intrusion in protecting the interests that are put forward to justify the limiting of another right. In the recent case of *R v Mahanga*[38] the Appeal Court held that the privacy interests of a convicted person were a legitimate factor to include in the balancing process when prohibiting access by a television company of a videotaped interview of the defendant that had been played during the course of a trial.

Although the question of balancing rights is referred to in some of the several Canadian Supreme Court decisions on competing rights,[39] the way in which this is to be approached was first considered in *Big M Drug Mart* case.[40] As Marguerite Russell says, the Court reached its decision in this case through a complex process of contextualising the rights involved and endeavouring to reach a conclusion based on the underlying core values of the Charter rather than on the basis of a hierarchical assessment of rights. In the recent *Aubry* case[41] involving the publication without consent of a photograph of

---

[38] [2001] 1 NZLR 641 (CA).

[39] For example, *Dagenais v CBC* [1994] 3 SCR 835, *Hill v Church of Scientology* [1995] 2 SCR 1130, *R v Mills* [1999] 3 SCR 668, *Trinity Western University v British Columbia College of Teachers* [2001] SCC 31.

[40] [1985] 1 SCR 295.

[41] *Aubry v Editions Vice-Versa* [1998] 1 SCR 591.

a teenage girl in an arts magazine, the court again emphasised the need to contexualise the competing rights. In particular, it directed that the balancing exercise depends on evaluating two factors: first, the nature of the information and, secondly, the situation of those concerned.

On the other hand in Australia, where the common law has a more important continuing role in the absence of a Bill of Rights, there is a series of relatively ad hoc balances between the public interest in freedom of expression and the protection of privacy. As David Lindsay says, it is arguable that in practice Australian courts have established an acceptable balance whereby, under the common law, personal privacy tends to prevail over the interest in freedom of expression, whereas in relation to government information, free speech is accorded greater importance than competing interests.

As these chapters show there are different ways to determining what is the "acceptable balance" between these two fundamental rights. As we go to press, the Court of Appeal in the case of *A v B and C*[42] has sought to provide a framework for just such an exercise in a case involving the publication of a prominent footballer's extra-marital affairs. The 15 guidelines do not give deference to either right, but require the drawing up of a "balance sheet" of respective interests in a context-based approach. While there is clear recognition of the principle of a right to privacy in UK law, the Court is at pains to point out that:

> It is not necessary to tackle the vexed question of whether there is a separate cause of action based upon on a new tort involving the infringement of privacy.

Some would say that such reluctance is misplaced; others that it correctly reflects the restraint on courts to make law. However, this decision does show that there continues to be the potential for significant development of the law in this area. We hope that this book will be an important source for all those who may participate in that development.

---

[42] *A v B and C* [2002] EWCA Civ 337, 11 March 2002. See also *Naomi Campbell v Mirror Group Newspapers Ltd*, QBD, Morland J, 27 March 2002.

2

Striking the Balance: Privacy v Freedom of Expression under the European Convention on Human Rights

Jemima Stratford[1]

INTRODUCTION

Articles 8 and 10 of the European Convention on Human Rights present a paradigm of the potential for conflict between competing rights. One person's right to private life may conflict with another person's right to freedom of expression; one person's right may be another person's wrong.

As Basil Markesinis has noted "[t]he protection of human privacy is a modern, difficult, intriguing problem".[2] Modern because increased technology for collecting, collating and disseminating information mean that intrusions into human privacy are increasingly effective and thus potentially harmful. Difficult because the solutions must be sought in a number of different branches of the law. And intriguing because the protection of privacy involves a process which strives to achieve a balance between two important social interests: the respect for human personality and the preservation of freedom of expression.[3]

The tension between the right to privacy and the right to freedom of expression arises most obviously in cases concerning the media. To

---

[1] This chapter is based on part of a paper given at the Bar European Group and Administrative Law Bar Association Millennium Conference, May 2000. I am most grateful to Professor David Feldman, David Anderson QC and Jason Coppel for their comments on an earlier draft of that paper.

[2] "The Right to be Let Alone versus Freedom of Speech" [1986] *PL* 67.

[3] Markesinis described these two interests as "equally important", but recognised that to attribute equal value to them is in itself a potentially controversial statement. The abstract ranking of rights is perhaps seldom necessary or helpful.

date, the cases which have come before the European Commission of Human Rights ("the Commission") and the European Court of Human Rights ("the Strasbourg Court") have very largely concerned this field. However, as cases from the English courts show, this balance may also be of central relevance in other fields as diverse as:

(1) cases concerned with reporting restrictions on court proceedings in the fields of employment law,[4] family law[5] and criminal law[6];

(2) cases concerned with disclosure of sensitive information by public bodies to third parties[7];

(3) cases concerned with secret or intrusive filming.[8]

---

[4] For example: *Chessington World of Adventures Ltd v Reed, ex parte News Group Newspapers Ltd* [1998] IRLR 56 (EAT) (restricted reporting order discharged in appeal concerning sex discrimination complaint brought by a transsexual—newspaper relying on Article 10 and Morison J concluding his decision to discharge the order with a reference to Article 8 and the desirability of a law protecting privacy).

[5] For example: *Re HS (Minors) (Protection of Identity)* [1994] 1 WLR 1141 (CA) (Order restricting comment which transsexual parent could make to the press varied to prevent any dealings by the parent with the media in the home where the children lived or elsewhere in their presence); *A v M* [2000] 1 FCR 1 (Fam Div) (Injunction granted against disclosure of information by mother concerning family proceedings, even of matters already placed in the public domain). See also Markesinis's discussion of the differing approach taken to protecting privacy in two earlier wardship cases *Re X* [1975] Fam 47 and *Re X* [1984] 1 WLR 1422 in [1986] *PL* 67 at 74–75.

[6] For example: *McKerry v Teesdale & Wear Valley Justices* (7 February 2000) (Div Ct) (Order dispensing in part with reporting restrictions made under the Children and Young Persons Act 1933 upheld).

[7] For example: *R v Chief Constable of the North Wales Police, ex parte Thorpe* [1999] QB 396 (CA) (police gave information about two long-term child abusers to owner of caravan site to which they had moved); *Woolgar v Chief Constable of Sussex Police and Anor* [2000] 1 WLR 25 (CA) (upholding refusal to grant injunction to prevent police disclosing material obtained during interview with registered nurse under caution to the regulatory body for nursing); *R v A Local Authority and a Police Authority, ex parte LM* (6 September 1999, unreported) (allowing application for judicial review of the Respondents' decision to disclose past allegations of sexual abuse of children to a County Council which was considering offering him employment as a teacher); *R v Secretary of State for Health, ex parte C* (*The Times*, 1 March 2000) (CA) (upholding dismissal by Richards J of application by unqualified social worker for judicial review of Secretary of State's decision to place his name on the consultancy service index of people thought to be unsuitable to work with children).

[8] For example: *R v Broadcasting Complaints Commission, ex parte Barclay and Anor* (*The Times*, 11 October 1996) (QBD) (unauthorised filming by BBC on applicants' island—no power for Broadcasting Complaints Commission to adjudicate upon complaints of infringement of privacy prior to broadcast. A complaint to the Strasbourg Commission was subsequently rejected as inadmissible); *R v Brentwood Borough Council, ex parte Peck* [1998] EMLR

Accordingly, it is likely that the jurisprudence of the Strasbourg Court will develop further, as that Court is faced with more varied circumstances in which there is a tension between the rights protected under Articles 8 and 10.

Following a necessarily summary and selective introduction to each of Articles 8 and 10, this chapter will consider some of the cases brought before the Commission and Court of Human Rights in which the right to privacy and freedom of expression have come into conflict.

Articles 8 to 11 of the Convention

Articles 8 and 10 are part of the group of qualified rights contained in Articles 8 to 11 of the Convention. Each protects against interference by the state with activities in which a person may or may not choose to engage. These rights are not merely derogable in times of emergency, they are also not expressed in absolute terms. The other qualified rights are:

—Article 9—freedom of thought conscience and religion;
—Article 11—freedom of assembly and association.

The structure of each of these four Articles is broadly similar. In the first paragraph the right protected is set out. The criteria upon which an interference with that right may be justified are identified in the second paragraph. To be justified the interference must be lawful, pursue a legitimate aim, and be necessary in a democratic society, which entails the requirement that it be proportionate to the aim which is sought to be achieved. Accordingly, when considering whether an alleged violation of any of Articles 8 to 11 of the Convention is made out, the analysis of the Strasbourg Court adopts the following pattern:

697 (QBD) (in a widely criticised decision, Harrison J refused application for judicial review of Council disclosure of CCTV footage showing applicant's suicide attempt which was subsequently shown on television—application for permission to appeal to CA refused and an application to Strasbourg has recently been declared admissible: Application No 44647/98). See also *R v Secretary of State for Culture, Media and Sport, ex parte Danish Satellite TV and Anor* (12 February 1999, unreported) (QBD) for a discussion of Articles 8 and 10 in relation to the proscription of a pornographic satellite television service.

(1) Does the subject matter of the alleged violation fall within the scope of the Article?

(2) If yes, has there been interference by a public authority?

(3) If yes, was the interference "in accordance with the law" (Article 8) or "prescribed by law" (Articles 9, 10 and 11), did it pursue a "legitimate aim" and was it "necessary" (ie did the interference correspond to a "pressing social need" and was it proportionate to that need)?

Each of the Articles in this part of the Convention therefore contains an in-built balance which must be achieved in every case, as well as on occasion having to be balanced with each other, right against right.[9]

ARTICLE 8

Article 8 provides that:

1) Everyone has the right to respect for his private and family life, his home and his correspondence.

2) There shall be no interference by a public authority with the exercise of this right except such as is in accordance with the law and is necessary in a democratic society in the interests of national security, public safety or the economic well-being of the country, for the prevention of disorder or crime, for the protection of health or morals, or for the protection of the rights and freedoms of others.

There are equivalent provisions governing respect for private life and related interests in other international human rights instruments including Article 12 of the Universal Declaration of Human Rights (1948) and Article 17 of the International Covenant on Civil and Political Rights (1966).[10]

Article 8 has been subject to some relatively dynamic interpretation by the Strasbourg Court.[11] This is in part because there is considerable

---

[9] Of course, Arts 8–11 of the Convention may also come into conflict with, and have to be balanced against, rights set forth in other parts of the Convention.

[10] See also Article 11 of the American Convention on Human Rights. There is no equivalent right to privacy in the African Charter on Human and Peoples' Rights.

[11] See among a number of excellent general surveys: DJ Harris, M O'Boyle and C Warbrick, *Law of the European Convention on Human Rights* (Butterworths, London, 1995), ch 9; K Reid, *A Practitioner's Guide to the European Convention on Human Rights* (Sweet &

room for disagreement about the values which privacy-related rights should protect. Article 8 has therefore been the focus of much inventive advocacy, some of which has succeeded in bringing within the scope of the Article interests which are otherwise inadequately protected by the Convention.[12]

At the first stage of its analysis under Article 8, a court must identify the interest of the applicant and decide whether it falls within one of the four nominated interests: private life, family life, home or correspondence. In *Niemietz v Germany*,[13] the Court stated generally:

> The Court does not consider it possible or necessary to attempt an exhaustive definition of the notion of "private life". However, it would be too restrictive to limit the notion to an "inner circle" in which the individual may live his own personal life as he chooses and to exclude therefrom entirely the outside world not encompassed within that circle. Respect for private life must also comprise to a certain degree the right to establish and develop relationships with other human beings.

The Court has therefore deliberately refrained from stating an exhaustive definition of the concept of "private life", but it is clear from the case law that it goes further than a right to privacy in the strict sense of control over personal information,[14] and is also linked with notions of personal autonomy and development.[15]

Maxwell, London, 1998) 323–34; D Pannick and A Lester (eds) *Human Rights Law and Practice* (Butterworths, London, 1999) 165–90; J Coppel, *The Human Rights Act 1998* (John Wiley, Chichester, 1999), ch 10; S Grosz, J Beatson and P Duffy, *Human Rights: the 1998 Act and the European Convention* (Sweet & Maxwell, London, 2000).

[12] See D Feldman, "The Developing Scope of Article 8 of the European Convention on Human Rights" [1997] EHRLR 265. Professor Feldman has pointed out that Article 8 does not purport to protect privacy as such, but rather the right to respect for a number of rather more concrete interests (private life, family life, home and correspondence) which are best described as privacy-related rights. These are not merely individualistic, but protect our ability to enter into worthwhile social relationships and co-operative activities of our choosing for the public benefit.

[13] (1993) 16 EHRR 97, para 29.

[14] The ever-widening scope afforded to the notion of privacy in many jurisdictions of the world is a controversial issue in itself. See, for example, R Wacks, "The Poverty of 'Privacy' " (1980) 96 *LQR* 73 where the author described privacy as a "large and unwieldy concept" which has "become almost irretrievably confused with other issues".

[15] See, for example, *X v Iceland* (1976) 5 D & R 86 and *Botta v Italy* (1998) 26 EHRR 241, concerned with the rights of disabled people to have access to sea bathing. See also *Clunis v UK* (pending).

In considering the meaning of "family life" under Article 8, the Court has taken a non-legalistic fact-based approach to the question whether family life exists from case to case. In the important early case *Marckx v Belgium*,[16] the Court held that Article 8 made no distinction between legitimate and illegitimate family ties, so that the relationship between an unmarried mother and her child amounted to family life, despite the requirement for a formal act of recognition under domestic law. The case also established that family life does not include only social, moral or cultural relations, but also interests of a material kind such as intestate succession.[17]

In contrast with the concepts of private and family life, there has been relatively little case law addressing the meaning of the term "home". Whether a place constitutes a person's home is a question of fact which is not dependent on establishing a proprietary interest.[18] The term may extend to a professional person's office, although a state's entitlement to interfere under Article 8(2) "might well be more far-reaching where professional or business activities or premises were involved than would otherwise be the case".[19] The right to a home has also been used to develop a right not to suffer severe environmental pollution.[20]

The term "correspondence" has been broadly defined to cover telephone conversations as well as written correspondence,[21] and there seems little doubt that it will be developed to cover other new forms of correspondence such as e-mail. The concept of correspondence covers commercial communications concerning products, as well as more obviously private personal correspondence.[22]

---

[16] (1979) 2 EHRR 330, para 31.

[17] See also *Keegan v Ireland* (1994) 18 EHRR 342; *Abdulaziz, Cabales and Balkandali v UK* (1987) 7 EHRR 471; *X, Y and Z v UK* (1997) 24 EHRR 143.

[18] *Mentes v Turkey* (1998) 26 EHRR 595; *Buckley v UK* (1997) 23 EHRR 101, para 54.

[19] *Niemietz v Germany* (1993) 16 EHRR 97, para 30. See also *Huvig v France* (1990) 12 EHRR 528.

[20] *Lopez-Ostra v Spain* (1995) 20 EHRR 277 (waste treatment plant); *Powell & Rayner v UK* (1990) 12 EHRR 355 (aircraft noise); *Guerra v Italy* (1998) 26 EHRR 357 (toxic emissions from a factory).

[21] *Klass v Germany* (1978) 2 EHRR 214, para 41.

[22] *Amann v Switzerland* (2000) 30 EHRR 843.

Article 8 Cases

Important areas in which Article 8 is capable of being successfully invoked include the following:

—Children (custody, public care and adoption[23]);
—Sex and sexuality[24];
—Immigration[25];
—Prisoners[26];
—Housing, including cases relating to planning enforcement action against gypsies[27];
—Environment[28];

---

[23] See, for example, *Hendriks v Netherlands* (1983) 5 EHRR 223; *Olsson v Sweden (No 1)* (1988) 11 EHRR 259; *Olsson v Sweden (No 2)* (1994) 17 EHRR 134; *Eriksson v Sweden* (1990) 12 EHRR 183; *Johansen v Norway* (1996) 23 EHRR 33; *EP v Italy* (Judgment of 16 November 1999); *Ignaccolo-Zenide v Romania* (25 January 2000); *Elsholz v Germany* (13 July 2000); *Scozzari & Giunta v Italy* (13 July 2000). See also *TP & KM v UK* (1998) 26 EHRR CD 84, one of the cases arising from the decision of the House of Lords in *X v Bedfordshire County Council* [1995] 2 AC 633, in which the Commission found an infringement of Article 8 due to the "careless" removal of a child into care. The case is currently pending before the Grand Chamber of the Court.

[24] See, for example, *Dudgeon v UK* (1981) 4 EHRR 149; *Sutherland v UK* (Commission Decision of 1 July 1997) [1998] EHRLR 117; *Cossey v UK* (1991) 13 EHRR 622 (no violation) but see *B v France* (1993) 16 EHRR 1; *Modinos v Cyprus* (1993) 16 EHRR 485; *Smith & Grady v UK* [1999] IRLR 734 (the homosexuals in the military case); *Salgueiro da Silva Monta v Portugal* (2001) 31 EHRR 47 (homosexuality and custody of the applicant's daughter; violation of Art 8 taken together with Art 14); *ADT v UK* (2001) 31 EHRR 33 (prosecution and conviction of a man for engaging in non-violent homosexual acts in private with up to four other men was a violation of Art 8).

[25] *Uppal v UK (No 2)* (1981) 3 EHRR 399; *Abdulaziz, Cabales and Balkandali v UK* (1985) 7 EHRR 471; *Berrehab v The Netherlands* (1988) 11 EHRR 322; *Moustaquim v Belgium* (1991) 13 EHRR 802.

[26] See, for example, *Golder v UK* (1975) 1 EHRR 524; *Silver v UK* (1983) 5 EHRR 347; *Boyle and Rice v UK* (1988) 10 EHRR 425; *McCallum v UK* (1990) 13 EHRR 596; *Campbell v UK* (1992) 15 EHRR 137; *Demirtepe v France* (2001) 31 EHRR 28 (all concerned with prisoners' correspondence).

[27] See, for example, *Buckley v UK* (1997) 23 EHRR 101; a further group of cases including *Beard v UK* (1998) 25 EHRR CD 28 are currently pending before the Grand Chamber of the Court.

[28] See, for example, *Lopez-Ostra v Spain* (1995) 20 EHRR 277 (waste treatment plant); *Powell & Rayner v UK* (1990) 12 EHRR 355 (aircraft noise); *Guerra v Italy* (1998) 26 EHRR 357 (toxic emissions from a factory).

—Search and seizure[29];
—Surveillance and data collection[30];
—Media intrusion[31];

The last two of these areas—surveillance and data collection and media intrusion—are particularly likely to give rise to tensions with Article 10 rights to freedom of expression.

Positive Obligations

Although the Convention is mainly concerned with setting limits on the ability of public authorities to interfere with individual rights, the Strasbourg case law has also developed certain areas in which state authorities are obliged to take positive steps or measures to protect the rights in question.[32]

---

[29] *Funke v France* (1993) 16 EHRR 297; *Niemietz v Germany* (1993) 16 EHRR 97; *Chappell v UK* (1990) 12 EHRR 1 (Anton Piller orders, now search orders under CPR 25.1); *Camenzind v Switzerland* (1999) 28 EHRR 458 (search of residential premises for evidence of use of an unauthorised cordless telephone).

[30] See, for example, *Klass v Germany* (1978) 2 EHRR 214 (telephone tapping—adequate and effective guarantees found to exist); *Malone v UK* (1984) 7 EHRR 14 (telephone tapping—violation); *Halford v UK* (1997) 24 EHRR 523 (secret recordings made by the police of an employee's calls from police headquarters during employment tribunal proceedings); *Kopp v Switzerland* (1999) 27 EHRR 91 (unlawful tapping of a lawyer's telephone calls from his office by a post office official with no judicial supervision); *Leander v Sweden* (1987) 9 EHRR 433; *MS v Sweden* (1999) 28 EHRR 313 (disclosure of medical records); and *Z v Finland* (1997) 25 EHRR 371 (protection of medical data). Note that English law continues to grapple unsatisfactorily and in a piecemeal fashion with the problem of regulating covert surveillance; see, most recently, the Regulation of Investigatory Powers Act 2000.

[31] *Spencer v UK* (1998) 25 EHRR CD 105; *Winer v UK* 48 D & R 154 (Commission Decision); *Stewart-Brady v UK* (1997) 24 EHRR CD 38. These cases are examined in more detail in the section headed "The Tension Between Articles 8 and 10" below.

[32] See generally K Starmer, "Positive Obligations under the Convention", a paper presented to UCL/JUSTICE seminar, now published in J Jowell and J Cooper (eds), *Understanding Human Rights Principles* (Hart Publishing, Oxford, 2001). Keir Starmer discerns five general principles governing the scope of positive obligations under the Convention: (1) a duty to put in place a legal framework which provides effective protection for Convention rights; (2) a duty to prevent breaches of Convention rights; (3) a duty to provide information and advice relevant to a breach of Convention rights; (4) a duty to respond to breaches of Convention rights; (5) a duty to provide resources to individuals to prevent breaches of their Convention rights. In a written response to that paper, Professor Chris McCrudden argued that "there is, in fact, no coherent set of principles underpinning the jurisprudence of the European Court of Human Rights on this issue, in part because of a lack of any real theoretical underpinning for

Article 8 is unique in using the words "right to respect" for various interests.[33] From time to time states have sought to argue that this formulation imposes a less onerous burden, and limits the obligation to a purely negative one not to interfere excessively with the protected rights. However, the Court has rejected this narrow reading of Article 8, and stated in *X and Y v Netherlands*:

> [Article 8] does not merely compel the state to abstain from . . . interference: in addition to this primarily negative undertaking, there may be positive obligations inherent in an effective respect for private and family life . . . These obligations may involve the adoption of measures designed to secure respect for private life even in the sphere of the relations of individuals between themselves.[34]

Article 8 is therefore an important source of positive rights and obligations under the Convention. Such positive rights may require the State to ensure that respect for private life as between its citizens is properly protected under domestic law, as well as on occasion requiring the State itself to take positive steps where its inaction would otherwise violate a citizen's private life. A good example of the latter is *Gaskin v UK*[35] where the Court held that there was a positive obligation on the public authorities to allow Mr Gaskin access to records of his foster care.

Failure by a state to comply with a positive obligation to respect Article 8 rights has been limited by the Court by reference to concepts such as "the fair balance that has to be struck between the general interest of the community and the interests of the individual"[36] and by

that Court's approach to human rights in general. It is in areas such as the issue of positive rights that this absence is most keenly felt." Professor David Feldman, on the other hand, argues forcefully that there is a consistent and coherent test, namely whether the State has done what is necessary to secure the substantive right in question in the particular context. What may be less clear is how the Court will answer that question in any case. As Feldman has argued, the more significant (in human rights terms) are the interests which a right supports, and the greater the threat to those interests, the more the State will have to do in order to discharge its general obligation under Article 1 of the Convention to secure the right in question: see n 12 above.

[33] See A Connolly, "Problems of the Interpretation of Article 8 of the European Convention on Human Rights" (1986) 35 *ICLQ* 567, 584.

[34] (1985) 8 EHRR 235. See also *Marckx v Belgium* (1979) 2 EHRR 330, para 31.

[35] (1990) 12 EHRR 36.

[36] *Rees v UK* (1987) 9 EHRR 56, para 37.

affording states "a wide margin of appreciation in determining the steps to be taken to ensure compliance with the Convention with due regard to the needs and resources of the community and of individuals".[37] The Strasbourg institutions have been particularly generous in the margin of appreciation which they have allowed states in controversial areas where there is no generally shared approach among contracting states and in areas such as transsexualism where the law appears to be in a transitional stage.[38]

An Incoherent and Arbitrary Case Law?

There has been criticism, even from within the European Court of Human Rights itself, of the incoherent and arbitrary nature of some of its judgments under Article 8.[39] For example, in *Stjerna v Finland*,[40] which concerned the state's refusal to allow the applicant to change his surname, one of the concurring judges described the Court's differentiation between negative and positive obligations as part of "an established but still somewhat incoherent jurisprudence".[41] In arguing that a more coherent approach is possible, Colin Warbrick has noted:

> The tasks of the Court under Article 8(1) to decide what "respect" requires and under Article 8(2) to decide whether an interference is justified are similar but not identical. In each case the Court talks in terms of a fair balance and allows the State a margin of appreciation in striking it. In Article 8(1), what are to be balanced are the individual and public interests. The former and many of the latter will be invoked again in the Article 8(2) process. However, then it is the right of the individual which is to be weighed against only those aims denominated in Article 8(2) and any balance struck by the State must be measured against the pressing social need and the standard of proportionality. The Article 8(1) process is more favourable to the State than the Article 8(2) one. Incoherence arises when the Court collapses the examination of whether there is a positive obligation under Article 8(1) with the question of whether it has

---

[37] *Abdulaziz, Cabales and Balkandali v UK* (1985) 7 EHRR 471, para 67.
[38] For example, *Sheffield and Horsham v UK* (1999) 27 EHRR 163; *X, Y and Z v UK* (1997) 24 EHRR 143, para 52
[39] See C Warbrick, "The Structure of Article 8" [1998] *EHRLR* 32.
[40] Series A No 299–B (1994).
[41] *Per* Judge Wildhaber concurring.

been breached, an Article 8(2) matter. The approach is analytically misfounded because of the lack of substantive distinction between positive and negative obligations. It is, however, necessary to recognise that the consequences of this misconceived approach may be removed by characterising the duty of "respect" more narrowly. This may be criticised as harsh but it is neither incoherent nor arbitrary.[42]

ARTICLE 10

Article 10 of the Convention provides:

1) Everyone has the right to freedom of expression. This right shall include freedom to hold opinions and to receive and impart information and ideas without interference by public authority and regardless of frontiers. This Article shall not prevent States from requiring the licensing of broadcasting, television or cinema enterprises.

2) The exercise of these freedoms, since it carries with it duties and responsibilities, may be subject to such formalities, conditions, restrictions or penalties as are prescribed by law and are necessary in a democratic society, in the interests of national security, territorial integrity or public safety, for the prevention of disorder or crime, for the protection of health or morals, for the protection of the reputation or rights of others, for preventing the disclosure of information received in confidence, or for maintaining the authority and impartiality of the judiciary.

Freedom of expression is protected in other international human rights instruments including Article 19 of the Universal Declaration of Human Rights (1948), Articles 19 and 20 of the International Covenant on Civil and Political Rights (1966), and Articles 13 and 14 of the Inter-American Convention on Human Rights.[43]

---

[42] [1998] EHRLR 32 at 43. See also Harris, O'Boyle and Warbrick, *Law of the European Convention on Human Rights* (1995), 326–27.

[43] See also, Art 11 of the French Declaration of the Rights of Man. One of the most famous provisions to protect freedom of expression, the First Amendment to the United States Constitution, has a different structure from Art 10. Thus decisions of the US Supreme Court focus more than their Strasbourg equivalents on whether something comes within the protected sphere at all, in which case it is afforded a very high degree of protection, whereas the Strasbourg jurisprudence effectively includes all expression within Art 10(1) and focuses the enquiry on justification under Article 10(2). See further E Barendt, *Freedom of Speech* (1985).

As will be immediately apparent, Article 10(2) recites more potential grounds of limitation for this important right than attend Article 8, and indeed more than accompany any other article of the Convention.[44] Perhaps in part as reaction to this plethora of potential limitations, the Court has stressed the central place of freedom of expression in any democratic society:

> Freedom of expression constitutes one of the essential foundations of a [democratic] society, one of the basic conditions for its progress and for the development of every man. Subject to paragraph 2 of Article 10, it is applicable not only to "information" or "ideas" that are favourably received or regarded as inoffensive but also to those that offend, shock or disturb the state or any sector of the population. Such are the demands of that pluralism, tolerance and broadmindedness without which there is no "democratic society".[45]

Freedom of expression is therefore of high importance not only because of its role in the working of a democratic society,[46] but also because it is central to individual self-realisation.

The Court has taken a very broad approach to the content of expression which falls within Article 10(1), and in practice all forms

---

[44] See among a number of excellent general surveys of the case law on Art 10: Harris, O'Boyle and Warbrick, *Law of the European Convention on Human Rights* (1995), ch 11; Reid, *A Practitioner's Guide to the European Convention on Human Rights* (1998) 232–244; Pannick and Lester (eds), *Human Rights Law and Practice*, 197–206; Coppel, *The Human Rights Act 1998* ch 12; Grosz, Beatson and Duffy, *Human Rights: The 1998 Act and the European Convention* (2000), ch 10.

[45] *Handyside v UK* (1976) 1 EHRR 737, para 49. As well as containing this important early statement of the principles underpinning the importance of Art 10, the *Handyside* case recognised the unpredictable concept of "margin of appreciation", which has done much to undermine the strong principles of freedom of expression proclaimed by the Court. The case concerned a successful prosecution under the Obscene Publications Act against the publishers of *The Little Red Schoolbook*, a book which was said to encourage a liberal attitude to sexual matters among its young readership. The Court found no violation or Art 10, taking into account that the restrictions were imposed for the protection of morals of young people.

[46] It is this aspect of freedom of expression which has led Professor Conor Gearty to describe Art 10 as a secondary civil liberty (ie one of the freedoms essential to a properly functioning civil society). He distinguishes civil liberties from other rights (including the right to private life) which have in his view an "inherent tendency towards incoherence". Civil liberties are described as a bulwark against society as "a collection of autonomous individuals pursuing their own ends in a highly egoistic and frequently conflictual fashion" (JUSTICE Annual Lecture, 7 October 1999).

of expression are capable of protection under Article 10: political,[47] commercial[48] and artistic,[49] and including material which is obscene, blasphemous or racist.[50] "Expression" extends beyond the spoken or written word to include pictures, images and actions intended to express an idea or present information.[51] It is not only the expression which is protected, but also the means for its production and the medium for its communication. Existing media including print, radio, television broadcasting and film have all been recognised in the Strasbourg jurisprudence,[52] and there is no reason to believe that the Court will not continue to expand its horizons to take account of newly developed technologies including the internet.

Since almost all forms of expression fall within Article 10(1), the onus will almost always be on the State under Article 10(2) to justify interference with the freedom, although the task of such justification may not be a difficult one depending upon the type of expression at issue, the medium through which it is delivered, and the audience at which it is directed. This is because the wide powers of limitation which Article 10(2) permits may be applied differently (but not in a discriminatory manner) depending upon the type, form and media of expression at issue. For example, political speech has been

---

[47] See, for example, *Lingens v Austria* (1986) 8 EHRR 407, para 42.

[48] See, for example, *Cascado Coca v Spain* (1994) 18 EHRR 1, paras 35–36.

[49] See, for example, *Müller v Switzerland* (1991) 13 EHRR 212, para 27.

[50] See, for example, *Otto-Preminger Institute v Austria* (1994) 19 EHRR 34 (blasphemous material) and *Jersild v Denmark* (1994) 19 EHRR 1 (film including racist speech). However, in *Glimmerveen and Hagenbeek v The Netherlands* (1979) 4 EHRR 260 the Commission declared inadmissible as being outside the scope of Art 10 a complaint by extreme right-wing Dutch politicians concerning their conviction for distributing leaflets advocating racial discrimination and the repatriation of non-whites. The Commission relied upon Art 17 of the Convention, which precludes reliance on the Convention to protect activities "aimed at the destruction of any of the rights or freedoms set forth". Art 17 has been relatively rarely relied upon, and may be described as an exception of "almost last resort" (Harris, O'Boyle and Warbrick, at n 11 above, 374). Other Art 17 cases include *Kommunistishce Partei Deutschland v Germany* (1955–57) 1 Yearbook 223, *Lawless v Ireland* (1960–61) A 3, *Christians against Racism and Facism v UK*, 17 D & R 93, *Schimanek v Austria* (1 February 2000).

[51] For example, *Chorrer v Switzerland* (1993) A 266–B (images) and *Stevens v UK* (1986) 46 D & R 245 (dress capable of falling within Art. 10); *Steel and others v UK* (1999) 28 EHRR 603 (demonstrations capable of amounting to expressions of opinion).

[52] For example, *Groppera Radio AG v Switzerland* (1990) A 173 (radio), *Autronic v Switzerland* (1990) A 178 (television), *Otto-Preminger-Institut v Austria* (1994) A 295–A (film).

prioritised over other forms of speech such as commercial or porno-graphic expression.[53]

Claims to justification under Article 10(2) will be examined according to the same three tests as are applied under Article 8(2): is the interference with freedom of expression prescribed by law; is the interference in pursuance of one of the legitimate purposes listed in Article 10(2); was the interference necessary and proportionate?

No Article 10 Right of Access to Information

Article 10 guarantees the right to receive, as well as to impart, information and ideas without interference by a public authority.[54] However, unlike Article 19(2) of the ICCPR, the Convention does not expressly confer a right to seek information, or impose upon the State a duty to provide information. The Court has deliberately steered away from developing such a right under Article 10. Thus in *Leander v Sweden*,[55] the Court held that:

> the right to receive information basically prohibits a government from restricting a person from receiving information that others wish or may be willing to impart to him. Article 10 does not . . . confer on the individual a right of access to a register containing information on his personal position, nor does it embody any obligation on the government to impart such information to the individual.

This restrictive judicial approach leaves a lacuna in the rights pro-tected under the Convention which has only partly been filled by

---

[53] In "Is the Privileged Position of Political Expression Justified?" in *Essays in Honour of Sir David Williams QC* (Clarendon Press, Oxford, 2000) Ivan Hare argues that resolving free speech issues by reference to *a priori* categorisation of types of expression is dangerous, and that it may in fact be more legitimate to limit or regulate some forms of political speech than other forms of expressive activity, precisely because they are so important to the proper functioning of government and the democratic process.

[54] For a recent example of a finding of violation in relation to the freedom to impart information, see *Thoma v Luxembourg* (29 March 2001) (journalist quoting accusations formulated by fellow journalist).

[55] (1987) 9 EHRR 433, para 74. In *Z v Austria* (1988) 56 D & R 13, the Commission stated that the freedom to receive information which is protected by Art 10 is "primarily a free-dom of access to general sources of information which may not be restricted by positive action of the authorities."

resort to Article 8. In the *Gaskin*[56] case the Court held that Article 8 imposes a positive obligation upon the State to ensure that the interests of an individual seeking access to confidential records relating to his private and family life (childhood years spent in care) is secured when a contributor to the records either is not available or improperly refuses consent to access to those records. The Court noted that:

> This finding is reached without expressing any opinion on whether general rights of access to personal data and information may be derived from Article 8(1) of the Convention . . . in the circumstances of the present case, Article 10 does not embody an obligation on the state concerned to impart the information in question to the individual.

The case can be explained on its facts, which naturally focussed attention on the importance of the information to Mr Gaskin's understanding of his childhood years (and hence Article 8), but later cases have not reoriented the case law towards Article 10.[57] This is to be regretted; not only is Article 10 the more natural starting point for the development of a right of access to information, but the role of Article 8 must inevitably be limited to cases where the information held by public authorities is closely linked with private and family life.[58] Writing extra-judicially, Lord Justice Sedley has observed:

> There is something odd about discovering a right to information in the entrails of Article 8, which says nothing about information, and refusing to discern it in Article 10 which explicitly integrates "freedom . . . to receive . . . information and ideas without interference by public authority" in the right of free expression. Yet in its recent jurisprudence the

---

[56] *Gaskin v UK* (1990) 12 EHRR 36. The decision in this case led to the enactment of the Access to Health Records Act 1990, which permitted access to health records made after November 1991. This has now been repealed and replaced by the Data Protection Act 1998.

[57] For example, *McMichael v UK* (1995) 20 EHRR 205 (social work reports required in legal proceedings relating to children), *Guerra v Italy* (1998) 26 EHRR 278 (information about risks from fertiliser factory emissions), *McGinley and Egan v UK* (1999) 27 EHRR 1 (records concerning nuclear testing in the Pacific required for medical reasons; no violation due to failure to exhaust domestic remedies by requesting documents in pension proceedings).

[58] Even in such cases, the scope of right to access information is not a broad one: see *Martin v UK* (1996) 21 EHRR CD 112 where the Commission declared inadmissible an application relating to medical records where there was no blanket refusal to disclose (disclosure to a medical adviser had been offered), where it had not been demonstrated that the records were the only source of the information sought, and where the records related to a shorter period of adulthood, rather than to childhood as in *Gaskin*.

Court has stayed with its early decisions that the words I have quoted are included in Article 10 not to accord any right to information but simply to stop governments interfering with "information that others wish or may be willing to impart". It is not trite to ask why, in that case, the framers bothered to put them there at all.[59]

It is to be hoped that the right of access to information as a facet of Article 10 may yet be discerned by the Strasbourg Court.

Article 10 Cases

Important areas in which Article 10 issues have arisen include the following:

(1) Political debate[60];
(2) Discussion of non-political matters of public concern[61];
(3) Health information[62];

---

[59] "Information as a Human Right" (*Essays in Honour of Sir David Williams QC*, forthcoming).

[60] See, for example, *Lingens v Austria* (1986) 8 EHRR 407 (conviction of a journalist for defaming the Chancellor—violation); *Castells v Spain* (1992) 14 EHRR 445 (conviction and disqualification of an MP for insulting the Government—violation); *Ceylan v Turkey* (one of 11 cases decided on 8 July 1999 in which Turkey was held to have violated Art 10 by placing restrictions on political speech which were not necessary in a democratic society); *Dalban v Romania* (2001) 31 EHRR 39; *Erdogdou v Turkey* (15 June 2000) and *Sener v Turkey* (18 July 2000) (conviction of journalists for making separatist propaganda—violation in both cases); and *Aksoy v Turkey* (10 October 2000) (convictions of politician for disseminating separatist propaganda—violation).

[61] See, for example: *Thorgeirson v Iceland* (1992) 14 EHRR 843 (conviction of a journalist for defaming the police force following an article reporting allegations of police brutality—violation); *Bladet Tromsø and Stensaas v Norway* (1999) 29 EHRR 125 (convictions of newspaper for defamation against a group of seal hunters—finding of violation on basis that convictions were disproportionate to legitimate aim of protecting hunters' reputations given, in particular, vital importance of informed public debate); *Barthold v Germany* (1985) 7 EHRR 383 (availability of emergency veterinary service—newspaper article contained public justification of a matter of general interest and conviction under unfair competition law therefore violated Art 10). See also *Goodwin v UK* (1996) 22 EHRR 123 (order that journalist disclose source of confidential information could not be said to be "necessary in a democratic society"(para 39)).

[62] See, for example: *Hertel v Switzerland* (1999) 28 EHRR 534 (injunction restraining repetition of statements concerning health risks from microwaved food—violation); *Open Door and Dublin Well Woman v Ireland* (1993) 15 EHRR 244 (injunctions restraining provision of information to Irish women about abortion facilities abroad—violation given absolute nature of the injunctions which were disproportionate to the legitimate aim of protecting morals).

(4) The electoral process[63];
(5) The courts and administration of justice[64];
(6) The civil service[65];
(7) Advertising and other commercial speech[66];

[63] See, for example: *Bowman v UK* (1998) 26 EHRR 1 (restrictions on electoral expenditure aimed at maintaining equality between candidates legitimate, but restriction on distribution of pre-election leaflet by third party disproportionate and contrary to Art 10).

[64] See, for example: *Sunday Times v UK (No 1)* (1979–80) 2 EHRR 245 (injunction preventing publication of article concerning thalidomide as part of campaign during on-going court proceedings on basis that publication would be a contempt of court—violation on basis that the interference with freedom of expression was not necessary in a democratic society, in particular because it is incumbent on the mass media "to impart information and ideas concerning matters . . . of public interest. Not only do the media have the task of imparting such information and ideas: the public also has a right to receive them" (para 65)); *Barfod v Denmark* (1989) 13 EHRR 493 (attack on the impartiality of judges who had decided controversial tax case—no violation). In *Observer and Guardian Newspapers v UK* (1992) 14 EHRR 153 and *Sunday Times v UK (No. 2)* (1992) 14 EHRR 229 (The Spycatcher litigation) the Government initially argued that the injunction was necessary "for maintaining the authority and impartiality of the judiciary" during the course of proceedings to determine whether there was legal right to keep the information confidential; this argument lost any force when the information came into the public domain as a result of its publication abroad. See also *Tolstoy v UK* (1995) 20 EHRR 442 (libel damages must be subject to sufficient judicial control to offer adequate and effective safeguards against disproportionately large awards) and the discussion of that case by the Court of Appeal in *Victor Kiam v The Sunday Times* (17 July 1996, *The Times* 26 July 1996).

[65] See, for example: *Janowski v Poland* (2000) 29 EHRR 705 (conviction and fine for criticism of municipal guards—no violation on basis that civil servants do not knowingly lay themselves open to close scrutiny of their every word and deed to the extent to which politicians do); *Glasenapp v Germany* (1987) 9 EHRR 25 (applicant dismissed from job as school teacher for refusing to dissociate herself from the German Communist Party—no interference with the right guaranteed under Art 10(1) on the basis that the public authority took account of her opinions merely in order to satisfy itself as to whether she possessed the necessary qualifications for a civil service post); *Ahmed and others v UK* (1998) 29 EHRR 1 (restrictions on political activities of certain categories of local government officials were justified in the interests of preserving their political neutrality in order to safeguard effective local democracy).

[66] See, for example: *Markt Intern v Germany* (1989) 12 EHRR 161 (injunction against a trade magazine prohibiting it from publishing information about an enterprise operating in its market sector—no violation by very narrow majority, applying a less strict test of necessity to commercial communications and invoking a wide margin of appreciation); *Casado Coca v Spain* (1994) 18 EHRR 1 (disciplinary proceedings against lawyer for distribution of professional advertising—no violation taking into account the wide margin of appreciation allowed to States where there is no uniformity of practice among the parties to the Convention); *Jacubowski v Germany* (1994) 19 EHRR 64 (injunction preventing further distribution of a circular criticising applicant's former employer and addressed to employer's clients—no violation (again by majority)).

(8) Broadcasting[67];
(9) Artistic expression[68];
(10) Obscene, blasphemous and racist speech[69];

A Weakened Supervision in Practice?

Although the Court has re-stated on a number of occasions the strong importance attached to freedom of expression in the *Handyside* case, its decisions in particular cases have often failed to live up to this democratic ideal. This is apparent even from the short summary of some of the case law set out above, from which it is often difficult to discern principled reasoning, which is characterised by a high proportion of majority decisions and which often resorts to the doctrine of margin of appreciation. Commentators have criticised the erratic and sometimes inconsistent case law of the Commission and the Court,[70]

---

[67] See, for example: *Autronic AG v Switzerland* (1990) 12 EHRR 534 (prohibition on re-transmission of television signals from a Soviet satellite—violation); *Groppera Radio AG v Switzerland* (1990) 12 EHRR 321(prohibition on re-transmission by cable of radio signals from unlicensed Italian station—no violation taking into account the requirements of protecting the international communications order, noting that there had been no censorship directed against the content of the programmes concerned, and concluding that the authorities had not over-stepped their margin of appreciation); *Informationsverein Lentia v Austria* (1993) 17 EHRR 93 (refusal of a broadcasting licence pursuant to a state broadcasting monopoly—violation).

[68] See, for example: *Müller v Switzerland* (1991) 13 EHRR 212 (confiscation of paintings judged to be obscene—no violation invoking in particular the wide margin of appreciation in relation to the public morals exception); *Otto Preminger-Institute v Austria* (1994) 19 EHRR 34 (forfeiture of blasphemous film due to be screened to adults at private institute—no violation by majority).

[69] See, for example: *Handyside v UK* (1976) 1 EHRR 737 (see n 45 above); *Wingrove v UK* (1996) 24 EHRR 1 (refusal of classification for a video on grounds of blasphemy—no violation on basis that others might justifiably feel their religious beliefs to be under unwarranted attack in an offensive manner); *Jersild v Denmark* (1994) 19 EHRR 1 (television journalist convicted of aiding and abetting the dissemination of racial insults after a programme he had made broadcast racist remarks by a group of young people—violation on basis that the conviction was not proportionate to protecting the rights of others, ie those attacked in the racist insults).

[70] For example, A Lester, "Freedom of Expression" in Macdonald, Matscher and Petzold (eds) *The European System for the Protection of Human Rights* (Martinus Nijhoff, Dordrecht, 1993) 490–91, and Harris, O'Boyle and Warbrick, (see n 11 above, at 375–76 and 414–15). Some of the judgments of the new Court, established on the coming into force of the 11th Protocol to the Convention, suggest that the tide may be turning in favour of freedom of expression; see, for example, the finding of a violation of Art 10 in *Bladet Tromsø and Stensaas v Norway* (1999) 29 EHRR 125.

and this is one of the areas in which the Strasbourg Court could develop a stronger and more coherent rights jurisprudence.

THE TENSION BETWEEN ARTICLES 8 AND 10: THE STRASBOURG CASE LAW

One of the first, but still much quoted articles in support of a general right to privacy was published by SD Warren and LD Brandeis in 1890.[71] It was prompted by the intrusive behaviour of the local press on the occasion of the wedding of Mr Warren's sister, and called for the recognition of a self-standing "right to privacy" to combat a press which was:

> overstepping in every direction the obvious bounds of propriety and decency. Gossip is no longer the resource of the idle and of the vicious, but has become a trade, which is pursued with industry as well as effrontery[72]

Whilst such comments could equally well be applied to some of the worse excesses of the media today, few would question the importance of a free and vigorous press, or suggest that the balance towards protection for privacy should be tilted all one way.

This part of the chapter examines some of the cases in which the Strasbourg Commission and Court have sought to achieve a proper balance between freedom of expression and privacy. There is a relatively small but important body of cases in which the Strasbourg Court or Commission has expressly acknowledged the tension which exists between Articles 8 and 10. Of course, Articles 8 and 10 do not always conflict with each other. There are many instances in which Articles 8 and 10 are jointly invoked by the applicant, for example in cases concerning prisoner correspondence.[73] In some cases a

---

[71] "The Right to Privacy" (1890) 4 *Harvard LR* 193.

[72] *Ibid*, 196.

[73] For example: *McCallum v UK* (1990) 13 EHRR 596; *Schönenberger and Durmaz v Switzerland* (1989) 11 EHRR 202; *Silver v UK* (1983) 5 EHRR 347. A topical example of a case in which Arts 8 and 10 could be jointly invoked is provided by section 28 of the Local Government Act 1988 which prohibits local authorities from promoting homosexuality: see David Pannick QC, "Europe Will Have the Final Word in Section 28 Debate", *The Times*, 29 February 2000.

violation of both articles has been found,[74] but more often the Court having found a violation of one article, declares that there is no need to examine separately complaints made under the other article. For example, in *Smith and Grady v UK*,[75] the Court held that the investigations conducted into the applicants' sexual orientation together with their discharge from the armed forces constituted grave interferences with their private lives, which were not justified within the meaning of Article 8(2). Having reached that conclusion, the Court held that the freedom of expression element of the case was subsidiary to the applicants' right to respect for their private lives which was principally at issue, and therefore found that it was not necessary to examine the complaints under Article 10, either alone or in conjunction with Article 14.[76] In other cases the Court has found a violation of Article 10 and concluded that there was no need to examine the complaint made under Article 8.[77] Yet cases are often communicated to the Respondent Government under both Articles 8 and 10,[78] and the Court will on occasion of its own motion raise Article 8 or 10 as relevant where the applicant has only sought to rely on one of them.[79]

---

[74] For example, *Herczegfalvy v Austria* (1993) 15 EHRR 432 (Austrian law which allowed a mental patient's curator to decide whether his correspondence should be sent on).

[75] [1999] IRLR 734.

[76] Interestingly, the Court did go as far as to state that it would not rule out that the silence imposed on the applicants as regards their sexual orientation, together with the consequent and constant need for vigilance, discretion and secrecy in that respect with colleagues, friends and acquaintances as a result of the chilling effect of the MOD policy, could constitute an interference with their freedom of expression. The other two applicants, Lustig-Prean and Becket, whose cases were heard at the same time as the *Smith and Grady* case did not rely on Art 10.

[77] For example, *Hertel v Switzerland* (1999) 28 EHRR 534.

[78] See, for a relatively recent example, *Albayrak v Turkey* (No. 38406/97, admissibility decision of 16 November 2000) concerning disciplinary investigations against a judge of Kurdish origin who was accused *inter alia* of displaying sympathy for the PKK, of being a regular reader of a pro-Kurdish newspaper and of having watched in his home a satellite television channel allegedly controlled by the PKK. Communicated under Arts 8, 10, 13 and 14.

[79] See, for a relatively recent example, *Stacey v UK* (No 40432/98, admissibility decision of 19 January 1999) which concerned a single parent's refusal to provide information about the mother's whereabouts to the Child Support Agency. The applicant had relied upon Art 8, but the Court noted that Art 10 might also be considered as relevant in the context of a complaint about an obligation imposed with respect to the communication of information. The application was declared inadmissible as manifestly ill-founded.

The United Kingdom Cases

The United Kingdom cases decided in Strasbourg which address the tension between Articles 8 and 10 have been dominated by the important and much discussed question as to whether there is a right to privacy in English law, and have also considered whether the absence of such a right constitutes a breach of Article 8. Two Commission Decisions, dating from 1986 and 1998 respectively, exemplify the developments in this debate and merit particular scrutiny for the approach which the Strasbourg institutions took to the balance between Articles 8 and 10.

Winer v UK[80] concerned the publication of a book entitled *Inside BOSS* (the South African Bureau of State Security) which contained allegations that the applicant had been subject to "a campaign of denigration aimed at smearing him as a BOSS spy". The book also contained intimate references to the applicant's private life and his relationship with his former wife. The applicant submitted that some of the allegations in the book were true, of others he could not prove their untruth and others were false, but that all were inextricably interwoven so as to constitute a gross invasion of his and his former wife's privacy, a matter not generally protected under English law. Mr Winer had attempted to bring defamation proceedings against the publishers of the book (Penguin) in respect of those matters which were clearly defamatory, but those proceedings were settled by payment of a sum of £5,000 to the applicant after he had been advised that the proceedings, in which he acted in person due to the non-availability of legal aid, were inadequately pleaded. Before the Commission, the applicant complained of the absence of a remedy in English law for gross invasions of privacy arising from matters published in book form and which are not necessarily defamatory or untrue.

In its observations to the Commission the UK had denied that English law inadequately protected a right to privacy. The Government pointed to the balance which must be struck between, on the one hand, the individual's right to privacy and, on the other

---

[80] (1986) 48 D & R 154. The case was originally known only by the initials of the applicant (WSW) but has since been referred to by the Commission in other decisions by reference to the applicant's full name. It is still sometimes cited as *W v UK*.

hand, other individuals' right to freedom of expression. It emphasised that Article 8(2) provides for restrictions on the grounds, *inter
alia*, of the protection of "the rights and freedoms of others", and that
the remedy sought by the applicant could have a "substantial effect
on the right to freedom of expression guaranteed by Article 10 of the
Convention". The Government also noted that as well as defamation, an action for breach of confidence could have been brought by
the applicant.

The Commission accepted the Government's submissions that in
relation to those parts of the complaints which were included in the
settled defamation case the applicant could not claim to be a victim.
However, the Commission did not accept that the remedy of breach
of confidence, taken alone or in conjunction with an action in
defamation constituted an adequate or effective remedy which the
applicant should have exhausted before making his application. The
Commission went on to note that:

> there is no question in the present case of any involvement by the respon-
> dent Government in the publication of *Inside BOSS*. The applicant is
> therefore complaining about a lack of restriction on a third party, and is
> alleging that this omission involves the respondent Government's
> responsibility. In this regard the applicant is, in effect, calling for a posi-
> tive obligation to be imposed on States to interfere with other individu-
> als' right to freedom of expression, a right guaranteed by Article 10 of the
> Convention. However, the Commission considers that Article 10 must
> be taken into account when establishing the positive obligations which
> may be imposed by Article 8 of the Convention.[81]

Having decided in the applicant's favour that he had not failed to
exhaust his domestic remedies by failing to bring an action for breach
of confidence, the Commission nonetheless went on to hold that the
application was inadmissible as manifestly ill-founded:

> the Commission does not consider that the absence of an actionable right
> to privacy under English law shows a lack of respect for the applicant's
> private life and his home. Whilst it is true that this state of the law gives
> greater protection to other individuals' freedom of expression, the appli-
> cant's right to privacy was not wholly unprotected, as was shown by his

---

[81] (1986) 48 D & R, 170.

defamation action and settlement, and his own liberty to publish. The Commission, therefore, concludes that the case does not disclose a failure to respect the applicant's rights under Article 8 of the Convention.[82]

The *Winer* case is therefore an important and relatively early example of the Commission acknowledging the balance which must be struck between Articles 8 and 10, and applying a wide margin of appreciation to the state's exercise of its positive obligations to ensure respect for private life so that even "the absence of an actionable right to privacy" did not show a lack of respect for the applicant's private life in the circumstances of the case.

By the time *Spencer v UK*[83] was decided in 1998, the approach taken by the Commission had changed. In April 1995 the News of the World had published an article entitled "Di's Sister-in-Law in Booze and Bulimia clinic", which was accompanied by a photograph of Victoria Spencer, wife of Earl Spencer, taken with a telephoto lens while she walked in the grounds of a private clinic. The photograph was captioned "SO THIN: Victoria walks in the clinic grounds this week". Similarly intrusive articles and photographs were published in other newspapers over the following few days, and after a complaint by Earl Spencer to the Press Complaints Committee (PCC), certain newspapers attacked him alleging hypocrisy on the ground that he had previously used the media to gain publicity for himself. The PCC concluded that the Code of Practice relating to privacy had been breached, and apologies were published by the offending newspapers. Following the PCC rulings, solicitors for Earl Spencer and his wife threatened proceedings for breach of confidence against two former friends who were believed to be the source of the published information, but following service of a statement of claim seeking an injunction and damages, the claim was settled by consent. They did not threaten or bring proceedings against the newspapers concerned.

Earl Spencer and his wife lodged applications with the Commission complaining that the UK had failed to comply with its obligations under the Convention to protect their right to respect for private life in that it had failed to prohibit the publication and dissemination of information (and in the case of the second applicant

---

[82] *Ibid*, 171.
[83] Joined Applications 28851/95 and 28852/95 (1998) 25 EHRR CD 105.

of photographs) relating to their private life, or to provide a legal remedy whereby they could have prevented such action or claimed damages thereafter for the loss and distress caused. The Commission, having reviewed the law relating to actions for breach of confidence in some detail,[84] summarised the parties' arguments:

> The applicants essentially submit that the Government is under a positive obligation to provide effective protection for the rights guaranteed by the Convention. Given the terms of Article 10 of the Convention, the absence of an effective domestic remedy as regards invasions of privacy by the press constitutes a failure to effectively respect their right to respect for their private lives as guaranteed by Article 8 of the Convention.
>
> The Government argues that the domestic system as a whole (including remedies in breach of confidence and against trespass, nuisance, harassment and malicious falsehood together with the Press Complaints Commission) provides adequate protection to individuals and an appropriate balance between the often competing rights guaranteed by Articles 8 and 10 of the Convention.[85]

Picking up on the applicants' reference to Article 10, the Commission made the following hypothetical, but nonetheless potentially significant, statement:

> On the facts as presented by the parties, the Commission would not exclude that the absence of an actionable remedy in relation to the publications of which the applicants complain could show a lack of respect for their private lives. It has regard in this respect to the duties and responsibilities that are carried with the right of freedom of expression guaranteed by Article 10 of the Convention and to Contracting States' obligation to provide a measure of protection to the right of privacy of an individual affected by others' exercise of their freedom of expression.[86]

---

[84] Certainly in considerably more detail than had been included in its earlier decision in *Winer v UK.* The *Spencer* case refers to: *Kaye v Robertson* [1991] FSR 62; *Coco v AN Clark Engineers Ltd* [1969] RPC 41; *Bernstein v Skyviews Ltd* [1978] 1 QB 479; *Malone v Metropolitan Police Commissioner* [1979] Ch 344; *Francome and Anor v Mirror Group Newspapers Ltd and ors* [1984] WLR 892; *AG v Guardian Newspapers (No 2)* [1990] AC 109; *Shelley Films Ltd v Rex Features Ltd* [1994] EMLR 134; *Hellewell v Chief Constable of Derbyshire* [1995] 1 WLR 804; *Barrymore v News Group Newspapers Ltd* [1997] FSR 600; *X and Y* [1988] 2 All ER 648; *Argyll v Argyll* [1967] Ch 302; *Stephens v Avery* [1988] 1 Ch 449; *Seager v Copydex Ltd* [1967] 1 WLR 923. Only some of this case law post-dated *Winer.*

[85] CD 112.

[86] CD 112.

Thus the Commission emphasised the "duties and responsibilities" which attend the Article 10 right of freedom of expression, and contemplated that if there were no "actionable remedy" through which the applicants could obtain redress for the invasion of their privacy which they had suffered, this could be in breach of Article 8.

In the event, and particularly taking account of the clarification of the scope and extent of actions for breach of confidence since the time of the Decision in the *Winer* case, the Commission concluded that the applicants had failed to exhaust their domestic remedies by failing to pursue their action in breach of confidence.

The Decisions in *Winer* and *Spencer* therefore differ in two important respects: (1) in the former the Commission held that the applicant had exhausted his domestic remedies since an action for breach of confidence did not constitute an adequate or effective remedy, whereas in the latter the applications failed on the ground that the applicants should have brought a claim for breach of confidence against the newspapers; and (2) in the former the Commission held that the absence of an actionable right to privacy under English law did not show a lack of respect for the applicant's private life and his home, whereas in the latter the Commission indicated that the absence of an actionable remedy in English law to protect the applicants could indeed constitute a breach of Article 8, but that breach of confidence at least potentially offered such protection. It is striking that in *Spencer* the UK Government relied on cases such as *Hellewell* and *Shelley Films* [87] in order to found a successful argument that actions for breach of confidence were now capable of offering a remedy, for example, where unauthorised photographs were taken using a telephoto lens. The differences between the *Winer* and *Spencer* cases may be partly explicable on the basis of their different facts, the *Spencer* case arising out of a particularly crude invasion of privacy by tabloid newspapers without any public interest justification.[88] Nonetheless, the Decision in

[87] See n 84 above.

[88] Of course, merely because an action for breach of confidence or in defamation fails on its facts does not signal absence of an adequate actionable remedy to protect privacy. See, for example, *Stewart-Brady v UK* (1997) 24 EHRR CD 38 where the Commission declared inadmissible a complaint brought by Ian Brady arising out of a newspaper article. Brady had no prospect of success in an action for defamation (because he had no reputation to protect) or malicious falsehood (because he could show no financial loss). The fact that in his particular circumstances those causes of action were bound to fail did not, however, cause the Commission doubt their effectiveness in protecting privacy.

Spencer does represent both a fuller and more up to date understanding of existing protection for privacy under English law, and an indication that the margin of appreciation allowed by Strasbourg in relation to the balance which national law draws between Article 8 and 10 is not quite as wide as the *Winer* case may have suggested.

Although the new Court has not yet endorsed the approach of the Commission in *Spencer v UK*,[89] the case is likely to encourage further development of the common law (notably actions for breach of confidence) so as to provide a comprehensive "actionable remedy" in relation to invasions of privacy. This has been given another spur by the decision of the Court in *Smith and Grady v UK*,[90] which held that the applicants did not have an effective domestic remedy in relation to the violation of their right to respect for their private lives where judicial review proceedings placed the irrationality threshold so high that it effectively excluded any consideration of whether the interference with their private lives had answered a pressing social need or was proportionate to the national security and public order aims pursued by the Government. *Smith and Grady* did not, of course, involve any tension between Articles 8 and 10; nonetheless the case is a reminder that an "actionable remedy" for at least gross invasions of privacy may be required for all claimants, whether proceedings are brought in public law by way of judicial review or by private cause of action.

Non-United Kingdom Cases

It is instructive also to consider the way in which the Article 8/Article 10 balance has been addressed by Strasbourg in cases from countries whose laws already contain a more comprehensive right to privacy. Four cases—from Sweden, Spain, the Netherlands and Norway—offer some insight into how that balance is drawn in other states

---

[89] The case was referred to in the summary of the applicants' contentions in *Barclay v UK* (35712/97, admissibility decision of 18 May 1999) and has been referred to with approval in the dissenting opinion of five members of the Court (Mr Weitzel, Mr Soyer, Mrs Liddy, Mr Birsan and Mr Herndl) in *Bladet Tromsø and Stensaas v Norway* (1999) 29 EHRR 125 which stated: "The countervailing interest in protection of reputation may necessitate positive measures to protect the right to privacy under Art 8 even in circumstances where something less serious than an unsubstantiated allegation of criminal misconduct is at stake" (161).

[90] [1999] IRLR 734.

and the degree to which that balance is scrutinised under the Convention.

In *KVN v Sweden*[91] the Commission rejected a complaint by the owner of a handmade carpet business arising from articles which had appeared in a local daily newspaper allegedly insinuating that he was a swindler who had sold fake carpets and musical instruments. The newspaper claimed that the affair concerned millions of Swedish crowns. Proceedings brought against the editor of the newspaper failed, and the applicant complained to the Commission that the Swedish courts had failed to protect his right to respect for his private and family life. Having noted that the respondent state had no responsibility for the content of the articles, the Commission reiterated its jurisprudence to the effect that states are under a positive obligation in regard to respect for private and family life which may involve the adoption of measures in the sphere of relations of individuals between themselves. However:

> where a question arises of interference with private life through publication in mass media, the State must find proper balance between the two Convention rights involved, namely the right to respect for private life guaranteed by Article 8 and the right to freedom of expression guaranteed by Article 10 of the Convention.[92]

In holding that this balance had not been improperly struck by the Swedish courts, the Commission noted in particular that the articles concerned "a matter of some public interest", that the applicant's name was not mentioned in the articles and that Swedish law offered protection for a person's honour. The Commission concluded:

> The fact that the applicant was not successful in bringing proceedings against the editor of the newspaper does not mean that the respondent State has failed in its obligation to provide adequate protection for his rights under Article 8 of the Convention. As stated above, it is necessary in a case of this kind to strike a balance between the rights protected under Articles 8 and 10 of the Convention, and the Commission finds no indication that, in striking this balance, the court gave inadequate consideration to the applicant's rights under Article 8.[93]

---

[91] (1987) 50 D & R 173.
[92] *Ibid*, 175.
[93] *Ibid*, 175.

The courts must therefore give *adequate* consideration to Article 8 rights in striking the balance, and factors including anonymity and the degree to which the matter is one of proper public concern are relevant to whether this balance has been appropriately struck.

Lopez-Fando Raynaud and Pardo Unanua v Spain[94] concerned a series of controversial articles which had been published in the newspaper *El Pais* attacking the judges of the central employment tribunal. In one of the articles the two applicant judges were named, and were accused of being members of the extreme right wing. Proceedings were brought in the Spanish courts against the director of the newspaper, the journalist who had written the articles and against the editor. Initially the judges were successful, and the court fined the defendants and ordered publication of their findings in a number of Madrid newspapers. However, following an unsuccessful appeal to the Supreme Court, the newspaper and journalists brought a constitutional challenge before the Constitutional Court alleging violation of their freedom of expression. The Constitutional Court overturned the decision of the Supreme Court, noting the interests in play, but recalling the particular importance which must be accorded to freedom of expression and freedom of information in a democratic society. The Constitutional Court concluded that in spite of the severe nature of the criticism made by the journalists, those criticisms had not overstepped the bounds of what was constitutionally protected under the rights of freedom of expression and information. The Court noted in particular that the remarks could not be characterised as abusive, and did not entail allegations of corruption.

Before the Commission the two judges complained that the decision of the Spanish Constitutional Court breached their right to respect for their private life and failed to take proper account of the restrictions on freedom of expression provided for under Article 10(2) of the Convention. Using very similar words to those employed in *KVN v Sweden*, the Commission declared the complaint inadmissible as manifestly ill-founded, concluding that it could not be said that in striking the balance between the interests in play the Constitutional Court had failed to have sufficient regard to the

---

[94] Appl No 31477/96 (15 January 1997, available (in French) on the Council of Europe's HUDOC internet database at <www.echr.coe.int>).

applicants' Article 8 rights. The fact that the applicants' claim had failed did not mean that their right to private life had been inadequately protected, in particular having regard to the facts that the articles concerned a matter of public interest and that, although wounding and shocking, the articles represented journalistic criticism which could not be considered to have overstepped the boundary in undermining the applicants' right to respect for their private life.[95]

The Commission had rather more difficulty with a recent case brought by journalists and a newspaper in which the applicants sought to argue that Dutch law had given too much protection to the right to private life and had inadequate regard to freedom of expression. *Middelburg, Van Der Zee and Het Parool BV v The Netherlands*[96] arose out of a series of articles published by the applicants calling into question the circumstances surrounding the death in 1944 of a German Jewish man who was hidden in Amsterdam by the Dutch resistance. X, now a well-known Dutch film maker, had been convicted of killing the man, but pardoned in 1946 on the basis that the man had threatened to compromise the safety of a resistance group. The articles challenged X's account of the death, and concluded that the killing was premeditated murder and robbery. The Dutch Board of Journalism condemned the articles, and X brought civil proceedings against the applicants for damages. X's claim failed at first instance on the basis that although the articles damaged X's honour and good reputation, they concerned matters which still constituted an issue of important general interest. The Dutch Court of Appeal and Supreme Court overturned that decision, balancing the right of individuals not to be exposed to "rash accusations" in the press and "the interest of the press in its informative, opinion forming and alerting activities in the interest of the general public". The Court of Appeal and Supreme Court balanced a number of criteria including:

---

[95] The Commission contrasted this case with another case involving criticism of judges, *De Haes and Gijsels v Belgium,* in which the applicant journalists had been convicted for more severe criticism. In that case the Court went on to find that the necessity for the interference with the journalists' freedom of expression had not, on the facts, been established: (1997) 25 EHRR 1.

[96] Appl No 28202/95 (admissibility decision of 21 October 1998).

—the nature of the suspicions published and the seriousness of the probable repercussions for the person to whom the suspicions related;

—the seriousness—from a public interest point of view—of the injustice which the publication sought to expose;

—the extent to which the suspicions were supported by factual material available at the time of publication.

The Supreme Court considered that X's rights weighed particularly heavily in the balance given that he had already been punished for the act in question which had taken place many years previously.

After a very careful analysis of the requirements of Article 10(2), the Commission concluded:

> having regard to the duties and responsibilities inherent in the right of freedom of expression guaranteed by Article 10 of the Convention and to Contracting States' obligation to provide a measure of protection to right of privacy of an individual affected by others' exercise of their freedom of expression . . . , the Commission cannot find it unreasonable that, after having examined and balanced the interests at issue, the domestic courts rejected the argument that the applicants' right to freedom of expression should outweigh X's right to protection of his good name and reputation and reached the opposite conclusion.

The Commission drew support from the fact that the Netherlands Press Council had concluded that the articles had exceeded the bounds of acceptable behaviour in professional journalism, and concluded that "the interference at issue was justifiable and proportionate to the legitimate aim pursued". Nonetheless it appears from the relatively lengthy consideration given by the Commission to the factors which must be weighed in the balance, and to the emphasis placed on the merely "supervisory function" of the Strasbourg organs, that this case fell closer to the outer limits of what constitutes an acceptable balance between the rights to privacy and freedom of expression under the Convention.

In the case of *Bladet Tromsø and Stensaas v Norway*[97] the majority of the Court held that the articles in question and the subsequent defamation proceedings brought successfully against the newspaper

---

[97] (1999) 29 EHRR 125.

and its editor fell on the other side of the line, and accordingly the Court found a violation of Article 10. The newspaper had reported (without first independently verifying) critical findings of an official inspector's report into seal hunting. The majority of the Court did not expressly refer to the balance required between Articles 8 and 10, but it did emphasise the "duties and responsibilities" attaching to the exercise of freedom of expression under Article 10(2) which are liable to assume significance when, as in that case, there is a question of attacking the reputation of private individuals and undermining the "rights of others".[98] By reason of those duties and responsibilities, the safeguard afforded by Article 10 to journalists in relation to reporting on issues of general interest is subject to the proviso that they are acting "in good faith in order to provide accurate and reliable information in accordance with the ethics of journalism".[99] Interestingly, the Respondent Government is recorded as having relied on Article 17 of the ICCPR, but not Article 8 of the Convention. However, the Court concluded that the convictions for defamation were disproportionate to the legitimate aim of protecting the seal hunters' reputations, and accordingly found a violation of Article 10.[100]

CONCLUSION

The Convention provides no obligatory point at which the balance must be struck between Articles 8 and 10. However, both rights may

---

[98] Para 65 of the judgment. See also *Wabl v Austria* (2001) 31 EHRR 51 (no violation because injunction prohibiting applicant from repeating statements alleging that a newspaer article about him was "Nazi-journalism" was "necessary in a democratic society" for the protection of the reputation and rights of others (para 45)). And see: *Contantinescu v Romania* (27 June 2000) (no violation because conviction of trade union president for defamation was proportionate to the legitimate aim of protection the reputation or rights of the three defamed teachers); *Tamner v Estonia* (6 February 2001) (no violation—conviction of journalist for using insulting words in relation to the wife of a well known politician).

[99] Para 65, citing *Goodwin v UK* (1996) 22 EHRR 123, para 39 and *Fressoz and Roire v France* 21 January 1999, para 54.

[100] See also recent findings of violations of Art 10 in: *News Verlags GmbH & CoKG v Austria* (2001) 31 EHRR 8; *Fuentes Bobo v Spain* (2001) 31 EHRR 50; *Ozgur Gundem v Turkey* (2001) 31 EHRR 49; *Bergens Tidende & ors. v Norway* (2001) 31 EHRR 16; *Lopes Gomes Da Silva v Portugal* (28 September 2000); *Jerusalem v Austria* (27 February 2001).

only be interfered with to the extent that such interference is capable of justification within the terms of Article 8(2) and 10(2) respectively. In other words, there is no obligation on any State party to the Convention to draw the line between Articles 8 and 10 at any particular point, but any interference with a right must be justified by reference to the principles of legality, pressing social need and proportionality.

It is striking how few of the cases decided to date by the Strasbourg Commission and Court in which the tension between the right to privacy and the right to freedom of expression has arisen have expressly referred to the potential for conflict between Articles 8 and 10. Instead, the Court has generally confined its reasoning to one or other Article, and most often has analysed such cases under Article 10 and by reference to the Article 10(2) justification of "protection of the reputation or rights of others". Yet, as the summary of the Article 8 case law above has shown, privacy-related rights within the umbrella of Article 8 go further than protection of reputation or the right to privacy in the strict sense of control over personal information. Thus there may well be scope in future cases for inventive and express recourse to Article 8 or 10 as a potentially powerful balance to whichever right is being invoked.

There are undoubtedly lacunae in the rights protected under the Convention. Of particular relevance to Articles 8 and 10 is the absence of a "right vesting in citizens to know what is done in their name".[101] The illogical placing of a right of access to information under Article 8 rather than Article 10, and its limited extent have been discussed above. The words of Article 10 offer creative possibilities in this regard, and the development of a "right to know" under the Convention would be a valuable addition to Strasbourg jurisprudence.

---

[101] Per Lord Steyn, speaking extra-judicially at the Liberty/JUSTICE Human Rights Awards 1999 (Law Society, 10 December 1999).

3

The Protection of Private Life versus Freedom of Expression in French Law

Catherine Dupré[1]

INTRODUCTION

The notion of private life has been elaborated by the french case law since the end of the nineteenth century in order to respond to the increasing number of breaches caused, in particular, by the publication of photographs. The Act of 17 July 1970[2] provides for the general mechanism for the protection of private life, especially against the media. Article 22 of this act was incorporated in the Code Civil under Article 9. It provides that everyone has a right to have their private life respected and that judges can put an end to a breach of intimate private life by any measure, such as seizure or sequestration of the contested publication. Furthermore, these measures can be ordered through "emergency interim proceedings" (*référé*)[3] and they can be ordered within a few hours. Since then, numerous statutes have been enacted for the protection of private life in specific circumstances, but they will be disregarded for the purpose of this study because they do not directly involve freedom of expression.[4]

---

[1] Jean Monnet Research Fellow in Law, European University Institute, Florence, Italy. This study was originally done at the request of *Justice*.

[2] Loi No 70–643 du 17 juillet 1970, "tendant à renforcer la garantie individuelle des droits des citoyens", *Journal Officiel*, 19 juillet 1970, 6751.

[3] Article 9 Code Civil: "Chacun a droit au respect de sa vie privée. Les juges peuvent, sans préjudice de la réparation du dommage subi, prescrire toutes mesures, telles que séquestre, saisie et autres, propres à empêcher ou à faire cesser une atteinte à l'intimité de la vie privée; ces mesures peuvent, s'il y a urgence, être ordonnées en référé".

[4] The Loi du 11 juillet 1979, "de la liberté d'accès aux documents administratifs", *Journal Officiel*, 12 juillet 1979, loi du 6 janvier 1978, "relative à l'informatique, aux fichiers et aux libertés" are probably the two main statutes. A list of all specific provisions involving private life is presented by the *Jurisclasseur*, Article 9. They concern, among others, professional secrecy (Article 226–13 Nouveau Code Pénal) and secrecy of correspondence (Article 226–15

Article 22 of the Act of 1970 is phrased in very broad terms. At the same time, it endeavours to restrict the scope of private life to the concept of "intimate private life" (*intimité de la vie privée*) when measures of urgency can be ordered by judges, such as seizure or sequestration. The Act of 1970, however, does not contain any definition of private life; as a result this notion has been developed by courts on a case-by-case basis.

Following case law and under Article 9 Code Civil, everyone has a right to a private life. Therefore, disclosure of elements belonging to private life can only be permitted on the basis of consent, which is interpreted by the courts in a restrictive manner. Nevertheless, judges have elaborated case law which covers a variety of situations. However, when judges are asked to order drastic measures that restrict other rights, and in particular freedom of expression, they require that the breach of private life be particularly serious or unavoidable by other means.

Freedom of expression in French law derives from the Act of 29 July 1881 (subsequently modified)[5] that set out the principle of freedom of the press and marked the end of a preventive system, that is, the requirement of specific authorisation prior to publication and the existence of censorship. Limitations to this freedom were precisely defined and did not permit the interference with the expression of political opinions. Restrictions were imposed mainly through the criminal law because it was considered to give better protection to freedom of the press.

Under the Act of 1881, freedom of expression had traditionally been mainly considered from the perspective of the newspapers, that is the organisation of this profession and the freedom to print.[6] The Conseil constitutionnel extended this conception to the right of the

---

Nouveau Code Pénal), genetic tests (Loi 29 juillet 1994), and closed circuit television (Loi 21 janvier 1995).

[5] As most breaches of private life occur in the press, the legal framework of other media, such as radio, television, cinema and theatre, or simply books will not be considered here. JCl Colliard, *Libertés publiques*, 7th edn (Dalloz, Paris, 1989) provides a good historical section on the development of freedom of expression.

[6] This explains the fact that freedom of expression is usually presented in textbooks as a description of the organisation, production and distribution of the press. See for instance J Robert, *Libertés publiques et droits de l'Homme*, 4th edn (Montchrestien, Paris, 1988).

readers on the basis of Article 11 of the Déclaration des Droits de l'Homme et du Citoyen (DDHC) of 1789[7] in a famous decision of 10–11 October 1984 concerning the Act on "concentration and financial transparency and pluralism among the press companies".[8] In this decision the Conseil also declared that freedom of expression is one of the essential guarantees for the respect of other freedoms as well as of national sovereignty.[9] Moreover, the Conseil ruled that the principle of pluralism was a "constitutional objective" (*objectif à valeur constitutionnelle*). That is that readers, who are the main beneficiaries of Article 11 DDHC, should be able to exercise freely their choice of a newspaper.[10] The importance of pluralism was confirmed in a second decision following the modification of the 1984 Act by the right-wing majority in 1986.[11] The Conseil constitutionnel extended the meaning of Article 11 of the 1789 Declaration to radio

[7] Article 11 DDHC reads: "La libre communication des pensées et des opinions est un des droits les plus précieux de l'homme, tout citoyen peut donc parler, écrire, imprimer librement, sauf à répondre de cette liberté dans des cas déterminés par la loi." In the absence of fundamental rights in the 1958 constitution, the Conseil consitutionnel has generally used this famous Declaration to protect constitutional rights since its ruling of 1971.

[8] Loi du 23 octobre 1984, "visant à limiter la concentration et à assurer la transparence financière et le pluralisme des entreprises de presse" *Journal Officiel*, 24 octobre 1984, 3323. This statute was enacted by the new socialist parliament in an attempt to modernise the Ordonnance of 1944 as well as to limit the financial concentration of press companies. The opposition was particularly active during the debates which eventually led to the Act being referred to the Conseil once it was adopted, but before its promulgation following the procedure of preventive norm control.

[9] Conseil constitutionnel: "s'agissant d'une liberté fondamentale [Article 11 DDHC] d'autant plus précieuse que que son existence est l'une des garanties essentielles du respect des autres droits et libertés et de la souveraineté nationale."

[10] Conseil constitutionnel: "qu'en définitive l'objectif à réaliser est que les lecteurs qui sont au nombre des destinataires essentiels de la liberté proclamée à l'art. 11 de la Déclaration de 1789 soient à même d'exercer leur libre choix sans que ni les intérêts privés ni les pouvoirs publics puissent y substituer leur propre décision, ni qu'on puisse en faire l'objet d'un marché." 10–11 octobre 1984.

[11] Loi du 1 août 1986, "portant réforme du régime juridique de la presse", *Journal Officiel*, 2 août 1986, 9529. Décision du Conseil constitutionnel 29 juillet 1986, *Journal Officiel*, 30 juillet 1986: "Considérant que le pluralisme des quotidiens d'information politique et générale est lui-même un objectif de valeur constitutionnelle, qu'en effet, la libre communication des pensées et des opinions garantie à l'art. 11 DDHC de 1789 ne serait pas effective si le droit public auquel s'adressent ces quotidiens n'était pas à même d'imposer un nombre suffisant de publications de tendances et de caractères différents."

and television and specified that everyone is free to choose the words best expressing their thoughts.[12]

However, the principle of freedom of expression is still subjected to some statutory limits. One of them is the need to protect young people; it involves both publications for young people and adult publications that represent a danger for young people and is regulated by an Act of 16 July 1949. The other restriction concerns publications in a foreign language and allows very generally the Ministre de l'Intérieur to prohibit the distribution of publications of foreign origin.[13] Moreover, there is a large number of press offences (*infractions de presse*) which are inserted in the Code Pénal and the Code de la Santé Publique.

Freedom of expression also applies to other media, such as radio and television. However, claims of breach of private life concerning those media are rare and therefore this study will focus on the press.[14] Finally, it has to be noted breaches of private life can be committed on the internet. Due to the fairly recent use of the internet in France, no specific statute regulates this matter. However, a first instance court decided in 1996 that the Act of 1881 applied to publications on the internet. This case concerned serious accusations made against two

---

[12] Décision du Conseil constitutionnel, 29 juillet 1994 sur la loi "relative à l'emploi de la langue française". The *Conseil* ruled that freedom of expression also applied to "collective expression of ideas and opinions" DC 18 janvier 1995 on "la loi d'orientation et de programmation relative à la sécurité". These rulings are available on the web site of the *Conseil Constitutionnel*: www.conseil-constitutionnel.fr.

[13] Décret-loi 6 mai 1939. This text, adopted in the particular circumstances of the war, has been interpreted in a very wide manner by courts and it is still applicable. See JCl Colliard, *Libertés publiques*, n 5 above, 560. In 1997, the Conseil d'État found that this provision complied with Article 10 and 14 ECHR. Therefore, it ruled that the collective book entitled *Euskadi en guerre* had been legally prohibited: "Considérant qu'il appartient au juge administratif de rechercher si la publication interdite est de nature à causer un dommage justifiant l'atteinte portée aux libertés publiques; que le pouvoir ainsi exercé, sous le contrôle du juge, par le Ministre de l'Intérieur, n'est pas, conrtairement à ce que soutenait l'association requérante, incompatible avec les stipulations combinées des articles 10 et 14 de la Convention Européenne des Droits de l'Homme" (1998) *Dalloz* 317.

[14] For the organisation of radio and television see J Robert, *Libertés publiques et droits de l'Homme*, n 6 above. In 1997, the Cour de cassation ruled, against the appeal court, that the caricature in the form of a puppet of the manager of a car company in a parody information programme on television constituted a harm for the real person. In other words, Article 1382 civil code could be used for restricting freedom of expression. Cour de cassation 2 Civ 2 avril 1997 "SA automobiles Citroen c. SA Canal Plus" (1997) *Dalloz* 411, annotated by B Edelman.

banks that the manager of a company had put on the internet, as well as sending them, by post, to several people. The banks asked the court for an injunction to stop publication on the internet. The court of Paris, following the normal rules of territorial jurisdiction, decided that it was competent to rule on this matter because the contested information was available for anyone in Paris. Consequently, the judge ordered the person who had put the contested accusations on the internet to stop their diffusion by all appropriate means.[15] This first instance ruling, if confirmed on appeal and possibly by the Cour de cassation, raises the important question of inventing appropriate means of protection against the use of (personal) information on the internet.

The protection of private life from the media is also provided by criminal remedies.[16] These involve only very specific and acute breaches and they are rarely used by plaintiffs who prefer the speedy intervention of a judge to prevent or to stop the damage. As a result, these criminal remedies will only be mentioned as minor elements of comparison with the civil remedies provided by Article 9 of the Code Civil.

THE STATUS OF PRIVATE LIFE

The presentation of the development of the right to a private life follows a chronological order that emphasises the importance of the role

---

[15] Tribunal de Grande Instance Paris, réf 16 avril 1996, (1997) *Dalloz* 72, with a short note by JY Dupeux.

[16] The offence of defamation was introduced in Article 35 of the Act of 1881 on the press, as amended by the *Ordonnance* of August 1944, contained in Article 368 of the *Code Pénal*. As a principle, producing evidence that the defamatory allegations were based on true facts led to the exoneration of the offence. This principle, however, did not apply to private life for which, even if defamation was based on true facts, it was still constituted. Defamation, however, has not been used very often for the protection of private life for a number of reasons. First, private life can be breached by mere disclosure of private facts whereas defamation corresponds to a much narrower definition. Secondly, the protection granted by defamation was limited to the seizure of at most four copies of the publication. This might have been impressive then, but in the era of mass media, this limited number has sometimes appeared to plaintiffs to be ridiculously small. Finally, defamation is obtained through criminal proceedings that are long and burdened by formalism and can in no way act in a preventive manner. Following the reform of the *Code de Procédure Pénale*, a new offence was introduced to protect intimate private life, under Art 226 –1 to 15.

played by case law for the definition, as well as for the protection of private life, before the Act of 1970. This approach also reveals that in French law, private life was granted a constitutional status by the Conseil constitutionnel only in 1995.

A Right Constructed by Case Law

The notion of private life was elaborated at the turn of the century and was first linked to the development of photography. In the absence of a special legal provision on private life, judges relied on the principle of delictual liability under Article 1382 of the Code Civil. Following this provision, whoever causes harm to somebody else must repair it. Legal commentators, more or less at the same time, created the new category of the rights of personality in which private life is usually inserted. These rights were considered as having no financial aspect (*droit extra-patrimonial*) and were developed on the basis of Article 1382 to protect various aspects of the personality such as honour and reputation, private life and the "right to one's own image".[17]

The "right to one's own image" (*le droit à l'image*) was the first approach of the courts to protect private life, long before the Act of 1970[18] and it is still used even after the enactment of this specific provision on private life. Legal commentators disagree as to whether the "right to one's own image" is an aspect of the right to a private life[19] or whether it is an autonomous right.[20] Case law has developed this right both as a property right to one's own image, as well as an extension of the personality. Legal commentators formulate this in saying

---

[17] The first reflection on personality rights is probably the article of EH Perreau, "Les droits de la personnalité" published in (1909) *Revue Trimestrielle de Droit Civil* 501. R Nerson, *Les droits extra-patrimoniaux* (Thèse, Lyon, 1939). More recently, R Lindon has tried to present personality rights as they have appeared in case law in *La création prétorienne en matière de droits de la personnalité et son incidence sur la notion de famille* (Dalloz, Paris, 1974). See also C Bigot, *Protection des droits de la personnalité et liberté d'information* (1992) *Dalloz* chr 2.

[18] The first case to grant protection of the image is probably the *Rachel* ruling decided by the Tribunal de la Seine 16 June 1858 (1858, 3, *DP*, 62). In this case judges awarded damages to the sister of Rachel, a deceased actress, of whom a newspaper had published a portrait on her deathbed without authorisation. On "the right to one's own image" see R Lindon, n 17 above, 28–45.

[19] See R Lindon, n 17 above.

[20] See Badinter, "Le droit au respect de la vie privée" (1968) I *Jurisclasseur Périodique* 2136.

that this right as two aspects: one that can be evaluated in money (*droit patrimonial*) and the other that cannot be evaluated in money (*droit extra-patrimonial*).[21] The "right to one's own image" is linked with the development of photography and is very often invoked in support of a breach of privacy, in particular by the tabloid press which relies more on images than on text. Furthermore, one can only agree with R. Lindon when he says that one's own features are part of private life and therefore should be protected as such. However, the "right to one's own image" protects situations which do not strictly belong to private life, such as professional life.[22] In other instances, claimants have sought protection against a commercial or a political use of their own image.[23] Therefore, this right will not be developed in this paper which is mainly concerned with the 1970 Act.

The Act of 17 July 1970

The Act of 1970 was adopted in the context of efforts by the legal commentators to name and, probably as well, to rationalise the protection granted by case law without a specific statutory basis. It is interesting to note that, rather than looking at existing international conventions, such as the European Convention on Human Rights or the International Covenant for Civil and Political Rights, legal scholars looked at foreign legal systems. In particular, the American conception of private life was always mentioned.[24] Moreover, in the late 1960s and early 1970s the notion of private life drew the attention of academia and international conferences were organised on this topic. One of them had an immediate and direct, if limited, impact on case law. Very shortly before the new Act was adopted, the

---

[21] E Gaillard, *La double nature du droit à l'image et ses conséquences en droit positif francais* (1984) *Dalloz* chr 16.

[22] A first instance court protected a prostitute against the publication by a German weekly magazine of photographs which clearly represented her waiting for clients on a street, Tribunal de Grande Instance 28 Février 1974, (974) *Dalloz* 531. In a later case the Tribunal de Grande Instance de Paris (réf 14 novembre 1980) protected a doctor against the publication of his image in his professional activity in a wide audience magazine. Similarly, an "avocate" was protected against the publication of her photograph illustrating a dossier on her profession in a weekly magazine (Tribunal de Grande Instance Paris, réf 27 mars 1981).

[23] See R Lindon, n 17 above.

[24] Nowadays, when the notion of private life is better developed and studied in French law, the American example is the favourite reference for scholars writing on private life.

appeal court of Paris, in the *Jean Ferrat* case,[25] defined private life as "the right for one person to be free to lead her own existence as she wishes with a minimum of exterior interferences". This definition was directly inspired from the presentation by Professor Strömholm at the Franco-Nordic conference, held in May 1970.[26] Courts did not follow this definition, but it is still mentioned in legal writing. As if to reinforce the need for an Act on private life, the annual report of the Cour de cassation for the year 1968–1969, which presents the latest evolutions in its case law noted the increasing role played by personality rights in judicial reasoning.

The purpose of the Act of 1970 was to reinforce the individual guarantee of citizens' rights. It is a long and detailed statute which is generally concerned with criminal law and in particular conditions of custody and punishment. Its third part is entitled "the protection of private life" and is mainly concerned with "false testimony, slanderous accusations and revelation of secrets". However, it is headed by a general provision, which was inserted in the Code Civil under Article 9. It reads:

> Everyone has a right to the respect of his private life. Judges can without prejudice to the determination of the harm suffered, order all measures, such as seizures, sequestrations and other provisions, as appropriate to prevent or to stop a breach of intimate private life; in urgent situations these measures can be ordered under emergency interim proceedings.[27]

The essential impact of this provision was to confirm the existence of a right to a private life. Moreover this right can be protected without relying on the heavy mechanism of "delictual liability" requiring the existence of a wrongful conduct, a resulting harm and the proof of a causal link between the two. Finally, the violation of private life could be prevented or stopped by a powerful measure, such as seizure by a single judge.

---

[25] Cour d'appel Paris 15 mai 1970, (1970) *Dalloz* 466.

[26] S Stromhölm, "La vie privée et les procédés modernes de commnunication, droit nordique" (1971) *Revue Internationale de Droit Comparé* 765–92.

[27] Art 9: "Chacun a droit au respect de sa vie privée. Les juges peuvent, sans préjudice de la réparation du dommage subi, prescrire toutes mesures, telles que séquestres, saisies et autres, propres à empêcher ou faire cesser une atteinte à l'intimité de la vie privée; ces mesures peuvent, s'il y a urgence, être ordonnées en référé."

This statute, however, did not contain any definition of private life. This has usually been interpreted as a confirmation of elements developed by preceding case law. By contrast, the notion of "intimate private life" was generally taken, following parliamentary debates, as being more restrictive than "private life". This was intended by Parliament so as to make sure that freedom of the press would not be unduly reduced by seizures, sequestration and other measures. Indeed, these measures can only be ordered under two conditions: first, there must be a breach of "intimate private life" and secondly, the situation must be urgent, ie no other measure can remedy the damage. However, the Act of 1970 does not clarify the meaning of "intimate private life". As a result, the full nature of this right, as well as its scope, is still the object of much speculation among commentators.[28] B Edelman, an avocat who has widely studied the developments of the case law on private life, summarised the situation of the right to private life in an eloquent manner:

> The nature of the right possessed by an individual over his private life has always been problematic. No one knows exactly whether it is a property right, a personality right or an extra-patrimonial right and no argument has been convincing. As always when the law attempts to codify the individual's relations with himself—whether it be a question of private life, of the right to one's image or more generally all the attributes of personality—lawyers are at bay. On the one hand, they fear making human beings "legal objects" and treating humans like things. On the other hand, they recognise that the individual is never so well protected as by property law. Their wish, which is impossible to fulfill, would be for the individual to be as well protected as private property, but without having to assume the same status.[29]

Since then, the legal definition has not been clarified. If anything, it is becoming more complex with the creation of a new criminal

---

[28] See for instance J Carbonnier, *Droit civil, Les personnes*, 20th edn (Thémis, Paris, 1996) 132–43, or G Cornu, *Droit civil, introduction, les personnes*, 8th edn (Montchrestien, Paris, 1997) 188–99 or F Terré and D Fenouillet, *Droit civil, les personnes, la famille, les incapacités* 6th edn (Dalloz, Paris, 1996) 9–47.

[29] B Edelman, case note under Cour de cassation 1ch civ 3 décembre 1980 "Affaire du pullover rouge", (1981) *Dalloz* 221.

offence prohibiting the violation of "intimate private life".[30] This expression reproduces exactly the one contained in Article 9 of the Code Civil and raises the interesting question of whether the criminal law will follow the civil law approach of "intimate private life".

Recent Constitutional Status: An Element of Personal Freedom

The constitution of 1958 does not list any fundamental right, nor does it refer to private life. Constitutional rights have been gradually recognised by the Conseil Constitutionnel since its famous case of 1971. The Conseil declared that it could refer to the preamble of the 1946 constitution and, in particular, to the "fundamental principles recognised in republican statutes" (*principes fondamentaux reconnus par les lois de la République*) among which was the 1901 Act on freedom of association.

A report, written in 1992, in the perspective of a substantial amendment of the 1958 constitution, proposed to insert the right to private life in the 1958 constitution. Interestingly, this report did not suggest including private life in a special section on fundamental rights, nor in the preamble of the constitution. Instead of this the report proposed to insert private life under Article 66 on the judiciary stating that "every body has a right to the respect of her private life and to the dignity of her person".[31] The subsequent constitutional reform, however, did not enact this proposition. As a result, private life is still not contained in the 1958 constitution.

---

[30] Art 226–1 Nouveau Code Pénal: "Est puni d'un an d'emprisonnement et de 300,000F d'amende le fait, au moyen d'un procédé quelconque, volontairement de porter atteinte à l'intimité de la vie privée d'autrui: 1—en captant, en enregistrant ou transmettant, sans le consentement de leur auteur, des paroles prononcées à titre privé ou confidentiel 2—en fixant, enregistrant ou transmettant, sans le consentement de celle-ci, l'image d'une personne se trouvant dans un lieu privé. Lorsque les actes mentionnés au présent article ont été accomplis au vu et au su des intéressés sans qu'ils s'y soient opposés, alors qu'ils étaient en mesure de le faire, le consentement de ceux-ci est présumé". The application of this provision will not be studied here beyond the example of the protection against publication of photographs of dead people, below.

[31] Rapport remis au Président de la République par le Comité consultatif pour la révision de la constitution le 15 février 1993, also called "Rapport Vedel": "Chacun a droit au respect de sa vie privée et de la dignité de sa personne" in JL Favoreu (ed), *La révision de la constitution* (Economica, Paris, 1993).

This lack of a constitutional basis is, to a certain extent, compensated by recent Conseil constitutionnel case law. After seemingly ignoring the issue of private life, the Conseil acknowledged it in a case on closed circuit television in 1995. In that decision, the Conseil associated the notion of private life with the notion of personal freedom (*liberté individuelle*) under Article 66 of the 1958 constitution. The constitutional judges noted that breaching private life could lead to a breach of personal freedom. This reasoning was confirmed in a ruling of 1997, in which the Conseil constitutionnel stated that a serious failure to respect private life may breach nationals' and foreigners' personal freedom.[32] However, in a ruling on the Loi de finance for 1999, constitutional judges did not find that the use of a personal identity number, for the purpose of checking identities and addresses of tax payers, by three sections of government, that is, public accountancy, tax and customs, was a breach of private life and personal freedom.[33]

The status of private life in French law is strengthened by the European Convention on Human Rights. The Convention was ratified in 1974 and has formed part of French law since then, but French judges were, at first, reluctant to refer to it explicitly in their reasoning. The French legislature also rarely refers to the ECHR in statutes despite the fact that MPs may well be aware of its terms.[34] For instance, it is said that the Act of 1970 and, in particular the new

---

[32] See F Luchaire, *Le Conseil constitutionnel, Jurisprudence, l'individu* (Economica, Paris, 1998) 34–5.

[33] Conseil constitutionnel 29 décembre 1998. This ruling held during festivities of the end of the year raised only a mild concern in newspapers and has not been yet commentated in legal journals.

[34] On this matter, see C Dupré, "The Effect of the ECHR on the Legal and Political Systems of Member States" in R Blackburn and J Polakiewicz (eds), *Fundamental Rights in Europe* (OUP, Oxford, 2001) 313–35. The ECHR, however, had two decisive impacts on the French notion of private life but they are not directly related to this study. The first impact was the enactment of a statute on phone tapping after the two *Kruslin* and *Huvig* cases of 24 June 1990. The second was the acknowledgement by the Cour de cassation, departing from previous case law, that it follows from the respect for private life that the new sexual identity of a transsexual should be registered by the *état civil*, Cour de cassation, assemblée plénière, 11 décembre 1992. In this case the Cour de cassation explicitly mentions Art 8 of the ECHR but ignores the recent ruling of the European Court of Human Rights (*B v France*, 25 March 1992). In this case the European Court ruled that the new sexual identity of a transsexual should be registered in official records. As a result, the Cour de cassation seems to have followed the *B v France* ruling but does not mention it.

Article 9 of the Code Civil, was inspired by the ECHR. However, the statute itself does not refer to it at all. Similarly, a recent statute on the control of immigration is thought to have been drafted in compliance with the ECHR requirements on private life, but it does not refer to the Convention in an explicit manner.[35] Recently, French judges have started to refer to the ECHR in their reasoning in relation to private life.[36] In one ruling, in particular, the Cour de cassation referred to Article 8 of the ECHR together with Article 9 of the Code Civil. The court found that the posthumous publication of information about the emotional life that had already been disclosed by the person in his lifetime was not a breach of private life.[37] In this case, however, it is difficult to assess the impact of Article 8 of the ECHR since the court does not distinguish it from Article 9 of the Code Civil.

PRIVATE LIFE: NUMEROUS ASPECTS CONSTRUCTED BY CASE LAW

The notion of private life generally encompasses personal identity,[38] health[39] and maternity,[40] emotional and family life, domicile and address, correspondence and disclosure of wealth. This section, however, will only provide examples of private life in cases where it conflicts with freedom of expression.[41] Everyone can be protected

[35] Art 5 of Loi du 11 mai 1998 "relative à l'entrée et au séjour des étrangers en France et au droit d'asile" *Journal Officiel*, 12 mai 1998, 7087

[36] Cour de cassation crim 12 février 1997, *Jurisdata* No 001382. In this case the court ruled that the recording of the registration plate of cars exceeding the speed limit by a special instrument was not a breach of Art 8 of the ECHR.

[37] "C'est dans l'exercice de son pouvoir souverain d'appréciation que la cour d'appel a relevé que les faits rapportés par l'hebdomadaire étaient déjà connus et que, peu de temps avant son décès, le défunt avait lui-même laissé complaisamment révéler des éléments de sa vie sentimentale, de sorte que le préjudice invoqué par sa dernière compagne n'est pas établi. L'atteinte à la vie privée, au sens de l'article 9 code civil et de l'article 8 CEDH, suppose l'existence d'une référence ou d'une allusion à la vie de la personne qui entend se prévaloir de cette atteinte". Cour de cassation 2 civ 22 mai 1996, (1996) IV *Jurisclasseur Périodique* 1571.

[38] See the *Jean Ferrat* case mentioned below and the latest case of the Cour de cassation on transsexuals' identity, n 34 above.

[39] Cour de cassation 1 civ, 6 juin 1987, on the photograph of an actress leaving a hospital, *Bulletin*, I, No 191.

[40] Cour de cassation 1 civ, 5 janvier 1983, *Bulletin*, II, No 4.

[41] Private life has had an interesting impact on working conditions, see O de Tissot, "La protection de la vie privée du salarié" (1995) *Droit Social* 222.

against intrusions into their private life by the media,[42] even persons who enjoy a certain celebrity, such as actresses or singers. Indeed, anonymous life, be it private or not, is of little interest for tabloids and, as a result, most private life cases involve well known persons or persons who also have a public life.[43] Courts seem to be particularly sensitive to the protection of private life of vulnerable people, such as children[44] and the mentally disabled.[45]

Disclosure Based on Consent

One idea that can perhaps bring some clarification to the massive case law on private life in relation to freedom of expression is that the disclosure of facts concerning private life should always be based on explicit consent. Indeed, consent is so important for the definition of private life that one legal commentator traced this notion to the principle of the autonomy of the will that is at the basis of French civil law.[46] Without theorising this aspect, it can be noted that consent is an element that is always considered by judges determining whether there has been a breach of private life. A general principle of the case law on private life is that everyone is free to determine the extent of their own private life. In other words, everyone is free to disclose, or not to disclose certain aspects of their private life.

As a result, case law does not distinguish between the private life of private persons and the private life of so called "public persons", that

---

[42] Cour de cassation 1 civ, 23 octobre 1990, *Bulletin*, I, No 222.

[43] This was presented as the "paradox of private life" by R Badinter, "Le droit au respect de la vie privée", (1968) I *Jurisclasseur Périodique* 2136.

[44] One of the first cases concerned the son of a famous actor, Gérard Philippe, who had been photographed lying on his hospital bed (Cour d'appel Paris, 13 mars 1965). In another instance, the court ordered the seizure of a magazine publishing photographs and information about Alain Delon's latest liaison within the neighbourhood where his son, aged ten, might come across it, Tribunal de Grande Instance Paris réf, 28 Juin 1974, (1974) *Dalloz* 751.

[45] Cour d'appel Toulouse, 1ch 15 janvier 1991, (1991) *Dalloz* 600 and Cour de cassation, civ 24 février 1993 (1993) *Dalloz* 614.

[46] See P Kayser, *La protection de la vie privée*, 3rd edn (Economica, Paris, 1995) No 139. The author goes on then to analyse the notion of private life as a contract: "Il semble plus exact de considérer le consentement comme donnant naissance à un contrat. Il consiste en effet dans l'acceptation, par une personne, de la proposition d'une autre de s'immiscer dans sa vie privée ou de la divulguer, de réaliser ou de publier son image. Mais ce contrat peut être aussitôt exécuté que formé ou donner naissance à des obligations dont l'exécution est successive".

is, persons who are more exposed to the public in their everyday life such as actors, singers or politicians.[47] Indeed, the first case on private life granted compensation for the publication of Marlène Dietrich's personal memoires in a weekly magazine. This case emphasised the fact that the famous actress had not consented to this publication. It went on to state that anecdotes and stories about private life, especially those concerning intimate life, could only be written with the consent of the person.[48] The consent to publication of private facts has to be express and clear. For instance, an appeal case confirmed that a magazine had to prove that it had received the express and unequivocal consent of the actor Jean Louis Trintignan for the publication of photographs of him with his wife and daughter, supported by a text revealing his alleged affair with Brigitte Bardot. The court added that only the private person can determine the limits of what can be published about their intimate life, as well as the circumstances and conditions of this publication.[49] Judges have usually given consent a strict interpretation. In other words, publication of elements of private life cannot be based on consent given to previous publications. For instance, in a famous case, the singer Jean Ferrat was granted damages on appeal for the publication of his real name, his address and phone number in Paris, as well as some indication of his country house. Appeal judges ruled that it did not matter that some of this information had previously been disclosed with the singer's consent. In other

[47] Private life is not accepted by judges as a means to protect professional life. In certain cases, however, where particulial professions abide by a code of ethics excluding publicity, such as *avocats* or doctors, judges sanction the publication of photographs of professional activity, especially when patients are involved, or the information produced is confusing and not accurate.

[48] Cour d'Appel Paris 16 mars 1955, *Marlène Dietrich c. Soc. France Dimanche* (1955) *Dalloz* 295: "Mais considérant surtout, ce qui est très important, qu'il appert des documents fournis à la cour d'appel que Marlène Diétrich n'a jamais donné la moindre autorisation à *France Dimanche* pour publier ses soi-disant souvenirs . . . considérant . . . Que les anecdotes et les récits de la vie privée, surtout ceux touchant à la vie intime, ne peuvent être écrits qu'avec le consentement de l'intéressé".

[49] Cour d'appel Paris 17 mars 1966, *La France continue et dame de Montfort c Trintignan* (1966) *Dalloz* 749: "la personne privée a seule le droit de fixer les limites de ce qui peut être publié ou non sur sa vie intime, en même temps que les circonstances et les conditions dans lesquelles ces publications peuvent intervenir". This principle was reiterated by the Cour de cassation 5 mars 1997, quoted by B Beignier, "La protection de la vie privée" in R Cabrillac, MA Frison Roche, T Revet (eds), *Droits et libertés fondamentaux* 4th edn (Dalloz, Paris, 1997) 146.

words, that prior consent did not mean that the singer had given up the right to oppose publication about his public life.[50]

However, judges might consider the previous behaviour of the person involved when deciding what sanction to impose for the breach of private life. The kindness of a singer towards the press and his previous tendency to accept or even provoke intrusions into his private life did not imply that he has given up the right to respect for his private life. In that case the judges pointed out that the singer could not obtain seizure of a magazine which published photographs of him in the company of his new fiancée because this publication was not considered to be an "unbearable breach of his intimate life".[51]

Furthermore, in recent case law, judges have tended to give a less strict interpretation of the private life of persons who, by birth or because of their function or profession, are exposed to public curiosity.[52] As a result, first instance courts have considered that giving birth, the christening of a princess's children, or a famous person's divorce cannot be protected against the press.[53]

As an exception to the protection of private life, judges have usually ruled that private facts that have become known to the public because the person has played a historical role do not form part of the person's private life any longer. This distinction was first made by the Tribunal de la Seine in 1854, in a case about the erection of a monument by A Dumas to the memory of Honoré de Balzac. His widow opposed this idea, but the court ruled that the erection of this

---

[50] Cour d'appel Paris 15 mai 1970, *Soc FEP c Epoux Tenenbaum* (1970) Dalloz 466: "Considérant que c'est fort justement que les premiers juges ont fait observer qu'il importait peu que certains renseignements ou clichés eussent antérieurement été divulgués dans la presse, même avec l'accord de l'intéressé, dès lors que la société FEP ne justifiait pas avoir obtenu de lui une autorisation expresse et spéciale pour faire paraître l'article litigieux . . . ; que ce n'est pas, en effet, parce que Jean Ferrat avait autorisé expressément ou tacitement les publications antérieures qu'il avait ce faisant renoncé au droit de s'opposer à toute publication ultérieure".

[51] Cour d'appel Paris 14 ch 21 décembre 1970, *Société SFP c. Muraccioli dit Antoine* (1971) II *Jurisclasseur Périodique* 16653.

[52] Tribunal de Grande Instance de Nanterre, 13 janvier 1997: "les limites de la protection de la vie privée, lorsqu'elles s'appliquent au profit d'une personne que sa naissance ou encore les fonctions ou la profession qu'elle a accepté d'exercer exposent à la notoriété et donc à la curiosité du public, ne peuvent s'apprécier aussi strictement que lorsqu'il s'agit d'un citouen anonyme éloigné des médias par son mode devie." Quoted by C. Bigot, Avocat, *Protection des droits de la personnalité et liberté de l'information* (1998) *Dalloz* chr 238

[53] See C Bigot, n 52 above.

monument was a public homage and the expression of public admiration for a man who had honoured his country.[54] Courts have maintained this distinction since then and have usually based it on the need to research and write history.[55] However, judges do not accept that history is a justification for the violation of private life when the person has just died.[56]

Following a similar logic, persons who have been involved in judicial proceedings can not claim that the facts revealed in these circumstances belong to their private life. For instance famous swindlers, such as Papillon or Stavinsky, could not oppose the publication of a book or a film about their past behaviour.[57] However, courts protect the private life of less famous people who have been at the centre of judicial proceedings.[58] Even if cases are usually published, courts have found, for instance, that disclosure of the divorce of a famous actor is a breach of his private life or that a specialised periodical, when reporting a divorce case involving details of the claimant's sexual conduct, should not reveal his identity.[59]

---

[54] Tribunal de la Seine 3 mai 1854, quoted in R Lindon, *La création prétorienne en matière des droits de la personnalité et son incidence en matière de famille* (Dalloz, Paris, 1974) 15. See also Cour d'appel Paris 39 juin 1961 (1962) *Dalloz* 208: "L'oeuvre de l'historien bat en brèche le secret de la vie privée de ses personnages."

[55] See R Lindon, n 59 above, Tribunal de Grande Instance Paris 17 ch 13 janvier 1997 (1997) *Dalloz* 255.

[56] The first instance court decided that the publication of the photograph of the former President on his deathbed could not be justified by history. Tribunal de Grande Instance Paris 13 janvier 1997 (1997) Dalloz 255.

[57] Generally, see H Blin, "Publication des décisions de justice et atteinte à l'intimité de la vie privée" (1972) *Jurisclasseur Périodique* I, 2470. Also see Tribunal de Grande Instance de Paris, réf 27 Février 1970, *Charrière dit Papillon c Ménager et autres* (1970) II *Jurisclasseur Périodique* 16293 and Tribunal de Grande instance de Grasse réf 22 mai 1974, *Stavisky c Belmondo* (1974) *Dalloz* 571.

[58] The Art 9–1 of the civil code also protects the presumption of innocence against publication assuming the culpability of the person involved. An injunction can than be obtained from the judge and a notice has to be inserted in the publication. Cour de cassation 1 civ, 6 mars 1996, *Bulletin civ*, I, No 123.

[59] In one case in particular, judges were very sympathetic to a hairdresser divorced by his wife because, among other things, he kept insisting on having sexual relations with her. The hairdresser, who worked in a small provincial town, nonetheless obtained from the judge an order that his identity should not be revealed in the case report, (1972) I *Jurisclasseur Périodique* 2470. Case reports are usually careful to mention only the initials of people involved when matters become too private, despite the fact that the identity of the person involved can be obvious and that it can be relevant to the case.

Over the past couple of years, first instance and appeal courts have ruled that important current cases can be reported by journalists despite the fact that they concern very private matters (such as a criminal case about a person infected with the HIV virus). Judges, however seem to allow this publication only for cases decided in public hearings. Moreover, photographs of the parties can be published to illustrate an article related to a particular case, as long as they do not breach the private life of the person involved and the person was aware of being photographed.[60]

Finally, information related to personal wealth is considered by courts as being an element of private life.[61] However, since the early 1990s the Cour de cassation has developed a strict interpretation of the disclosure of personal wealth of persons influencing economic life. In 1993, it confirmed that the disclosure of information on personal wealth, in the absence of indications about life or personality, is not a breach of private life. The court specified that there is no breach of private life when the publication only contains information on wealth and does not contain any allusion to the life or the personality of the person involved[62]. Wealth is also becoming one of the few accepted restrictions on politicians' private life.

The Private Life of Politicians

The private life of politicians is protected by the courts as much as anybody else's.[63] Publication of photographs of politicians is based on their implicit consent, but the "right to their own image" has been used by courts to provide protection against commercial use of the

[60] Most of these cases have not been reported. They are mentioned by C Bigot, *Protection des droits de la personnalité et liberté de l'information* (1998) *Dalloz* chr 236.

[61] Cour de cassation 1 civ, 12 octobre 1976, *Bulletin civ*, I, No 292.

[62] Cour de cassation 1 civ, 20 octobre 1993, *SA Groupe Expansion c Bich et autre* (1994) Dalloz 594: "Attendu que pour accueillir ces demandes la cour d'appel (CA Amiens 9 septembre 1991), statuant sur renvoi après cassation, a énoncé que la fortune personnelle est un élément de la vie privée et qu'elle ne peut être portée à la connaissane du public;—attendu qu'en se déterminant ainsi, alors que la publication de renseignements d'ordre purement patrimonial, exclusifs de toute allusion à la vie privée et à la personnalité des intéressés, ne porte pas atteinte l'intimité de leur vie privée la cour d'appel a violé le texte sus-visé [Art 9]."

[63] The private life of politicians is usually of less interest for the French press than it can be in anglo–saxon countries.

image of the President of the Republic.[64] The private life of politicians is only regulated by the common principles of the protection
of private life.[65]

However, legal commentators have repeatedly expressed the need
for a lesser protection of some aspects of politicians' private life. In
1974, R Lindon, one of the main writers on private life, in his anno-
tation of two particularly strange cases on the private life of politicians, noted that some elements could be disclosed to the extent that
they reveal attitudes incompatible with the politician's claimed political doctrine.[66] Some authors express the more extreme view that
politicians should be completely transparent, following the anglo-
saxon tradition.[67] More recently, some authors have noted that the
particular function of politicians gives rise to a legitimate interest for
citizens to be informed about their representatives' private life, and in
particular on their wealth and the use they make of public funds.[68]

[64] Tribunal de Grande Instance, Paris, réf 4 avril 1970, *Georges Pompidou c l'Express* (1970)
II *Jurisclasseur Périodique* 1328. Against the use of the photograph of G Pompidou in a motor-
boat as an advertisement.

[65] The Act of 1881 on the press contains a special provision related to causing offence to
President of the Republic (and other foreign heads of state). Charles De Gaulle, who often felt
offended by the publication of his image, used this provision fairly frequently. For instance see:
Cour de cassation, crim 5 avril 1965 (cartoon), (115) *Bulletin*, Cour de cassation crim 31 mai
1965 (despising expression), (1965) *Dalloz* 645, Cour de cassation crim 21 décembre 1966
(photomontage) (1967) *Dalloz* somm 15, Cour de cassation, crim 12 avril 1967 (defamation),
(1967) *Dalloz* 372. Quoted by G Lebreton, *Libertés publiques et droits de l'Homme*, 3rd edn
(Armand Colin, Place, 1997) 395. However, this provision has not been used since then.

[66] R. Lindon, case note of Tribunal de Grande Instance de Paris, 2 mai and 25 avril 1974,
(1974) Dalloz 697. These two cases were decided in the context of the political campaign for
the presidency of the Republic in 1974. In the first case, the court ordered the seizure of a
pseudo personal diary of Georges Marchais, revealing that he had been a voluntary worker in
Germany during the Second World War, on the basis that it was an "unbearable breach of
intimate private life". In the second case, the court ordered the seizure of a fake journal from
the following year, publishing an article criticising the catastrophic results of the election of
F Mitterrand to the presidency of the Republic. Protection was granted to the candidate
Mitterrand on legal grounds that are not clearly identifiable.

[67] JM Cotteret and C Emeri, "Vie privée des hommes politiques" in *Mélanges offerts à
J. Ellul* (PUF, Paris, 1983) 674: "à l'évidence, l'homme politique doit être nu, transparent.
Aucun de ses faits et gestes, voire ses pensées n'échappe au contrôle social. On constate ce point
de vue remarquablement exprimé dans la tradition anglo-saxonne."

[68] P Kayser expresses this wish in his casenote under Cour de cassation 28 mai 1991, (1991)
Dalloz 216: "Le droit au respect de la vie privée comporte une limitation qui est imposée par
le caractère de leurs fonctions. La liberté d'information et le droit à l'information du public
n'ont pas seulement pour objet leurs activités publiques: ils s'étendent à leur vie privée quand

Currently, certain aspects of politicians' private life can be legally disclosed to the public. In particular, the Electoral Code requires that all candidates publish details of their private fortunes, before the elections. At the end of their mandates, they also have to produce a similar declaration.[69]

Moreover, the health of Presidents of the Republic is usually disclosed to the public following political practice since the presidency of Georges Pompidou. François Mitterrand decided to follow this practice during his two mandates.[70] Nevertheless, in 1998 the Cour de cassation confirmed the prohibition of a book related to the health of the president. This book, written by the president's personal doctor, describing his disease and was published almost immediately after his death. In this case, the protection of medical secrecy, the confidence of the patient in his doctor and the relatives' concern were given priority by the judges over the possible implications of the disease on the president's performance of his duties.[71]

Protection of Private Life of the Dead

The first example of protection of private life by a court is the ruling of the Tribunal de la Seine in 1858 that declared that the right to oppose the publication of a portrait of the famous actress, Rachel, on her deathbed, was absolute. It was grounded on the principle of the respect for the grief of the family and that its breach would hurt the most intimate and the most respectable and natural feelings and

---

celle-ci porte atteinte à l'intérêt général. . . . Cette limitation de la vie privée s'étend à leur patrimoine. La presse peut divulguer l'enrichissement de leur patrimoine qui a une origine illicite. Leur droit au respect de la vie privée a un contenu plus restreint que celui des autres hommes, mais cette inégalité est justifiée à la fois par le caractère de leurs fonctions et par l'intérêt du public."

[69] The loi organique No 88–226 of 11 mars 1988 on the financial transparency of political life applies to the President of the Republic and the MPs. A similar statute applies to members of government, members of Consel régional, members of Conseil général and mayors of communes inhabited by more than 30,000 persons.

[70] It appeared later that François Mitterrand had given a flexible interpretation to this practice. He did publish regularly information on his health but did not seem to consider that this information had to be absolutely accurate.

[71] Case quoted and criticised by P Wachsmann, *Libertés publiques* 2nd edn (Dalloz, Paris, 1998) 382. Cour de cassation 16 juillet 1997, (1997) III *Légipresse* 137.

domestic piety.[72] Since then, the notion of private life has been developed and inserted into the theoretical frame of personality rights, that is, rights which cannot be seized, given up, transmitted or acquired or lost by prescription.

As a result, the protection of the private life of the dead raises at least two questions. The first is about the immediate contradiction in terms when the notion of private life applies to dead persons. The second question is that since obviously the dead person cannot act, on which legal grounds can the relatives act for the protection of the dead, considering that the right to private life cannot be transmitted?

Legal commentators, in general, do not recognise the existence of a posthumous right to private life. Judges, however, have granted protection against the unauthorised publication of a photograph of a dead person. In particular, in 1977, first instance judges ordered the seizure of the magazine *Paris Match* that had published the photograph of the actor Jean Gabin on his deathbed.[73] This case was confirmed by the Cour de cassation, reasoning not on the basis of Article 9 of the Code Civil, but on Article 368 of the old criminal code.[74] The same magazine, however, disregarding this ruling, published twenty years later, in similar circumstances, the photograph of the President of the Republic on his deathbed. His widow and children acted on the basis of Article 226–6 of the Nouveau Code Pénal. The Cour de cassation interpreted this provision as meaning that taking a photograph of a person's mortal remains was definitely a breach of the "right to private life of others" as well as a breach of the respect due to the human person, dead or alive.[75] In this ruling, the court is

---

[72] Tribunal civil de la Seine, 16 juin 1858, (1858) 3 DP 62. Quoted by R Lindon, *La création prétorienne en matière de droits de la personnalité et son incidence sur la notion de famille* (Dalloz, Paris, 1974) 10.

[73] Tribunal de Grande Instance de Paris réf 11 janvier 1977 (1977) II *Jurisclasseur Périodique* 18711 with a case note by D Ferrier.

[74] Cour de cassation crim, 21 octobre 1980 (1981) *Dalloz* 72: "attendu en effet que la fixation de l'image d'une personne vivante ou morte, est prohibée sans autrisation préalable des personnes ayant pouvoir de l'accorder et que la diffusion et la publication de ladite image sans autorisation entre nécessairement dans le champ d'application des articles précités [Art 368, 369, 370 Code pénal]".

[75] Cour de cassation crim. 20 octobre 1998, (1998) II *Jurisclasseur Périodique* 10 044, annotated by G Loiseau: "Attendu que . . . les juges . . . énoncent que le fait de prendre des photographies d'une dépouille mortelle porte incontestablement atteinte à la vie privée d'autrui, le respect étant dû à la personne humaine, qu'elle soit morte ou vivante, et quel que

vague as to determining whose private life is protected, but it does not explicitly disagree with the *Jean Gabin* ruling. Instead of this, the court seems to emphasise the importance of the respect due to a human person, dead or alive.[76] As a result, it seems that a better protection of "posthumous private life" is granted under the new criminal code than under Article 9 of the Code Civil according to which following case law, the protection of private life cannot be transmitted to heirs.

JUDICIAL REMEDIES

Very generally, the civil judge is in charge of the protection of private life. Article 9 of the Code Civil made "emergency interim proceedings" (*référé*) available for the protection of breaches of intimate private life and as a result reinforced the trend to use such proceedings more frequently. This emergency remedy allows a single judge (the president of the court) to order a measure to prevent or to stop the breach of private life. These measures can be executed within a few hours. Largely, and theoretically, these rulings (*ordonnance de référé*) cannot bind a subsequent examination of the merits of the case. Finally, the requirement of "urgency" is assessed by judges and depends largely on the thought that only a particular measure ordered through this remedy can prevent or stop the damage.

Before the Act of 1970, the protection of private life was developed on the basis of "delictual liability". This principle is set out in Article 1382 of the Code Civil and it reads:

---

soit son statut." This case confirms the appeal ruling, Cour appel 11 ch 2 juillet 1997, (1997) *Dalloz* 596, annotated by B Beignier, and the first instance ruling, Tribunal de Grande Instance, Paris, 17 ch 13 Janvier 1997, (1997) *Dalloz* 255, annotated by B Beignier.

[76] In an earlier case the same year, the Cour d'appel followed the *Rachel* ruling to decide that the publication of a photograph of the "préfet" of Corsica lying in the street immediately after his assassination was a breach of private life. The publication of photographs "au cours de la période de deuil des proches parents de Claude Erignac, constitue, dès lors qu'elle n'a pas reçu l'assentiment de ceux-ci, une profonde atteinte à leurs sentiments d'affliction, partant à l'intimité de leur vie privée." Cour appel Paris 24 Février 1998, (1998) *Dalloz* 225, annotated by B Beignier.

Any human deed whatsoever which causes harm to another creates an obligation in the person by whose fault it was caused to compensate it.

In order to obtain damages for a breach of their private life, plaintiffs had to prove that the damage suffered was caused by the wrongful behaviour of somebody else. For private-life-related breaches, judges have developed a fairly flexible interpretation of this principle. They have usually admitted that the causal link between the wrongful behaviour and resulting harm was obvious. Furthermore, they have usually ruled that the breach of private life related interests consisted solely in the disclosure to the public. Finally, the notion of damage was interpreted fairly broadly so as to include "moral damage" as well as physical or financial damage.[78] Judges could then grant damages by way of compensation, the amount of which they were free to determine on the basis of the particular circumstances of the case (*appréciation souveraine des juges du fond*).

The novelty of the Act of 1970 was to suppress the requirement of a particular harm, that is the breach of private life *per se* could be compensated in the form of the allowance of a certain amount of money. Furthermore, Article 9 of the Code Civil made the prevention of breaches of private life possible in specific circumstances, namely, an urgent situation and a breach of "intimate private life". Following Article 9, a single judge can then take different sorts of measures to stop or to prevent the breach. Two of the most drastic measures are listed in Article 9: sequestration and seizure. As in most cases plaintiffs prefer to prevent or stop a breach to their "intimate private life" happening, the emergency remedy has become the general remedy for the protection of private life, as opposed to normal procedures where judges award damages after the breach has happened.

This trend was reinforced by the existence of another emergency remedy applicable very generally under Article 809 of the Nouveau

---

[78] A breach of private life almost never materialises in the form of physical damage. Financial damage, however, has very often been the support for a breach of the "right to one's own image". This trend was criticised by legal commentators and in particular by R Lindon, n 72 above. Recent commentators, however, have accepted that the "right to one's own image" could have these two aspects.

was confirmed by the phrasing of Article 9 in 1970 that made the distinction between "private life" and "intimate private life".

Early case law did not refer to freedom of expression, focussing instead on the need to protect private life. The *Jean Ferrat* case, decided shortly before the Act was adopted, ruled that if the right to freedom of expression was certain, it was limited the right to respect for private life.[86] After the Act of 1970, judges have started emphasising the importance of freedom of expression. More specifically, when judges are asked to order particularly drastic measures against freedom of expression, such as seizure, they are particularly careful in assessing the breach of private life. They regularly stress the exceptional gravity of seizure that can breach the right to freedom of expression or freedom of information.[87] Since then, they have also applied this reasoning to lesser restrictions on freedom of expression, such as the suppression of contested parts of a book that can constitute a real censorship and noted that freedom of expression is a fundamental principle.[88]

The Requirement of an "Unbearable Breach" of Private Life

Before restricting freedom of expression by emergency measures protecting private life, judges have required that the breach of private life be of an "unbearable degree" (*caractère intolérable*) or constitute an "unbearable interference" (*immixtion intolérable*) with private life. For instance, in a case where the famous singer Antoine required the immediate seizure of a magazine that had published photographs of him with his new fiancée, he could only obtain a limited seizure. Judges did not find that there was such an unbearable interference

---

[86] Cour d'appel 15 mai 1970 *Soc FEP c Epoux Tenenbaum* (1970) *Dalloz* 446: "Considérant que si le droit à la liberté d'expression est certain, il n'est pas sans limite et ne peut s'exercer qu'à la condition de ne porter atteinte au droit au respect à la vie privée".

[87] Cour d'appel Paris, 14 ch 21 décembre 1970 *Sté France Editions et Publications c Muraccioli dit Antoine* (1971) II *Jurisclasseur Périodique* 16653: "Considérant . . . que la saisie d'une oeuvre de l'esprit, mesure d'une exceptionnelle gravité, pouvant léser le droit à la liberté d'expression et d'information, doit être envisagée avec circonspection".

[88] Cour d'appel 14 ch 14 mai 1975 *SARL Editions J-Cl Lattès et J Baynac c cons Cance* (1975) *Dalloz* 688: "Considérant, cependant, que le séquestre ou la saisie d'une publication ou encore la suppression de certains passages d'une publication, assimilable à une véritable censure, ne peuvent être ordonnées qu'avec une grande circonspection, ces mesures aboutissant nécessairement à infléchir *le principe fondamental de la liberté de la presse*." (emphasis added).

with his private life because the singer very often let the press report it.[89] By contrast, in relation to another singer, Jean Ferrat, appeal judges ruled that the publication by the press of photographs and his phone number and address were an "inopportune interference". In this case, despite the fact that some of the information had already been disclosed, judges noted that the journalist was aware that the singer and his wife "were hiding well", led a normal life and refused to behave like other singers.[90] When the publication of private information affects a child, judges have usually found that there was an "unbearable breach" of private life. In one of the very first cases (1965) on private life, judges ruled that the publication of photographs of a famous actor's son on his hospital bed was an "unbearable interference" with private life. As a result, they ordered the seizure of all copies of the magazine in question.[91] By contrast, judges ruled in the *Papillon* case that there was no such unbearable breach of private life of the famous swindler Papillon because the facts published in the contested book had already been legally disclosed.[92]

The Breach of "Intimate Private Life" under the 1970 Act

The Act of 1970 introduced the requirement of a breach of "intimate private life" before judges could order seizures or sequestration. "Intimate private life" was clearly understood as meaning a more restrictive aspect of private life.[93] Judges, however, do not seem to

---

[89] Cour d'Appel Paris, 21 décembre 1970, *Sté Editions et Publications* c *Muraccioli dit Antoine* (1971) II *Jurisclasseur Périodique* 16653, n 87 above.

[90] *Jean Ferrat*, n 86 above.

[91] Cour d'appel Paris 13 mars 1965: the fact that several photographers came "dans la chambre d'hôpital où se trouvait l'enfant d'un acteur célèbre qui n'avaient pas hésité, malgré sa frayeur et ses protestations, à prendre des clichés' as well as 'la reproduction, dans un but purement commercial, de clichés non autorisés et les indications données sur l'état de santé réel ou supposé du mineur ainsi que les soins dont il fait l'objet constituent une immixtion intolérable dans la vie privée de la famille de l'intéressé."

[92] Tribunal de Grande Instance Paris, réf 27 février 1970, *Charrière dit Papillon c. Ménager et autre* (1970) II Jurisclasseur Périodique 16293: "Attendu qu'en l'espèce, le caractère intolérable de l'atteinte ne se justifie pas puisque l'ouvrage de Ménager est, . . . 'presqu'exclusivement' composé de documents extraits du dossier de l'information judiciaire qui a été suivie contre Charrière en 1930, que ces documents ont donné lieu devant la cour d'assise à des débats publics, que les faits qu'ils relatent ont donc été légalement révélés."

[93] In the parliamentary debates the Garde des Sceaux made clear that: "il s'agit par cet article de résoudre équitablement pour tous le conflit latent entre le droit à l'information et le

find this notion easier to apply. Consequently, they have tended to interpret it in reference to the seriousness of the interference with private life as they had done before. In an attempt to clarify the notion of intimacy, judges have also tended to link it to the notion of secrecy. For example, first instance judges ruled in 1974 that the breach of intimate private life implied that the facts disclosed had a certain character of secrecy.[94] According to an appeal ruling of 1995, the disclosure of the contents of a dustbin on the day after Christmas is definitely a breach of "intimate private life".[95]

On other occasions, judges have used the criteria of "intimate life" and "unbearable breach" simultaneously. For instance, in 1974, a court ordered the seizure of magazines publishing information about the alleged affair of Alain Delon with his baby sitter on the basis that it was an "unbearable breach to the intimate private life". In support of this ruling, the court noted, in particular, that the ten-year-old son of Delon was becoming curious about publications concerning his father.[96]

It soon became apparent, that there was a risk in basing restrictions to freedom of expression on purely subjective grounds. Indeed, judges very often considered the feelings of the applicants, in particular in cases related to the publication of photographs of loved ones. In this respect, the notion of "intimate private life" might be understood as

respect de la vie privée, on ne doit pas risquer de porter atteinte au principe de la liberté de la presse. Aussi, le projet de loi tend-il à fixer une limite au domaine de la vie privée, objet de la protection légale, en précisant que seules les atteintes à l'intimité de la vie privée seraient sanctionnées sur le plan civil ou sur le plan pénal. Cette notion d'intimité devra, évidemment être appréciée par les tribunaux qui auront à appliquer le texte, mais elle marque, d'ores et déjà, une restriction par rapport à celle de la vie privée employée sans autre précision." *Journal Officiel, Débats parlementaires,* 1970, 2068.

[94] Tribunal de Grande Instance Marseille 18 Janvier 1974, (1974) 1 *Gazette du Palais* 282. Judges noted that Art 9§2 tends to "protéger, non la vie privée, mais d'une façon plus restrictive, l'atteinte à l'intimité de la vie privée, ce qui suppose que les faits doivent avoir un certain caractère secret."

[95] Cour d'appel Paris 30 mars 1995 (1995) *Dalloz* IR, 140: "Le fait que des objets aient été jetés en vue de leur destruction implique nécessairement le refus par leur propriétaire de les présenter à la presse. Dès lors, un hebdomadaire porte incontestablement atteinte à l'intimité de la vie privée d'une personnalité en dressant l'inventaire de ses poubelles au lendemain du réveillon de Noel et du jour de l'An et en montrant à ses lecteurs les bas qu'elle portait, les médicaments qu'elle prenait, les dessins effectués par ses enfants pour elle-même ou ses amis, ainsi que les menus qu'elle préparait."

[96] Tribunal de Grande Instance Paris réf 28 juin 1974, *Alain Delon et Mireille Darc c Soc, France Editions Publications* (1974) *Dalloz* 751.

an improvement on "unbearable breach". That is, whereas the latter is almost based exclusively on the subjective perception of the breach of an individual's private life, the former could be understood as being more objective, ie easier to assess for judges. More importantly, before 1970, the Cour de cassation did not control the legality of the "unbearable interference with private life" because it belonged to the merits of the case, which by definition the Cour de cassation never examines.[97] After the 1970 Act, the Cour de cassation could extend its control to the notion of "intimate private life" because it is from then on a legal notion.[98]

As a result, in a ruling of 1980, the Cour de cassation endeavoured to make the assessment of private life more objective, in the sense that it should be based on facts rather than feelings. This case arose after the murder of a young girl, whose murderer was subsequently sentenced to death. Following these events, a film was made about the whole story. The appeal court had ordered the suppression of four scenes of this film on the basis that they were a breach of the "intimate private life" of the parents even though the facts of this sad story had been widely debated in the media at the time. The appeal court based its decision on the grounds that the scenes represented with the strength particular to the cinema the behaviour of the parents and the expression of their feelings of profound grief.[99] The case went before the Cour de cassation which ruled that the disclosure of the parents' feelings did not qualify as a breach of the "intimate private life".[100] This case was subsequently heard by another appeal court that ruled that only one of the four contested scenes was a breach of private life: the scene representing the parents' grief when they were told about their daughter's death.[101] On a different matter,

---

[97] It may be recalled here that the Cour de cassation, which intervenes after the ruling of an appeal court, only controls the legality of the appeal decision and does not consider the facts, nor the merits of the case for which only first instance and appeal judges are competent. This is sometimes expressed by the distinction between "juge du fond" (on the merits), as opposition to the Cour de cassation that only rules on the interpretation of the law ("juge du droit").

[98] Cour de cassation 2 civ 14 novembre 1975 (1976) *Dalloz* 421.

[99] Cour d'appel Paris 9 Novembre 1979 (1981) *Dalloz* 109.

[100] Cour de cassation 1 ch civ 3 décembre 1980 (1981) *Dalloz* 221, annotated by B Edelman.

[101] The court ruled that: "en donnant de la sorte un spectacle la douleur des époux R, MD heurtait chez ceux-ci un sentiment de pudeur morale élémentaire qui appartient à ce qu'il y a de plus intime chez tout individu, qu'il était donc tenu de soumettre à leur accord la réalisation de semblables séquences, dès lors qu'elles étaient, ainsi que la cour a été en mesure de

the Cour de cassation decided in 1993 that a television film representing mentally disabled persons in their every day life inside the establishment where they lived was a breach of their "intimate private life".[102] In so doing, the Cour de cassation considered the elements of this breach and confirmed the appeal ruling.

The Cour de cassation, however, does not assess the amount of damages, it only checks the legal arguments used by a judge to refuse or to grant a particular measure for the protection of private life.[103]

The Use of Article 10 of the ECHR in Support of the 1881 Act

Finally, it must be noted that judges rarely refer to the 1881 Act on the press when they adjudicate on breaches of private life. Instead, they seem to prefer to use the *principle* of freedom of expression. In some cases, they have considered how the right to freedom of expression was exercised and whether the elements disclosed really contributed to the information of the public or were driven by other considerations, such as financial gains.[104] This is an element put forward by courts, in particular, in cases concerning the publication of mortal remains of famous persons. In the *Jean Gabin* case, the court ruled that by the journal had exceeded its duty of information and that the breach of private life could not be justified by the necessity of journalism.[105] More recently, a similar argument was used in the *Mitterrand* case and confirmed by the appeal court.[106] In the *Erignac* case about the publication of photographs of the assassinated

---

le constater, sans réelle utilité pour la compréhension de l'affaire." Cour d'appel Paris 1 ch 6 octobre 1982, (1983) *Dalloz* 186.

[102] Cour de cassation 1 civ, 24 février 1993: "La reproduction d'images représentant des handicappés mentaux dans l'intimité de leur existence quotidienne à l'intérieur del'établissement où ils vivent, et ce, sans l'autorisation de leurs représentants légaux, constitue une atteinte illicite à l'intimité de leur vie privée."

[103] Cour de cassation 1 civ 17 novembre 1987, *Bulletin civ*, I, No 301.

[104] In the *Jean Ferrat* case, the court seemed to be concerned that: "la liberté de presse et le droit du public à l'information qui en est le corollaire ne sauraient justifier, même pour satisfaire une clientèle de plus en plus avide d'informations sensationnelles ou dans un esprit de lucre, des atteintes de plus en plus fréquentes au droit de chacun à la paix et la tranquillité." Cour d'appel Paris 15 mai 1970 (1970) *Dalloz* 466.

[105] Tribunal de Grande Instance Paris réf 11 janvier 1977 (1977) II *Jurisclasseur Périodique* 18711.

[106] Cour d'appel Paris 11 ch 2 juillet 1997 (1997) *Dalloz* 597.

préfet of Corsica, the appeal court explicitly referred to Article 10 of the ECHR and to Article 11 of the Declaration of 1789. In doing so the court might seek to reinforce the importance of freedom of expression by referring to norms with a higher rank than Article 9 of the Code Civil. However, appeal judges found that restrictions of freedom of expression under Article 9 complied with these provisions. At the same time, they ruled that the seizure required by the relatives could not stop the breach to the "intimate private life". As a result, they confirmed that the publication of a notice was sufficient to redress the harm suffered by the relatives.[107] It might be recalled here that, on the basis of the criminal code, the relatives of the former President of the Republic had obtained a seizure in a similar situation, that is, against the publication of the photograph of the deceased.

Finally, freedom of expression has also been limited on the sole basis of Article 1382.[108] Usually, first instance and appeal judges have interpreted freedom of expression in a fairly extensive manner, that is, they have considered that the wrongful behaviour under Article 1382 of the Code Civil had to be particularly serious to allow a restriction of freedom of the press. For instance, the appeal court had not found that erotic photographs of young men dressed in the scouts uniforms published by the magazine *New Look* could justify a restriction to freedom of expression. In this case, appeal judges referred to Article 11 of the Declaration of 1789 as well as to the Universal Declaration of Human Rights and ruled that Article 1382 could only be used in cases where the publication breaches fundamental rights of the person. The Cour de cassation, however, did not accept this restrictive interpretation and ruled that Article 1382 had to be normally interpreted in cases involving freedom of expression.[109] The appeal court that subsequently examined the case

---

[107] Cour d'appel Paris 1 ch A 24 février 1998 (1998) *Dalloz* 225: "Considérant, en droit, que selon l'art. 11 de la Déclaration des Droits de l'Homme et du Citoyen de 1789, tout citoyen peut écrire, imprimer librement sauf à répondre de l'abus de cette liberté dans les cas déterminés par la loi; qu'il résulte des dispositions de l'article 10 de la CEDH que l'exercice du droit à la liberté d'expression peut être soumis à certaines sanctions qui constituent des mesures nécessaires, dans une société démocractique, à la protection des droits d'autrui; qu'institue une sanction satisfaisant aux exigences des dispositions précitées l'art 9 al 2 du code civil."

[108] See on this matter, J Carbonnier, *Le silence et la gloire* (Dalloz, Paris, 1951) ch X, 119.

[109] Cour de cassation 2 civ, 5 mai 1993 (1994) *Dalloz* Som 193.

followed the Cour de cassation and ruled that the magazine had to redress the "moral damage" suffered by the scouts associations.[110] This ruling seems to encourage the tendency that anyone disturbed by the publication of information and image can obtain a measure restricting freedom of expression in cases where there is no breach of their private life nor a particular "press offence" under the 1881 Act.

CONCLUSION

The case law on breaches of private life through the media concerns only a few people who, moreover, are usually involved in (Parisian) public life.[111] Despite this, judges have always sought to protect private life in an efficient and appropriate manner. In this respect, the 1970 Act has probably been of little support to them since it lacked a definition of private life. As a result, courts have kept using their traditional approach, under the control of the Cour de cassation that has sought to rationalise their efforts.

The extent of restrictions to freedom of expression varies according to the remedy used by claimants and judges. It is very small under the specific "press offences" under the 1881 Act and it is also limited by case law under Article 9 of the Code Civil to particularly serious breaches of private life. By contrast, and following recent case law, it is much wider under the sole ground of Article 1382 of the Code Civil. Conversely, the protection of private life varies according to the type of remedy used by judges. Article 9 of the Code Civil allows an efficient protection, ie the seizure of the contested publication, for "unbearable breaches" of private life or for breaches of the "intimate private life". Article 1382 provides a wider protection of private life in that it protects private life-related aspects such as image, honour and reputation. Finally, criminal law protects the human person after death against publication of photographs of the deceased whereas Article 9 of the Code Civil does not.

The differences between these systems of protections of private life have led to a paradoxical situation. Some minor aspects of private life, in the sense that they involve very few people and do not affect

---

[110] Cour d'appel Versailles ch civ réun 17 mai 1995 (1997) *Dalloz* Som, 73.
[111] B Beignier, "La protection de la vie privée", n 49 above, 160.

very private elements of life, or rather, death are extremely well protected by the criminal code. At the same time, the Conseil constitutionnel did not find that the use of a national identity number by three branches of government, ie customs, accounts and tax, for the purpose of checking identities and addresses, was a breach of the private life of tax payers.[112] This amounts to distinguishing between different aspects of private life despite the fact that a human being is essentially one person with only one (private) life.

Finally, in France the current protection of private life relies very much on principles and methods of judicial reasoning dating from the last century. Nowadays, however, the nature of information produced by the media has changed. In other words it seems to be increasingly based on financial interests, as far as information about the private life of certain persons is concerned, and probably also far beyond this matter.[113] At the same time, the intimate private life is shrinking under the intrusion of new technologies, such as video surveillance, psychological and genetic tests that are used more and more commonly.[114] All this calls into question the current definition of private life as an exception to freedom of expression. In response to this, some French authors seem to favour a more general approach to private life such as a "right to tranquillity" following the American conception.[115] Others, maybe more imaginative, suggest a "right to difference and to indifference", that might reflect better the multicultural character of current societies.[116] There is little doubt that a more appropriate definition of private life to modern times needs to be linked to an understanding of the human person that embrace more aspects of the personalityas well as activity. This new conception of human beings might already have been phrased in 1998 by the Cour de cassation that focussed on "the respect due to the human person, be it dead or alive and no matter its status".

---

[112] Conseil constitutionnel sur la loi de finance pour 1999, 29 décembre 1998.

[113] See R Kapucsinski, "Les média reflètent-ils la réalité du monde?" *Le Monde Diplomatique*, August 1999, 8–9, translated by the *Guardian Weekly* in August.

[114] See D Duclos, "La vie privée traquée par les technologies" *Le Monde Diplomatique*, August 1999, 16–17.

[115] See B Beignier, "La protection de la vie privée", n 49 above, 145.

[116] G Koubi, "Le droit à la différence, droit à l'indifférence" (1993) *Revue Trimestrielle des Droits de l'Homme* 243.

4

Protection of Privacy and Freedom of Speech in Germany

Rosalind English

INTRODUCTION

Privacy law in Germany provides a useful model for the approach to be taken by courts in the United Kingdom to Article 8 of the European Convention on Human Rights (ECHR). In the absence of an express right to privacy even under constitutional human rights law, German privacy protection has developed case by case. However there is no doubt now that German citizens enjoy a highly developed law of privacy, both in their dealings with each other and with the state, thanks to a series of landmark rulings by the Federal Constitutional Court and the Supreme Court over the years.

Before looking in detail at the judicial development of privacy law in Germany, it is worth giving a very brief outline of the hierarchy of German law, which is constitution-based. There are essentially three types of law:

—The Basic Law (Grundgesetz): this was the constitutional settlement drafted at the end of the Second World War, and its provisions are interpreted and applied by the Federal Constitutional Court (Bundesverfassungsgericht), whether the case concerns a conflict between provisions of the Basic Law, or the conflict between the Basic Law and some other law or regulation lower on the hierarchy. It is the first source for privacy in Germany.
—The Civil Code (B(rgerliches Gesetzbuch) which sets out the rights and obligations between private parties.
—The Criminal Law Code (Strafgesetzbuch).

There are also a number of Federal and State laws relating to specific activities that have played an important role in the development of privacy.

Biefly, privacy has developed in three ways:

—The Constitutional Court has interpreted the rights set out in the Basic Law to inviolability of human dignity (Article 1) and free development of the personality (Article 2) to cover interests that would generally be recognised as privacy rights (see below).

—Gradually it has become accepted that privacy interests may be included as a protected interest in the provisions in the Civil Code imposing liability for negligent or intentional infliction of harm (equivalent to the torts of negligence and trespass under English law). A constitutional right to privacy is thus fed into private law via the interpretative obligation of the court.

—For infringements of these rights, the German Courts have often granted a remedy in damages, despite the fact that the Civil Code prohibits monetary damages for immaterial loss except where expressly provided for by law.[1]

DEVELOPMENT OF PRIVACY RIGHT

Constitutional and Statutory Provisions

German courts attempted to find remedies for breaches of privacy long before the Basic Law was drafted, in much the same way as English judges have over the years extended the tort of breach of confidence beyond the protection of commercial information to cover private information with no commercial value at all (*Prince Albert v Strange* (1849) 1 Mac & G 25). In the *Bismarck* case (RG 28 December 1899) photographers intruded into the room where the corpse of Bismarck was laid out and took photographs. The Court granted Bismarck's heirs an order that all the photographic negatives and plates should be destroyed. The order was based on unjust enrichment: the defendants should be liable to make restitution of unlawfully obtained profit.

---

[1] Art 253 of the Civil Code.

However, it has been the Basic Law, drafted in 1949, with its right to dignity and development of the personality that are the main source for the case by case development of the right to privacy. The Basic Law provides that:

Article 1: The dignity of the human being is inviolable [Schutz der Menschenwürde].

and

Article 2(1): Everyone has the right to the free development of his personality, insofar as he does not injure the rights of others or violate the constitutional order or the moral law.

Since the rights set out in the Basic Law represent fundamental norms which govern all forms of adjudication, even private disputes, the privacy interests which have been fashioned from Articles 1 and 2 have come to form part of the main tort provision in the Civil Code. Article 823 of this Code provides:

I. A person who intentionally or negligently injures the life, body, health, freedom, property or other right of another unlawfully is obliged to compensate the other for the harm arising from this.

II. The same obligation applies to a person who offends against a statutory provision which has in view the protection of another.

In addition Article 826 of the Civil Code comes into play when the harm to the plaintiff's privacy interests are intentional; this imposes liability for deliberate infliction of harm *contra bonos mores*:

A person who intentionally inflicts harm on another in a manner which offends against good morals is obliged to make compensation to the other for the harm.

It is not entirely clear from the case law or the academic literature whether privacy is one of the protected interests in paragraph I of Article 283, which require absolute protection, or paragraph II, which only imposes liability in respect of acts which breach other statutory obligations.[2] In any event the distinction between paragraph I and the

---

[2] See BS Markesinis, "Privacy, Freedom of Expression and the Human Rights Bill: Lessons from Germany" (1999) LQR 115, 47 and Stoll, "The General Right to Personality in German Law: an Outline of its Development and Present Significance" in BS Markesinis (ed) *Protecting Privacy* (Clarendon Press, Oxford, 1999), 29.

more limited protection afforded by paragraph II of Article 283 shades into insignificance in reality, since German courts have had no difficulty in finding some relevant statute which has been breached in privacy cases.

So, for example, the unauthorised publication of a photograph of an individual may disclose a breach of the statute dealing with copyright or the right to artistic creations. In celebrity cases it is often argued that non-consensual publication of pictures of "figures of contemporary history" (Personen der Zeitgeschichte) is expressly permitted by section 23(I) of the Law of Artistic Creations of 1907. However section 23(II) carves out an exception: if the individual in question has a legitimate expectation that their privacy will not be invaded, for example if they are in private surroundings, the action will be tortious.

Another example is where individuals have been misrepresented by the press. Each state (Land) in the Federal Republic of Germany has a press law which gives individuals a right to reply to any allegations made against them by the press. The person affected by the publication may obtain this right to counter-publication by means of an injunction, and the newspaper is bound to publish this counterstatement in the same part of the newspaper and in the same format as that carrying the original statement.

Of particular relevance in this context are the provisions in the Criminal Code which impose criminal liability for statements of opinion and fact which degrade a person or cause him to be contemptible in public opinion (the German equivalent of our law of defamation). Because of the overlap with Article 823 II mentioned above, the criminal offence of defamation or "insult" (*Beleidigung*) is also a tort. The person injured by the statement may lay a complaint against the author of it and this will trigger a criminal prosecution. The Federal Constitutional Court has held that a public body, such as active soldiers in the Federal Army, can be collectively insulted contrary to these provisions (*Soldiers are Murderers* BverfGE 266 (1995)). This approach differs markedly from that taken by the House of Lords in *Derbyshire County Council v Times Newspapers* [1992] 3 All ER 65, which effectively prohibits such bodies from taking proceedings in defamation at all. Indeed there is a special provision in the German Criminal Code (Article 187a) imposing criminal liability for defamation of persons in political life and providing a sanction of imprisonment of three months to five years. The fact that this provision can co-exist with the constitutional guarantee of free speech is evidence that German courts are prepared to deal with the tricky issue of political defamation on a case-by-case basis, rather than adopting the absolutist position of the US Supreme Court in *New York Times v Sullivan* US (1964) 254. To a certain extent this country occupies a middle ground between the US and German position in relation to the "public figure" defence, by refusing to grant blanket qualified privilege to "political information" concerning such a figure (see the House of Lords ruling in *Reynolds v Times Newspapers* [1999] 3 WLR 1010) but only granting it where all the circumstances justify this.

Whilst these articles of the Civil Code are assisting the development of privacy rights, as previously mentioned, Article 253 sets up a potential obstacle to indemnifying the victims of privacy violations. It prevents the granting of monetary awards for immaterial loss, unless expressly provided for by law. The Constitutional Court has surmounted this difficulty by relying on its own jurisdiction under the Basic Law to set aside any statutory provisions which do not correspond to the standards required by fundamental rights; if such a provision prevents the granting of a proper remedy for an infringement of Articles 1 or 2, it must be disapplied in that case.

Out of the general personality rights spring a range of other interests, which are effectively protected as privacy rights in German law: communication of medical reports without the patient's consent—BGHZ 24, 72; recording a conversation with the speaker without his knowledge and consent—BGHZ 27, 284; the right not to have private mail opened (whether or not it is read: BGH 20 February 1990); the right not to have intimate details published about one's own core sphere of privacy life (Kernbereich), even if those details are true (BGH 20 January 1965; see the *Gretna Green* case below); the right not to be photographed without consent (BGH 19 December 1995) and the right to a fair description of one's life. The scope of this last right was explored in the *Mephisto* case (BverfGE 30, 173 (1971)), where the heir to a famous German actor who had enjoyed considerable success under the Third Reich sought an injunction to prevent the publication of a novel charting the progress of a character which was a thinly veiled and highly critical representation of the plaintiff's father. The Court granted the injunction, basing the award on posthumous protection of the personality together with Article 22 of the Law of Artistic Creations which limits the circumstances in which the likeness of a person may be represented after his death.

Privacy may also be invaded by the publication of a completely fabricated interview, which in Basic Law terms is apt to restrict the plaintiff's freedom of social activity, and thus their personality contrary to Articles 1 and 2: the *Soraya* decision of 8 December 1994 (BGH; see p X below) and the *Caroline III* decision (BGH 15 November 1994; see p X below) are examples of this.

Case Law

As mentioned previously, the German courts were keen to find remedies for privacy breaches long before the Basic Law was drafted with its rights to dignity and development of the personality under Articles 1 and 2. It took only five years for the Federal Constitutional Court to apply these general personality rights to a situation which really concerned misrepresentation rather than breach of privacy (the cause of action under English law would be defamation by innuendo). However, this interpretation of the Basic Law provided fertile ground for a more direct application of personality rights to privacy cases in later years.

In *Schacht* (BGHZ 13, 334; BGH 25 May 1954) the lawyer plaintiff, acting on behalf of his client, the banker Dr Schacht, wrote a letter to a newspaper which had published a critical article about him, requesting the newspaper to publish a correction under his client's statutory right to reply. Instead of doing so the newspaper published a shortened and therefore distorted version of the plaintiff's letter in their letters column. The reproduction of this letter in this manner misrepresented the plaintiff in that it appeared to set out a mere expression of the opinion of a reader in relation to the preceding article about Schacht. Having failed to base his action on the provisions in the Criminal Code dealing with criminal defamation (see above),[3] the plaintiff complained that this was a violation of his personality (*Verletzung seiner Persönlichkeitsrechte*):

---

[3] The court below held that he had not been made contemptible in the eyes of the public by the publication.

in principle the authority to decide whether and in what form his writings are made accessible to the public belongs to the author alone; because every publication of the writings of a human being who is still alive which occurs under his name is correctly inferred by the general public to come from a corresponding direction of the will of the author . . . whilst an *unapproved* publication of private writings, as a rule, represents an impermissible encroachment into the protected private sphere (geschützte Geheimsphäre) of any human being, an *altered* reproduction of the writings violates the proper sphere of the legal personality (die persönlichkeitsrechte Eigensphäre) of the author.

It should be noted that the first type of unauthorised publication defined by the court in this case would in some circumstances be protected by the law of confidence under English law; the second may, again depending on the circumstances, be protected by defamation or copyright. In the German decision, the publishers were ordered to remedy the violation of the plaintiff's personality by publishing an article retracting the innuendo that the plaintiff had sent in a letter expressing his personal opinion. That protection of personality rights should cover misreprestation by misquotation was affirmed in the *Böll* case in 1975 (BverGe 34, 281) when the Constitutional Court awarded the author Heinrich Böll damages against a newspaper which attributed words to him that he had never spoken. Such misquotation, said the court "impairs [the speaker's] self-defined claim to social recognition."

Having thus opened an avenue for the application of constitutional rights in the private sphere (the newspaper after all was not an emanation of the state) the Federal Constitutional Court had given the green light to the lower courts to do the same; three years after *Schacht* came another landmark decision, the *Gentleman Rider* case. Here the plaintiff successfully argued in the Supreme Court that the unauthorised publication of his photograph in an advertisement for a drug which had claimed powers for increasing sexual potency violated his general personality rights under the Basic Law. Having upheld this claim, the Court proceeded to find that the defendant was liable in damages under the second paragraph of Article 823 of the Civil Code together with the Act on Artistic Creations (breach of the plaintiff's right to deal with his own portrait). Thus the Court had circumvented the prohibition on damages for immaterial injury set out in Article 823 of the Code (see above). They found the solution in Article 847 of the Code which allows equitable compensation in money for non-pecuniary loss in cases of "deprivation of liberty".

This line of reasoning provides a very clear example of the retrospective effect of the the Basic Law. The nineteenth century drafters of the Civil Code clearly had in mind the deprivation of *physical* liberty, a fact that the Supreme Court all too readily acknowledged. However, they could not have foreseen the greatly enhanced significance, in the immediate aftermath of the Second World War, of the individual's right to inner freedom of the personality, foremost in the constitutional settlement of the new Germany. Thus Articles 1 and 2 prevailed, once again, over the literal meaning of the Civil Code. The Supreme Court ruled (much in the way that UK courts are obliged to rule under section 3 of the Human Rights Act) that Article 847 of the Civil Code should be extended to provide a remedy for violations of personality rights under the Basic Law. DM 10,000 was awarded by way of compensation.

The lower courts had sought to find a remedy on the basis of a fictitious licence fee which the plaintiff might have charged had the advertising company sought his consent for publication of his portrait. This strained reasoning was rejected by the Supreme Court, emboldened by the Federal Constitutional Court's decision in the *Schacht* case. It is worth comparing this with the strenuous efforts by the Court of Appeal in this country to find a basis in law for remedying the gross invasion of the actor Gordon Kaye's privacy rights by newspaper photographers who pictured him lying unconscious in a hospital bed recovering from serious head injuries. The award against the paper was finally based on the strained construction of malicious falsehood—that publication of the photographs wrongly implied that Kaye had given his consent.[4]

The overriding of the limitation on damages for immaterial loss in the Civil Code was carried on by the Bundesgerichtshof in a later decision, similar to the *Gentleman Rider* case (BGHZ 35, 63), in 1961. The Court said, in terms, that just as the restriction of protection by the law of tort to specific legal interests of a human being had

---

[4] *Kaye v Robertson* [1991] FSR 62. This case, the "low water mark" of English privacy law, has now been overtaken by more recent developments: see *Michael Douglas, Catherine Zeta-Jones and Northern & Shell Plc v Hello! Ltd* [2001] 2 WLR 992, CA.

proved too narrow to afford the protection of personality required by the Basic Law, so the narrowing of immaterial damages to immaterial loss which cover only injury to specifically mentioned legal interest no longer conformed to the value system of the Basic Law and should thus be overruled.

Now that damages have become an established remedy for breach of privacy rights, in the absence of statutory or constitutional provision for either, the Supreme Court has taken the bold step of suggesting that punitive damages might sometimes ensue.[5]

In the *Caroline I* case (BGH 15 November 1994, BGHZ 128, 14 16), a ruling which has caused some controversy in legal and academic circles, the Court has suggested that whenever a newspaper intentionally encroaches upon another person's right to personality in order to make money, damages should be assessed, in such a way as to deprive it of the profits made from infringing the plaintiff's rights. Thus, motives are relevant; the wish to profit at the expense of the victim of the breach of privacy will mean that damages will be assessed in a way that would deprive the tortfeasor of his ill-gotten gains.

Like the *Soraya* case mentioned below, this case concerned the publication of a completely fabricated interview, this time with Princess Caroline of Monaco. The Supreme Court not only upheld the order made by the lower court to the publisher to withdraw the publications, but also referred the question of damages to the lower court for re-determination, taking into account the aim of deterrence. The award thus went up from DM 30,000 to DM 180,000, to take into account the profits of the defendant newspaper.

In quantifying damages in personal injury cases German judges rely on tables where awards for specific injuries are set out (similar to *Kemp on Damages*). Damages for immaterial injury to personality however are at large and until *Caroline I* there has been little in the way of guidance. Judges have sought guidance from a number of principles which depend more on the motive and the manner of the infringement than the injury to the complainant, particularly, as *Caroline I* specified, the intention to make profit. The direction given

---

[5] Compensation for non quantifiable injuries, such as interference with privacy interests, has an element of "satisfaction" (*Genugtuung*) about it in German law; the aim is to provide psychological satisfaction to an aggrieved person and to uphold the law (BS Markesinis, *The German Law of Obligations*, 3rd edn (Clarendon Press, Oxford, 1997) 921).

by the court—that in future cases judges should aim to skim off the profits made from the increase in sales—will inevitably lead to higher damages awards for celebrities (the rich) than those given in respect of violations of ordinary members of the public (the not so rich). Such a result may well be discriminatory, and would certainly be arguable as a violation of Article 14 of the ECHR (Convention rights are applicable in German law, although lower in the hierarchy to the Basic Law). The response to such a challenge however would be that the injury to a public figure is commensurately greater, thus the award reflects the damage done rather than the greater wealth of that figure.

PRIVACY V FREEDOM OF EXPRESSION

There is a constitutional right to freedom of expression, under Article 5 of the Basic Law, which provides:

(1) Everyone has the right to express and disseminate his opinion freely by word, writing and picture and to inform himself from generally accessible sources without restraint. Freedom of the press and of reporting by radio and film are guaranteed. Censorship is not to take place.

(2) These rights are limited by the provisions of general laws (*allgemeine Gesetze*), statutory rules for the protection of the young and the right to personal honour (dem Recht der pers ̄nlichen Ehre)

(3) Art, science, research and teaching are free. Freedom of teaching does not exonerate individuals from loyalty to the Constitution (this latter clause was included to prevent teachers from promoting ideas that undermine Constitutional values such as equality and dignity).

It did not take long for the newly developed personality right to come on a direct collision course with this constitutional right to freedom of expression. In 1973 the Federal Constitutional Court was asked to reconsider a decision by the court below that a television company's right under Article 5 of the Basic Law to freedom of expression should prevail over the right of the petitioner, who had been convicted some years before of armed robbery, not to have his personality rights invaded by having a film made about him without his consent. In considering where the balance lay, the Constitutional Court made the observation (quite familiar in freedom of speech cases) that the rights to an inviolate personality were limited to the extent that the individual places himself in the public arena (by, for example, tangling with the criminal law).

Again, in a manner which will be familiar to anyone who has studied the jurisprudence of the European Court of Human Rights in assessing the legitimacy of infringements of Article 10 ECHR, the Court considered the limitations on Article 5 of the Basic Law, particularly as it may be limited by general laws. The protection afforded by German copyright laws to the right to one's own likeness, enhanced by the Constitutional prohibition on violations of the personality, was just such a general law. Thus it was necessary to carry out a proportionality test. The damage to personality resulting from public representation must not be out of proportion to the importance of the publication upholding the freedom of communication. In this case, the Federal Constitutional Court decided that the general personality rights of the petitioner, along with the public interest in the rehabilitation of offenders, should outweigh the public interest in freedom of information in this case.

In fact the Court observed that, in solving the conflict between privacy and free speech:

> it must be remembered that according to the intention of the Constitution both constitutional concerns are essential aspects of the liberal democratic order . . . with the result that *neither can claim precedence in principle over the other.*

In the run up to the passing into force of the Human Rights Act concern was expressed in some circles that the press-saving provision of that Act, section 12, would distort similar efforts by UK judges to carry out the proportionality test. However in the *Michael Douglas* case,[6] the Court of Appeal observed that section 12 should not be treated like a trump card for those relying on freedom of expression. The better approach was to strike a balance between the merits of the right to privacy on the one hand, and the right to free speech on the other. Section 12(4) in turn would require the court to consider

---

[6] See n 4, above.

the compliance or otherwise of the party claiming freedom of expression with any prevailing privacy code such as the 1997 Press Complaints Commission Code of Practice (as amended).

It is worth noting that the German Court paid particular attention to the fact that the respondent was a television company, not, as one might expect, to boost the importance of its claim to freedom of expression, but to emphasise the greater damage it might do to the petitioner's personality rights (than might be inflicted by a medium attracting a more limited audience, such as the cinema or theatre): "it must be remembered that the *broadcast* performance of a documentary play entails specific dangers." Again, it will be noted that the English approach, whether the action is based on confidence or defamation, is to take account of the fact that the plaintiff has himself sought publicity, or has made some moral pronouncement and is found in his own private behaviour to be acting inconsistently with that standard. If he has (and the use of this personal pronoun is deliberate, since most of the cases in this context concern male Conservative politicians who have pinned their colours to the "Victorian values" mast) this is enough to justify the floodgates of intrusive media reports. Admittedly, the English courts have recently signalled in the *Douglas* case that, in the light of the adoption of the right to privacy in Article 8, even figures in the public eye do not by their very exposure forfeit that right to privacy but this is an early development.

The German approach is to acknowledge the fact that an individual has created his own problems by attracting public attention to himself, but nevertheless to maintain a sense of proportion about it:

> The invasion of the personal sphere is limited to the need to satisfy adequately the interest to receive information, *and the disadvantages suffered by the culprit must be proportional to the seriousness of the offence or its importance otherwise to the public.*

Some freedom of expression claims have been rejected on the basis of editorial confidentiality, indicating that freedom of expression and privacy are often merely opposing sides of the same coin. This was illustrated by the *Wallraff* case (BGH 20 January 1981, BGHZ 80, 25), in which a journalist who had infiltrated a right wing newspaper was injuncted from publishing a book about its internal practices. The illegal methods by which he discovered this confidential information clearly influenced the Constitutional Court to uphold the injunction which had been overturned by the Court below.

Application to Private Disputes

It will be noted that most of the cases surveyed above concern the application of constitutional values derived from Articles 1 and 2 of the Basic Law to essentially private disputes. German courts have developed a sophisticated system for the horizontal application of constitutional rights which is manifest in the case law on privacy rights, particularly where they conflict with freedom of expression.

The application of constitutional values in private disputes may work in two ways.

There has been a certain amount of discussion in academic and practitioner circles in the UK during the run up to the incorporation of the ECHR of the concept of *"unmittelbare Drittwirkung"*, the direct effect of constitutional rights on private law. Thus courts are under an obligation, because of the superior status of human rights, to determine the outcome of private disputes that in compliance with these rights. Such constitutional norms will therefore have an inevitable influence on *all* private litigation where they are engaged. In fact, at the time of writing, research conducted at the University of Oxford's Centre for Comparative and European Law has revealed only 166 invocations of Drittwirkung out of 2614 decisions of the German Constitutional Court.

The second avenue for horizontal application of constitutional rights, which has received less attention in this country, is the reciprocal relationship between constitutional rights and "general laws" (*allgemeine Gesetze*) that are found in private law. This "radiation effect" (*Ausstrahlungswirkung*) is dependent on the relevant private law including some reference to general principles through which the constitutional value can pass. Thus, unlike *Drittwirkung*, it does not have quite such a widespread effect on private disputes, and thus poses less of a threat to private autonomy.

A ruling that demonstrates the difference between the radiation effect (*Ausstrahlungswirkung*) and direct effect of constitutional norms (*Drittwirkung*), is the *Film Director* case. Here Veit Harlan, a film director who had associations with the Nazi regime, re-surfaced and started producing films. The journalist Luth called for a boycott of his films, on the basis that his pro-Nazi sympathies and anti-Jewish propaganda would upset the delicate process of post war rehabilitation between the German and Jewish communities (the war had ended only nine years previously). Harlan applied for an injunction on the basis of Article 826 of the Civil Code (intentional infliction of harm _contra bonos mores—gegen die guten Sitten_) and the state court awarded the injunction. The "_contra bonos mores_" element was relevant in the light of the fact that when Harlan had been acquitted of crimes against humanity in the de-Nazification process his acquittal meant that any limitations on his ability to pursue his vocation would be anti-democratic. Thus the action by Luth contravened the "democratic, legal and moral opinion of the German people" ("die demokratische Rechts und Sittenaffassung des deutschen Volks"). Luth sought a ruling from the Federal Constitutional court on the basis of Article 5 of the Basic Law, claiming that the state court as a public authority had violated this right in granting the injunction. The Constitutional Court, in considering this claim, stated that although the Basic Law was directed primarily against the state, it obviously influenced civil laws as well; no civil law provision could stand in contradiction to it and each such provision must be interpreted in the spirit of it (_in seinem Geiste ausgelegt werden_). To get the full flavour of this theory, it is worth quoting the Court's words at length:

> A dispute between private parties about rights and duties arising from such [constitutionally influenced] norms about behaviour (_grundrechtlich beeinflüssten Verhaltensnormen_) in the civil law, which is influenced by the Basic Rights, remains substantively and procedurally a civil law legal dispute. Civil law is interpreted and applied . . . from the Constitution . . .
>
> The influence of Basic Rights value yardsticks (_grundrechtliche Wertmassstäbe_) will arise primarily with those provisions of private law which contain compulsory law (zwingendes Recht) and thus form part of the public order (_des ordre public_) . . . that is, the principles which for reasons of public benefit (_gemeinen Wohls_) should also be binding for the formation of legal relationships between individuals and therefore are withdrawn from the control of the private will. These provisions have, in accordance with their purpose, a close relationship with public law, which they complement. That must expose them to a special extent to the influence of constitutional law.

What is interesting to the UK lawyer in all this is that public policy restrictions on private law—our equivalent of "zwingende Rechte"—may serve equally as a conduit for the flow of ECHR principles into private law; doctrines such as non-discrimination, for example, in the employment and services field, or the statutory prohibition on unfair contract terms, restraint of trade laws and so on.

The "general law" in question in Luth, then, was the reference to "gute Sitten", *bonos mores* or good morals made by the draftsmen of the Civil Code in Article 826. Because of the importance of constitutional rights, however, the reference in Article 5 of the Basic Law to limitations imposed by these general laws could only be justified if the general law itself was interpreted in strict compliance with the important right to freedom of expression. It is a kind of quid pro quo:

> if the constitutional right takes effect in private law matters, asserting for example the importance of freedom of expression against the private law interests of a private citizen, so then must the contrary effect of a private law norm limiting the basic right in certain circumstances be taken into consideration, insofar as the norm is intended to protect legal interests which are of higher rank ("soweit sie höhere Rechtsgüter zu shützen bestimmt ist"). *It could not be conceived why provisions of civil law which protect honour or other substantial interests of the human personality should not suffice to set limits on the exercise of the basic right of free expression of opinion, even without criminal provisions being enacted for the same purpose.* [Emphasis added.]

Because of this reciprocal effect of constitutional rights on private rights and vice versa, the Court was able to uphold Luth's (limited) right to freedom of expression. In other words, the limiting effect of the general law under Article 826 which authorised the injunction had in the circumstances been a disproportionate interference with his freedom of expression, given the seriousness of his fears of Harlan's potential effect on Christian–Jewish relations, and the non-coercive nature of his call for a boycott (which could not be said to have materially interfered with Harlan's Article 1 and 2 personality rights).

Legitimate Restrictions on Freedom of Expression

The press usually justifies its publications on the basis of the public interest in the dissemination of information, whether it relates to iniquitous practices, suspected crime, corrupt politicians or any other issue relevant to legitimate public debate. The German courts' balancing of these public interests against the individual's interest in an inviolate personality is a far more transparent exercise than that carried out by English courts in cases involving claims to press freedom, and arguably clearer and more principled than the lengthy judgments emanating from Strasbourg in cases concerning Article 10 of the ECHR. This is because the German courts make an effort to include in the balance specific relevant provisions, whether they be drawn from the Civil or Criminal Code, the Constitution, or other domestically applicable law such as the European Convention on Human Rights.

A good example is the *Syrian Bribery* case permits (NJW 1987, 2682). The Oberlandsgericht of Cologne was asked to consider whether a news article which alleged that the plaintiff, a city official, had been bribed by suspected Syrian terrorists to grant residence had violated the plaintiff's right to personality. One of the considerations the court took into account in determining the balance between freedom of the press and the plaintiff's personality interests was Article 6(2) of the ECHR, a provision which has equal status to domestic law in Germany but only against the state. The Court observed that the plaintiff was under suspicion at the time when the news article was published; he was therefore under the protection of the presumption of innocence, even though criminal proceedings had not been commenced.

> This has the effect that when the press alleges the guilt of such a person, and bases that allegation on substantial grounds of suspicion, it will not itself be acting on the basis of a legitimate interest.

On the application of Article 6 to the press, the Court said:

> the effects of the presumption of innocence extend into the realm of privacy and demand that this right is formulated in such a way as to protect the presumption of innocence and that consequently the presumption of innocence is seen as a protected interests for all persons. If the right of personality is understood in those terms, it places limits upon reports of criminal activities, as a counterbalance to the freedom of the press.

A similar incident occurred in this country on 14 February 1997, the five youths suspected but not convicted of the murder of the black teenager Stephen Lawrence were photographed on the front cover of the Daily Mail under the banner headline "MURDERERS . . . If we are wrong, let them sue us". Had this taken place in Germany, the line of reasoning in the *Syrian Bribery* case would have given them a very clear cause of action against the newspaper.

Public Interest Defence

Statements which do not contribute to political debate and speech which is pure gossip and motivated by greed, are not protected under Article 5 of the Basic Law. The publication of accurate but private details does not tend to attract constitutional protection under freedom of expression, even if the subject is a public figure. In *Caroline III* (BGH NJW 1996, 1128) the Supreme Court said, in relation to the publication of photographs of Princess Caroline of Monaco, taken without her consent in a restaurant where she was having dinner with her boyfriend:

> When balancing the competing interests, the informational value of the events depicted will be of crucial significance. The greater the need of the public to know, the more limited will be the rights of the person of contemporary history. By contrast, the need to protect this person's privacy will become greater as the information gained by the public becomes less valuable.

Another example of the German courts' distaste for press claims to constitutional protection for the publication of true but private facts is the *Gretna Green* case (BGH 20 January 1965). Here the plaintiff objected to the planned marriage of his daughter to a British corporal who had been stationed in Germany. The couple eloped to Scotland and the father asked his cousin there to discover their whereabouts. The cousin made an arrangement with a Scottish newspaper that their reporter would trace them in exchange for permission to publish their pictures and story. When this happened a German newspaper carried its own version of the story. The plaintiff successfully claimed damages against the newspaper for dragging an essentially private affair into the glare of publicity. The Supreme Court found that there had been serious disregard of the plaintiff's personality and rejected the defence that a similar article had already been published in Scotland. Under English law, any defamation action by the father would have been defeated by the defence of justification, and he would not have been able to take an action for breach of confidence, since the defendants would have been able to argue that the information was already in the public domain (*A-G v Guardian Newspapers Limited (No 2)* [1990] 1 AC 109 the "Spycatcher" case).

Publications with no basis in fact rarely enjoy the guarantees of Article 5. In the *Soraya* case, which arose as a result of a fabricated interview with the former Empress of Iran, the Court stated in terms that the publication of false information could not be saved by Article 5 of the Basic Law: "An invented interview adds not one iota to the formation of real public opinion".[7]

The Oberlandsgericht Hamburg granted damages for immaterial harm to the plaintiff against the defendant newspaper which published a headline suggesting that she had accepted a sum of money for being portrayed in the nude (OLG Hamburg AfP 1992, 367). The text of the article, in small print, explained that the plaintiff, a politician, was in fact claiming damages from another party for unauthorised publication of her image. The Court ruled that the informational value of these facts could not be invoked here, because it was "trivial". Such a clear distinction between meritorious and trivial information is rarely drawn by English judges, except on occasion in breach of confidence cases, where one of the conditions for confidentiality is that the information concerned must not be "trivial tittle-tattle"—*Stephens v Avery* [1988] 1 Ch 449.

There is another aspect of this judgment that contrasts starkly with the approach to similar issues in the UK. Far from being accorded less protection because she was a politician, the Court considered that her public status entitled the plaintiff to greater protection for her privacy interests, as the article in question had a much more damaging effect than it would have done on a private person.

Thus figures in the public sphere enjoy greater protection under German law than they do in the UK, even politicians. This was demonstrated in the *Telephone Conversation* case, where the Federal Court granted an injunction to restrain further publication of extracts from an illegally taped conversation between Helmut Kohl and another leading political figure, Kurt Biedenkopf (BGHZ 73,120):

---

[7] The plaintiff in this case later turned up in the Italian Courts, which awarded her compensation for the invasion of her privacy, following the lead of the German courts (see C von Bar, *The Common European Law of Torts*, Vol 1 (Clarendon Press, Oxford, 1998) para 587.

even politicians who are in the limelight, are entitled to have their privacy respected. This stems from articles 1 and 2 of the Constitution . . . and it is reinforced by section 201 of the Criminal Code which makes it illegal to record private telephone conversations without the consent of the persons involved.

CONCLUSION

The preceding survey of cases and statutes illustrates that German courts have developed a sophisticated and subtle system for the protection of privacy. Without the opportunity afforded by the inclusion of general personality rights in the Basic Law, privacy might have had only strained and somewhat piecemeal protection, similar to that offered by the patchwork of torts and statutes in this area in the United Kingdom. Nevertheless Articles 1 and 2 of the Basic Law have not proved to be a significant threat to free speech interests or press freedom, not only because of the weight given to the countervailing Article 5, but because of the careful appraisal of the circumstances in each individual case and the application of the proportionality test. This approach has been criticised (notably by Stoll) for sacrificing legal certainty to ad hoc fairness. But it may be that English courts could follow the German example whilst avoiding this Hobson's choice, since the law can be rendered calculable and therefore certain under the clear directions contained in Article 8 of the ECHR, a prop which the German courts have had to manage without. The case law also demonstrates how interlinked the conflicting interests of privacy and free speech often are, not in the sense that in upholding the one the courts must necessarily undermine the other, but that both are extensions of the inner freedom encapsulated in the constitutional right to free development of the personality. If Article 8 were interpreted along these lines, there should be no need for judges to follow the dictat of section 12 of the Human Rights Act, whose status is debatable and whose requirements should, in the future, be rendered superfluous.

There has been manifest reluctance to incorporate German law into UK ligitation, largely because of the difficulties presented by the language barrier. These difficulties are being considerably reduced by the efforts of research institutes such as the Centre for

Comparative European Law at Oxford University, to translate many landmark judgments and to reproduce much key German academic commentary in English; it is worth noting, too, that that archivists of German case law are providing an increasing number of head-notes and on occasion full judgments on the Internet (site details are given in the bibliography at the end of this report). The remaining objections to the use of German law in domestic litigation are targeted at the common law/civil law divide, which is of decreasing significance since the advent of European Community law and the obligation on our judges under the Human Rights Act to take account of the jurisprudence of the Court of Human Rights in Strasbourg, an institution whose determinations are dominated by civil law procedures and norms. German law, in other words, is not so different as not to offer some guidelines as to how to deal with the difficult business of balancing privacy against freedom of expression.

BIBLIOGRAPHY

Basil Markesinis, *The German Law of Obligations* Vol II, *The Law of Torts*, 3rd edn (Clarendon Press Oxford,1997)
—— (ed), *Protecting Privacy* (Clarendon Press, Oxford, 1999)
——, "Privacy, Freedom of Expression and the Human Rights Bill: Lessons from Germany" (1999) *LQR* 115, 47
Raymond Youngs *Sourcebook on German Law* (Cavendish Publishing, London, 1998)
Nigel Foster, *German Legal System and Laws*, 2nd edn (Blackstone Press London, 1993)
Christian von Bar, *The Common European Law of Torts* Vol 1 (Clarendon Press, Oxford, 1998)

INTERNET SITES

German Constitutional Court Decisions: http://www.uni.wuerzburg.de/glaw/indxbv95.html
German Law Archive: http://iecl.iuscomp.org/gla/
Human Rights Caselaw Update: http://www.lcor.com/

ABBREVIATIONS

BGH—Bundesgerichtshof (Federal High Court)
BverGe—Bundesverfassungsgericht (Federal Constitutional Court)
BGHZ—Entscheidungen des Bundesgerichtshofs in Zivilsachen (Decisions of the Federal High Court in Civil Cases)
NJW—Neue Juristischen Wochenschrift (New Legal Weekly Journal)
OLG—Oberlandsgericht (Upper State Court)

5

The Impact of the Charter of Rights on Privacy and Freedom of Expression in Canada

Marguerite Russell[1]

INTRODUCTION

Largely because of the Charter of Rights and Freedoms enacted in 1982, Canada has begun to emerge as a world leader in the constitutional protection of human rights. The legal conservatism elicited by the older, statute-based Bill of Rights has been displaced by substantive application of a wide range of Charter guarantees not unlike those of the Bill of Rights embedded in the United States Constitution. In a country that was for years characterised by the traditions of the colonial common law and civil law, the judiciary has begun the process of bringing Canadian law into line with the values expressed in the Charter.

Long before the adoption of the Charter of Rights, both courts and legislation had already granted some legal protection to privacy interests. As privacy law emerged, it was always recognised that "freedom of expression" might justify the invasion of privacy rights in some circumstances. The adoption of the Charter has raised new questions about the status and scope of privacy interests in Canada—especially in legal proceedings between "private parties". Although the Charter has been interpreted as protecting privacy interests, the express protection given to freedom of expression has created the possibility that the courts may place greater emphasis on freedom of expression and thus indirectly reshape privacy law.

Part I of this chapter outlines the recognition of privacy interests as they have been articulated in Canada. It begins with the recognition of the torts of invasion of privacy and appropriation of personality in

[1] I would like to thank Professor Kathleen Lahey and Queen's University for their invaluable assistance in the preparation of this chapter.

pre-Charter common law, and then examines the impact of statutory privacy provisions, human rights codes, and the Charter of Rights on the common law.

One of the conclusions that emerges from this discussion is that "privacy" interests have been in tension with expressive interests (freedom of expression, freedom of the press) from the outset. Thus, expressive interests have always played a role in shaping the common law recognition of privacy rights. However, as described in Part II, expressive interests have been given more definitive application as the result of the Charter of Rights. Part III looks directly at how the courts have reconciled apparently competing Charter values in recent cases. The full impact of the Charter on common law privacy rights has not yet been seen, particularly in cases involving private parties and non-state action. However, several leading decisions suggest that there is still considerable protection—perhaps even growing protection—afforded to privacy interests despite the fact that expressive interests are now expressly protected in the Charter of Rights.

RECOGNITION OF PRIVACY INTERESTS

Canada's legal roots are found in British and French colonialism, but United States law, which itself is a patchwork of British common law and Spanish and French civil law, has had a profound influence on the development of Canadian law. As the result of these diverse influences, almost every area of law reflects the influences of English, French, or US jurisprudence. [2]

In the case of privacy law, the most important direct influence has been the US jurisprudence inspired by the work of Warren and Brandeis, who published an article entitled "The Right to Privacy" in the 1890 *Harvard Law Review*.[3] In this article, they drew heavily on UK case law and on the political discourse of democratic liberalism associated with the guarantee of "life, liberty and the pursuit

---

[2] Canada has a federal/provincial political and legal structure. Each province and the federal sector have courts up to the appellate level. The top court in the country, the Supreme Court of Canada, hears both federal and provincial appeals. With the exception of Quebec, all jurisdictions in the country are common law jurisdictions. Quebec is a civil code jurisdiction.

[3] Samuel D Warren and Louis D Brandeis, "The Right to Privacy" (1890) 4 (5) *Harvard Law Review* 193.

of happiness". Warren and Brandeis' motivations for producing this work appear to have stemmed from their own experiences with intrusive press attention. Warren's wife had become increasingly upset with intrusions by the "yellow press" into what she and others of her social class considered to be their "private" social sphere.[4] Her irate husband turned to his famous former law partner (later appointed to the US Supreme Court), and together they wrote this article. Refraining from mentioning Warren's wife's concerns directly, the authors explained their interest in this area of law by asserting that "for some years there has been a *feeling* that the law must afford a remedy for unauthorized circulation of portraits of private persons" and suggested in terms that the press is "overstepping the mark".[5]

The Warren and Brandeis article is an excellent example of scholarly advocacy. Despite Warren's personal motivations for getting his partner interested in this area of legal policy, the authors managed to give "privacy" claims an ancient and venerable common-law lineage dating all the way back to the seventeenth century decision in *Semayne's* case.[6] Invoking the aura of the claim that "a man's house is his castle" and conveniently ignoring the fact that only the privileged classes owned single-family homes in which any sense of "privacy" as against the community or "the public" was even physically possible, Warren and Brandeis crafted the claim to "privacy" as "the right to be let alone". They then plumbed the evolution of the common law to find examples of how judicial understandings of "life, liberty, and the pursuit of happiness" had changed and expanded in keeping with the changes in society to support their contention that the time had come to recognise that the common law had always—implicitly if not expressly—given protection to "the right to privacy".

Warren and Brandeis minimised the public interest in "celebrity" figures. While they did admit that expressive rights such as free

---

[4] See William L Prosser, "Privacy" (1960) 48 *California Law Review* 383. In this article Prosser discusses the personal events that led to the writing of the Warren Brandeis text.

[5] It should be noted that the turn of the last century saw large scale technological changes in communications, eg photography, etc, just as the beginning of this century is confronting new technological issues with the internet, etc. See K Gormley, "One Hundred Years of Privacy" (1992) 92 *Wis L Rev* 1335.

[6] *Semayne's Case* (1604) 5 Co Rep 91 a (KB).

speech and freedom of the press were relevant to the scope of the
"right to privacy", this point was treated very much as an after-
thought. Unlike the discussion of the legal sources of privacy interests, which the authors claimed could be traced back to the
common-law doctrines of trespass and assault, Roman civil law, and
ecclesiastical law, the scope of the public's "right to know" or the
limitations on the "private sphere" were developed in far less detail
and left more to speculation than to analysis on the basis that those
interests would have to be articulated in practice.[7]

Not surprisingly, it would take another century before the class,
gender, and race biases inherent in this initial conceptualisation of
the "right to privacy" would become visible. For example, it was not
until the 1960s and 1970s that feminists in North America began to
connect state respect for the "private sphere" with women's difficulties in obtaining legal remedies for domestic violence. Even today,
it is perceived by feminists in Canada that the doctrine of family
privacy has impeded the recognition of women's equality under the
Charter of Rights. Because the Charter does not apply to abuses
committed by "private" persons, Madame Justice Bertha Wilson,
formerly of the Supreme Court of Canada, has concluded that the
fundamental sources of women's inequality continue to be perpetu-
ated behind the very closed doors that create the "private" realm.
From feminist perspectives, protecting the privacy of family life has
provided male privilege with a safe haven.[8]

Despite the hierarchical values around which the concept of "privacy" was initially constructed, "privacy" itself is usually considered
to be a "neutral" concept. In contrast, the tension between privacy
and expressive interests is often visible in the cases and statutes that
have come to define this area of law in Canada.

Pre-Charter recognition of "Privacy"

Legal recognition of "privacy" as a legal category in the US followed
very quickly after publication of the Warren and Brandeis' article
in 1890. In 1895, a New York court impliedly agreed that a public

---

[7] See, eg the discussion at page 220 of their article.

[8] Hon Bertha Wilson, "Women, the Family and the Constitutional Protection of Privacy"
(1991) 23 *Ottawa L Rev* 431.

figure could bring an action for misuse of their public image.[9] In 1905, a Georgia court recognised the tort of invasion of privacy when an insurance company had used the image of a "man on the street" in an advertisement and had falsely attributed enthusiasm for insurance coverage to him as well.[10] This aspect of privacy—the right to control the use of one's own name or likeness—has frequently been recognised as the basis for tort actions since then, particularly by famous personalities to protect against the unauthorised commercial exploitation of their fame.[11] Some US courts have gone so far as to classify this as the "right to publicity".[12]

Largely as the result of the degree of acceptance of "privacy" as a legal category in the US, "privacy" was recognised as a fundamental human right in the 1948 International Declaration of Human Rights, which provided that:

> No one shall be subjected to arbitrary interference with his privacy, family, home or correspondence, nor to attacks upon his honour and reputation. Everyone has the right to the protection of the law against such interference or attacks.[13]

---

[9] *Schuyler v Curtis*, 147 NY 434, 42 NE 22, 31 LRA 286, 4 Am St Rep 61 (1895). The action failed because it had been brought by the surviving members of Mrs Schuyler's family; the court held that the right to one's own image was not an interest that survived the death of the person such that other members of the family could sue on it. The plaintiffs objected to the display of Mrs. Schuyler's bust next to that of Susan B Anthony, a noted feminist activist, at the Chicago World Exhibition, saying that the necessary imputation of Anthony's politics to Mrs Schuyler was a misuse of the latter's image.

[10] *Pavesich v New England Life Insurance*, 122 Ga 10, SE 68–82 (1905).

The fact that it was a "good image" did not impede Mr Pasevich's claim to be compensated for having his privacy invaded. In 1902, a young woman was denied an almost identical claim in *Roberson v Rochester Folding Box Co*, 1 171 NY 538, 64 NE 442–52 (1902). Her image had been used to decorate flour bag bearing the legend "lour of the family". In this case, the finding that it was a "good likeness" was considered to be relevant to the legality of the claim.

[11] See American Law Institute, Restatement of the Law, Second, Torts (1977), para 652A.

[12] See *Martin Luther King Jr, Centre for Social Change v American Heritage Products*, 296 SE (2d) 67, 250 Ga 135 (1982). It is interesting to compare this decision with that of *Dworkin v Hustler Magazine Inc*, 867 F 2d 1188 (CCA 9, 1989), aff'g 634 F Supp 727 (Wyo DC,1986); cert den 110 S Ct 59 (USSC), in which it was held that Andrea Dworkin did not have a similar interest in her own image. In that case, freedom of expression was given priority over alleged invasion of privacy and defamation.

[13] United Nations Universal Declaration of Human Rights, G A Res 217A (III), UN GAOR, 3rd Session, Supp No 13, UN Doc A/810 (1948) 71, reprinted in [1948] UNYB 465, article 12.

The right to privacy was also included in Article 17 of the UN Covenant on Civil and Political Rights.[14] Although these international declarations were very influential in persuading Canadian courts to recognise the role of the courts in protecting human rights in some domestic contexts right away—such as the protection of Jewish people from discrimination[15]—these instruments had little impact on judicial recognition of privacy interests in Canada.

Common Law Doctrine

At the same time that US courts were energetically expanding the scope of privacy interests in tort litigation, Canadian courts were not only slower to recognise privacy as the basis for private actions, but initially seemed to be more comfortable when other grounds for liability were also pleaded. For example, in the 1976 *Motherwell* case, which dealt with harassing phone calls and letters, the judge made sympathetic comments about the idea of a common law tort of privacy, but decided the case on the much older tort of nuisance.[16] Other cases that appear to have recognised the common law tort of invasion of privacy left it unclear whether their findings were based on liability as an aspect of invasion of privacy or as an intentional economic tort.[17]

Thus, in Canada, although a number of common law tort actions[18] have been used to protect privacy interests, especially when property interests have been involved, privacy as a tort in its own right did not follow the US pattern until fairly late. In Ontario, it was not until 1981 that the court upheld a right of action for invasion of privacy, on this occasion holding the defendant liable for the unauthorised recording of a telephone call.[19]

---

[14] Adopted United Nations General Assembly Resolution 2200 A (XXI), 16 December 1966, Entry into force 23 March 1976.

[15] See, eg *Re Drummond Wren* [1945] OR 778.

[16] *Motherwell v Motherwell*, [1976] 6 WWR 550, 73 DLR (3d) 62 (Alta CA).

[17] See *Krouse v Chrysler Can Ltd* (1973) 1 OR (2d) 255 (CA); *Athans v Can Adventure Camps Ltd* (1977) 4 CCLT 20 (Ont HC).

[18] Eg trespass, nuisance, defamation, appropriation of personality or passing off, and breach of confidence.

[19] *Saccone v Orr* (1981), 34 OR (2d) 317, 19 CCLT 37 (Co Ct).

Two factors have moved the courts further in the direction of accepting claims for invasion of privacy. The first is the general effect that the provisions of statutory regimes such as the Quebec Charter of Rights and Freedoms have had on the status of privacy claims. The second is the impact of the national Charter on such claims. National Charter cases are discussed below, but it is worth noting that the provincial Quebec Charter was the first statute in Canada to recognise privacy as a legal interest.

Statutory Recognition of Privacy

As a province with a civil code jurisdiction, Quebec law is statutory in basis. Following the French law, liability for invasion of privacy is based on the two notions of fault and harm. The plaintiff may recover damages where the defendant has acted in a harmful manner towards them. The right to privacy is generally an accepted right in civil law, though it is difficult to set the limits of this right.[20] The first Canadian case that provided a remedy for invasion of privacy was in fact a Quebec decision.[21]

The concept of "privacy" as a value in Canada has also been increasingly reflected in legislation in those provinces with common-law jurisdictions. Both federal and provincial legislatures have passed statutes, sometimes designed to protect the privacy of individuals as against other individuals, and sometimes to protect individual information collected and held by government agencies. The federal government enacted the Access to Information and Privacy Acts on the same day in 1983.[22] These were followed by various provincial statutes. Today every Canadian province and territory[23] except Prince

---

[20] Liability, Code Civil Articles 35–41 du respect de la reputation et de la vie privee.

[21] *Robbins v CBC (Que)* (1957) 12 DLR (2d) 35 (Que Sup Ct). See also PA Comeau and A Ouimet, "Freedom of Information and Privacy: Quebec's Innovative Role in North America" (1995) *Iowa LR* 80 For a discussion the French civil law approach to privacy and how it differs from the English approach, see FP Walton, "The Comparative Law of the Rights to Privacy: The French Law as the Right to Privacy" (1931) 47 *LQR* 219.

[22] The Privacy Act, 1980–81–82–83, c 111, Sch 1. The current Federal Access to Information Act is RSC 1985, ch p–21, as amended. The Office of the Federal Privacy Commissioner can be reached via their web site at www.privcom.ca. A further Federal Act governing electronic data is being implemented in three stages, from 1 January 2001 to 1 January 2004: The Personal Information Protection and Electronic Documents Act.

[23] British Columbia: Freedom of Information and Protection of Privacy Act, RSBC 1996, ch 165; Alberta: Freedom of Information and Protection of Privacy Act, RSA 1994, ch F–18.5;

Edward Island has enacted legislation parallel to the federal Privacy Act and the Access to Information Act. These laws prevent the unnecessary distribution of personal information, and guarantee access to unrestricted government information.

Privacy has also emerged as an issue in criminal law. Crime falls in the federal sphere of legislative authority; thus the federal government has enacted a number of criminal provisions designed to protect privacy. Part VI of the Criminal Code entitled "Invasion of Privacy" deals with the interception of communications,[24] and Part VIII of the code deals with offences against the person and reputation.

Since the 1960s, Canada has developed extensive domestic human rights legislation. Today both federal and provincial human rights legislation exists in every province and territory.[25] Such legislation prohibits discrimination on the grounds of race, sex, age, sexual orientation, disability and religion in accommodation, employment and provision of services. Ironically, the concept of "privacy" has functioned to insulate some discriminatory clubs from human rights complaints by creating statutory exemptions from human rights legislation for "private" organisations. For example, the Yukon Territory human rights statute prohibits discrimination in associations, clubs, and trade unions, but then exempts those associations that are "private" in nature from regulation. To date, attempts to invalidate those privacy provisions when used to exclude women, for example, from clubs by appealing to the Canadian Charter of Rights and Freedoms have failed.[26]

Post-Charter Privacy Law

Privacy rights *per se* were not included in the Charter of Rights and Freedoms.[27] There were various attempts to include privacy rights,

Saskatchewan: Freedom of Information and Protection of Privacy Act, SS 1990–91, ch F–22.01; Ontario: Freedom of Information and Protection of Privacy Act, RSO 1990, ch F–31; Quebec's Charter of 1975 in S 5 enshrined a privacy right; Nova Scotia: Freedom of Information and Protection of Privacy Act, RSNS 1993, ch 5, s 1; Newfoundland: Freedom of Information Act, RSN 1990, ch F–25.

[24] RSC, C–34, ss 183–196; 297–303.

[25] For a useful web site with details of much of this legislation, see http://www.wwlia.org/ca-hr.htm.

[26] *Gould v Yukon Order of Pioneers* [1996] 1 SCR 571, discussed in the next section.

[27] Canadian Charter of Rights and Freedoms. The Charter is part of the Constitution Act of 1982. Because Canada has a written constitution originally enacted by the Parliament of the

evidenced in the discussion drafts of the Charter of Rights, but in the end, the right to privacy was excluded.[28] The rationale behind the exclusion of privacy rights appears to be that the legislators considered it dangerous to leave to the courts the determination of "reasonable" standards for application of such rights.[29]

The exclusion of "privacy" from the literal text of the Charter has not prevented privacy rights from being argued in Charter cases or from being recognised in Charter litigation. In the very first Charter case to reach the Supreme Court of Canada, the Court took the opportunity to declare that the "right to privacy" was among the fundamental rights and freedoms protected by the Charter.[30] Since then, privacy has played a growing role in the interpretation of several specific provisions of the Charter, chief among which are section 7 (security of the person) and section 8 (search and seizure).[31] The result is a constitutional jurisprudence that has come to echo Brandeis' view of the value of privacy as a core value:

> privacy is at the heart of liberty in a modern state . . . grounded in man's physical and moral autonomy, privacy is essential for the well-being of the individual.[32]

United Kingdom in 1867, patriation took place in 1982 by means of the Canada Act, 1982 (UK), ch 11; proclaimed in force April 17, 1982 (except s 23(1)(a) in respect of Quebec). Subsequent amendments are as follows: Constitution Amendment Proclamation, 1983; Constitution Act, 1985, (Representation) Constitution Amendment, 1987 (Newfoundland Act); Constitution Amendment, 1993 (New Brunswick); Constitution Amendment, 1993 (Prince Edward Island).

[28] See, eg Federal-Provincial First Ministers' Conference, 8–12 September 1980; Discussion Draft, 3 September 1980: Document 800–14/069 or Meeting of Officials on the Constitution, Ottawa, Ontario, 11–12 January 1979; Federal Draft, 8 January: Document 840–153/004.

[29] See, eg Federal–Provincial First Ministers' Conference, 8–12 September 1980; Discussion Draft, 3 September 1980: Document 800–14/069 or Meeting of Officials on the Constitution, Ottawa, Ontario, 11–12 January 1979; Federal Draft, 8 January: Document 840–153/004.

[30] *Hunter v Southam*, [1984] 2 SCR 145.

[31] S 7 of the Charter provides that "Everyone has the right to life, liberty and security of the person and the right not to be deprived thereof except in accordance with the principles of fundamental justice". S 8 provides that "Everyone has the right to be secure against unreasonable search or seizure".

[32] *R v Dyment* [1988] 2 SCR 417, *per* La Forest J, at 427–28. While sitting on the US Supreme Court, Brandeis J had written that "the right to be let alone [is] the most comprehensive of rights and the right most valued by civilized man". *Olmstead v United States*, 277 US 438, 478 (1928), *per* Brandeis J, dissenting.

The Canadian Charter applies only to governmental action[33]—that is, to state action rather than to private action.[34] Thus, it does not apply directly to the common law unless government action is involved. However, the position has been reached that, as a result of *obiter* comments in *Dolphin Delivery* and subsequent cases,[35] the courts have concluded that the common law must evolve consistent with "Charter values". Although the Charter does not apply directly to private litigants, it will apply indirectly as the common law doctrine is brought into line with "Charter values". According to one well-respected author, there is now little significance in the exclusion of the common law from Charter review.[36]

Common Law Doctrine

The enactment of the Charter has generally supported judicial recognition of privacy rights. Several lower court decisions in Ontario demonstrate that "invasion of privacy" is now developing as a tort in its own right,[37] particularly in cases concerning personal harassment. For example, in *MacKay v Buelow*,[38] the court held that an ex-husband who stalked and threatened his ex-wife and daughter by various intrusive means was liable for invasion of privacy. In *Roth v Roth*, a case involving a neighbour dispute over an access road[39] where there was verbal harassment, assaults and property damage, the court found, despite the existence of other torts, that the cumulative effect of the injuries suffered was an intolerable invasion of privacy rights rooted in the individual, rather than damage arising out of property rights.

---

[33] S 32.

[34] *Retail, Wholesale and Department Store Union v Dolphin Delivery* [1996] 2 SCR 573.

[35] See *Dagenais v CBC* [1994] 3 SCR 835 and *Hill v Church of Scientology* [1995] 2 SCR 1130.

[36] See Peter W Hogg, *Constitutional Law of Canada*, Vol 2 (Carswell, Toronto, 1997) at para 34.2(g) for a fuller discussion of these issues.

[37] See John DR Craig, "Invasion of Privacy and Charter Values: The Common-Law Tort Awakens" (1997) 42 *McGill LJ* 355.

[38] (1995) 11 RFL (4th) 403, 24 CCLT (2d) (Ont Gen Div).

[39] (1991) 4 OR (3d) 740, 9 CCLT (2d) 141 (Ont Gen Div).

Statutory Contexts

The privacy of medical records has been a significant area where privacy rights have been argued. In *Canadian Aids Society v Ontario*,[40] the Red Cross had blood donor samples tested for HIV, without the knowledge of the donors, and was required by provincial legislation to report HIV positive status to the donors and to the public health authorities. The court held that despite the donors' reasonable expectations of privacy under section 8 of the Charter, nevertheless the objectives of promoting public health outweighed the individuals' privacy rights. In *McInery v MacDonald*[41] the Supreme Court upheld a lower court decision that allowed a patient access to her medical records.[42]

In the criminal law context, privacy rights have been considered in relation to search and seizure,[43] the taking of blood samples,[44] police surveillance[45] and electronic surveillance.[46] One of the most significant areas where privacy as a Charter value in criminal law has emerged is in the area of sexual assault and legislative attempts to protect women from defence intrusion into prior sexual and medical history.[47] The most recent cases in this area are discussed in Part III.[48]

Privacy rights of women played an important role in the ruling that women have the right to choose whether or not to have an abortion: in *Morgentale*[49] the Supreme Court struck down the Criminal Code provisions on abortion completely.

Oddly, human rights provisions that insulate "private" discrimination from state regulation have withstood Charter scrutiny. In

[40] (1995) 25 OR (3d) 388 (Ont Gen Div).

[41] [1992] 2 SCR 138.

[42] Apart from the new Federal legislative proposals regarding electronic data referred to in n 22 above, various provinces have enacted statutes specifically relating to privacy and access to medical records: eg the Manitoba Personal Health Information Act 1997, see the website at www.ombudsman.mb.ca/phia-long.htm; the Alberta Health Information Act 2001, see the website at www.oipc.ab.ca.

[43] *Hunter v Southam* [1984] 2 SCR 145.

[44] *R v Dymet* [1988] 2 SCR 417.

[45] *R v Le Beau*, 25 OAC 1 (Ont CA), police surveillance in a men's lavatory.

[46] *R v Wise* [1992] 1 SCR 527.

[47] *R v Seaboyer* [1991] 2 SCR 577, *R. v O'Connor* [1995] 4 SCR 411.

[48] *R v Mills* [1999] 3 SCR 668.

[49] *R v Morgantaler* [1988] 1 SCR 30.

Lawrence v Canada (Dept of National Revenue, Customs)[50] a human rights tribunal held that the actions of a customs official who donned latex gloves and loudly commented on the applicant's medical condition (AIDS) was not discriminatory. In that case, the tribunal relied on a pre-Charter Supreme Court case concerning the level of privacy that could be expected on entering the country.[51] Similarly, the Supreme Court of Canada ruled in *Gould v Yukon Order of Pioneers* that a "men only club" was permitted to continue to exclude women.[52] The male members of the court supported the concept that the club offered to its members an intimate association, an opportunity to socialise in an all-male environment intended to enhance the emotional development of its members. The two women judges then on the Supreme Court were unimpressed by this appeal to male bonding, and dissented. Paradoxically, this case now actually strengthens the status of "privacy" rights under the Charter, so strongly did the majority express its views on the value of "intimate" association as a form of privacy.

FREEDOM OF EXPRESSION IN CANADA

Freedom of expression both from philosophical[53] and legal perspectives[54] is regarded as an essential requirement in a modern democratic state. It has thus received constitutional protection, most notably in the first amendment to the US constitution, and, more recently, in section 2(b) of the Canadian Charter, which guarantees: "Freedom of thought, belief, opinion and expression, including freedom of the press and other media of communications". This freedom is not absolute—section 1 of the Charter stipulates that rights and freedoms are guaranteed to individuals only to the extent that the government cannot "demonstrably justify" limitations on them.

Perhaps because Canadians have generally become inured to seeing the courts grant scant credit to freedom of expression, most

---

[50] [1997] CHRD no 2.

[51] *Simmons v The Queen* (1988) 45 CCC (3d) 296.

[52] *Gould v Yukon Order of Pioneers*, see n 26, above.

[53] See John Stuart Mill, *On Liberty* (Harvard Classics, Collier, 1860), vol 25.

[54] See *Irwin Toy v Quebec* [1989] 1 SCR 927 at 968–71, where in the majority judgment, the Supreme Court gave a three-part rationale for protecting freedom of expression.

Canadians generally believe that speech and expression are more constrained in Canada than in the US. Indeed many Canadians believe that the right to freedom of speech in the US is unlimited. In fact, as one constitutional expert has described, there are at least 13 or more exceptions to unlimited freedom of speech which the US courts and legislatures have recognised, and this list appears to be growing.[55] In Canada, however, the greater weight given to human rights provisions and prohibitions on hate speech appear to be offering new limitations on the expansive application of the speech and expressive rights guaranteed by the Charter.

Pre-Charter Freedom of Expression

In Canada, the position has been complicated by the federal/provincial division of powers. Whilst political speech may be considered to be a federal concern, advertising goods, etc., generally would be a provincial concern. Yet if advertising relates to a federally-controlled medium such as television, it would again be considered to be a federal matter.[56]

These jurisdictional issues are further complicated by the fact that the federal government also has jurisdiction over certain subject matter, such as criminal law. Thus to the extent that some types of speech—such as sedition or obscenity—are treated as criminal offenses, they fall under federal jurisdiction. Whilst provincial governments have regulated the tort of defamation and matters relating to "property and civil rights" such as advertising and consumer protection, there is tremendous scope for overlap and even confusion. In two significant pre-Charter cases, the Supreme Court upheld provincial censorship of films[57] and allowed a provincial temporary prohibition on demonstrations and protests in municipal parks and streets despite the fact that the federal government has considerable jurisdiction over both types of speech and conduct.[58]

---

[55] See Lawrence Tribe, *American Constitutional Law*, 2nd edn (Foundation Press, New York, 1988), ch 12.

[56] See Peter Hogg, *Constitutional Law of Canada*, 3rd edn (1997) at 40.1.

[57] *Nova Scotia Board of Censors v McNeil* [1978] 2 SCR 662.

[58] *A-G Can and Dupond v Montreal* [1978] 2 SCR 770.

Common Law Recognition of Expressive Interests

Canadian courts have not been reluctant to exercise their powers to protect freedom of speech or expression that has been considered to be political speech. Even before World War II, the Canadian Supreme Court struck down an Alberta statute that would have forced newspapers to print a government reply to any criticism.[59] Before the Bill of Rights was enacted, the Supreme Court of Canada showed a willingness to intervene to protect freedom of expression as a fundamental right.[60]

When balanced against legislation enacted to protect human rights, the courts have been less willing to give primacy to freedom of speech. In 1944, Ontario passed an anti-race discrimination statute that was widely denounced as interfering with free speech. The statute prohibited the publication or display of "signs, symbols, or other representations expressing racial or religious discrimination". This act was quasi-criminal, which meant that certain practices were illegal and sanctions for them were set out. Despite its impact on expressive interests, it was treated as valid legislation.

Statutory Recognition

As mentioned above in relation to privacy, during the late 1950s and well into the 1960s provincial legislatures began enacting domestic human rights legislation. This trend has continued to the present, with all provinces and territories having enacted similar legislation which is updated fairly regularly as new issues arise. Such legislation has usually resulted in the establishment of human rights commissions with enforcement via administrative tribunals rather than the courts. In 1978, the first federal human rights act was adopted, which established a federal Commission.[61] With the exception of the hate provisions of the federal statute, human rights codes typically do not concern themselves with matters of speech any more, but instead concentrate on discrimination in relation to employment, housing, public services, membership in public groups, and contract.

---

[59] *Re Alberta Statutes* [1938] SCR100.
[60] See *Samur v City of Quebec* [1953] 2 SCR 299; *Switzman v Elbling* [1957] SCR 285.
[61] Canadian Human Rights Act (RS 1985, c H–6).

In 1960, however, the federal parliament enacted a "quasi-constitutional" Bill of Rights[62] that recognised expressive rights under the heads of freedom of speech, freedom of association, and freedom of the press. The Canadian Bill of Rights was a singularly unsuccessful piece of legislation. The lack of constitutional entrenchment and judicial reluctance to use the Bill of Rights made it a tokenistic reform that attracted increasing criticism.[63] Eventually this criticism and the pressure for social change over the next two decades led to the enactment of the Canadian Charter of Rights and Freedoms, a constitutional document.

Expressive Rights in the Charter of Rights

The first Federal–Provincial Ministerial Conference on Human Rights was held in Ottawa in 1975. Canada had by now ratified the International Human Rights Covenants. The focus of this meeting was the shared responsibilities of both federal and provincial governments regarding human rights. Despite this "focus", by 1977, Sandra Lovelace, an Aboriginal woman, had won a ruling by the UN Human Rights Committee that Canada was in violation of Article 27 of the International Covenant on Civil and Political Rights (right of minority members to practice their culture). Even after this victory, and despite the passing of the first federal Human Rights Act,[64] it took until 1985[65] before the worst of the injustices faced by women like Sandra Lovelace under the Indian Act 1951 were rectified even partially.

In 1982, the Constitution Act, part of which is known as the Charter of Rights and Freedoms, was passed and entrenched.[66] Expressive rights are contained in section 2 of the Charter:

> Everyone has the following fundamental freedoms:
> (a) freedom of conscience and religion;
> (b) freedom of thought, belief, opinion and expression, including freedom of the press and other media of communication;

[62] An Act for the Recognition of Human Rights and Fundamental Freedoms, SC 1960, c 44.

[63] See WS Tarnopolsky, *The Canadian Bill of Rights* (McClelland and Stewart, Toronto, 1975).

[64] See n 61, above.

[65] 28 June 1985, Bill C–31.

[66] See n 25, above. S 15, the equality provision, did not come into force until 1985.

(c) freedom of peaceful assembly; and

(d) freedom of association."

The language of section 1 of the Charter is designed both to activate and give effect to the rights and freedoms guaranteed by the Charter, and, at the same time, to require federal and provincial/territorial governments that decide to place limitations on those rights and freedoms to do so only if they are "prescribed by law" and can be "demonstrably justified in a free and democratic society".

Many areas of law have been affected by these Charter expressive rights. Some cases, such as *Dolphin Delivery*,[67] have also raised questions about the scope of the application of the Charter to private litigants. In this case, the Supreme Court of Canada ruled that secondary picketing of premises involved some form of expression, but that the Charter did not apply to the case because the litigation was between purely private parties and did not involve any exercise of or reliance on governmental action. The Court went on to conclude that even had the Charter applied, section 1 of the Charter would justify granting of the injunction.

As in the US, expressive interests have not received unbounded protection even when given constitutional status as fundamental rights. Much of this litigation has centred on criminal regulation of expression. One of the most interesting tests of the limits on freedom of expression occurred in a Manitoba case concerning two sections of the criminal code that dealt with prostitution[68]—section 195.1(1)(c) (communications in public for the purpose of prostitution) and section 193 (the keeping of common bawdy-houses). It was suggested that these sections infringed section 2(b) (expression) and section 7 (life, liberty and security of the person) of the Charter.

While the Court had no difficulty in upholding the section 193 provision, three of the judges, however, including the then Chief Justice, found that the solicitation section 195.1(1)(c), represented a prima facie infringement of section 2(b) of the Charter. They went on to hold that the scope of freedom of expression extended to communication for the purpose of engaging in prostitution, but they also concluded that the elimination of street solicitation and the social nuisance that it created was a government objective of sufficient

---

[67] *RWDSU v Dolphin Delivery* [1986] 2 SCR 572.

[68] *Prostitution Reference* [1990] 1 SCR 1123.

importance to justify a limitation on the freedom of expression guaranteed by section 2(b) of the Charter.

Similar reasoning has been used in Charter challenges to Canada's criminal code provisions prohibiting "hate speech".[69] In *R v Keegstra*,[70] an Alberta high school teacher was charged with wilfully promoting hatred against an identifiable group by communicating anti-semitic statements to his students. The majority of the Supreme Court upheld his conviction. The majority accepted that section 319(2) of the Criminal Code infringed his Charter right to freedom of expression, but went on to hold that this section of the Code constituted a reasonable limit upon freedom of expression. In the same year, a human rights decision that found anti-semitic telephone messages was also vindicated as an appropriate limitation on freedom of expression.[71] Within two years, however, the Court in *R v Zundel*[72] refused to extend the "hate speech" rationale to a conviction under another section of the code[73] and held it to be unconstitutional.[74]

The Supreme Court has also had no hesitation in justifying limitations on speech and expression in the context of regulating obscene material that reinforces sexist stereotypes. In *Butler*,[75] the Supreme Court concluded that obscenity provisions in the Criminal

---

[69] Criminal Code, s 319(2).

[70] [1990] 3 SCR 697.

[71] *Canada (Human Rights Commission) v Taylor* [1990] 3 SCR 892. The appellants distributed cards inviting calls to a Toronto telephone number answered by recorded messages. The messages, while in part arguably innocuous, contained statements denigrating the Jewish race and religion. In 1979, complaints about these messages were lodged with the Canadian Human Rights Commission. The Commission established a tribunal which concluded that the messages constituted a discriminatory practice under s 13(1) of the Canadian Human Rights Act and ordered the appellants to cease the practice.

[72] [1992] 2 SCR 731.

[73] Criminal Code, RSC, 1985, c C–46, s 181— which provides that "[e]veryone who willfully publishes a statement, tale or news that he knows is false and causes or is likely to cause injury or mischief to a public interest is guilty of an indictable offence and liable to imprisonment."

[74] The charge arose out of the accused's publication of publication of a pamphlet entitled "Did Six Million Really Die?" The accused had added a preface and afterword to an original document, which had previously been published by others in the United States and England. The pamphlet, part of a genre of literature known as "revisionist history", suggests, *inter alia*, that it has not been established that six million Jews were killed before and during World War II and that the Holocaust was a myth perpetrated by a worldwide Jewish conspiracy.

[75] *R v Butler* [1992] 1 SCR 452.

Code infringed section 2(b) of the Charter but that this infringement was demonstrably justified under section 1 of the Charter. The majority of the Court emphasised the growing recognition that sexually exploitative material which may be said to exploit sex in a "degrading or dehumanising" manner will necessarily fail the community standards test, not because it offends against morals, but because it is perceived by public opinion to be particularly harmful to women and therefore harmful to society.[76]

The scope of the protection given to expressive interests in section 2(b) of the Charter has also been tested in other contexts. For example, the rights of the media to report proceedings and broadcast programs concerning trials have been considered by the Supreme Court in a number of decisions. In 1988, the Supreme Court held that protecting the anonymity of victims of sexual assault was a justifiable limit on press freedom.[77] In a strong decision, the Court pointed out that section 442(3) of the Criminal Code was intended to encourage complaints by victims of sexual assault by protecting them from the trauma of wide-spread publication resulting in embarrassment and humiliation. The Court found this objective to be of sufficient importance to warrant overriding a constitutional right. Not all publication bans have been upheld. In *Dagenais*,[78] the Supreme Court set aside a publication ban on a CBC mini-series that dramatised abuse of young boys in Catholic training schools in Newfoundland, despite the fact that criminal trials were ongoing regarding similar schools in Ontario. The Court stressed that a hierarchical approach to rights should be avoided. Two years later, the Court, confronted with a section of the Criminal Code that allowed a judge to exclude

---

[75] *R v Butler* [1992] 1 SCR 452.

[76] When confronted with Canada Customs having a dual standard regarding heterosexual or gay and lesbian censorship of erotic material, imposed on the lesbian and gay community in violation of Charter rights, the Supreme Court of British Columbia refused to find that the Customs Act itself violated the Charter but instead ruled that it was merely the discriminatory application of the Act by Customs that created the violation. On appeal to the Supreme Court, this approach was upheld, although a reverse-onus section of the Customs Act was struck down. *Little Sisters Book and Art Emporium v Canada (Minister of Justice)* [2000] 2 SCR 1120. For a fuller discussion of freedom of expression for lesbians and gays, see Kathleen A Lahey, *Are We Persons Yet?* (University of Toronto Press, Toronto, 1999).

[77] *Canadian Newspapers v Canada (AG)* [1988] 2 SCR 122.

[78] *Dagenais v CBC* [1994] 3 SCR 835.

the public and hear matters *in camera*, stressed that it was only in exceptional cases where there was clear evidence of undue hardship that such orders could be made.[79]

The government has had less success in defending limitations on advertising that have been challenged under section 2 of the Charter. In 1988, the Ford Motor Company succeeded in its attack on a Quebec Law that only allowed public signs to be in French.[80] A year later, the Supreme Court upheld a provincial law limiting advertising aimed at children under the age of 13.[81] The Court recognised that such a law infringed speech, but found that the limitation was justified under section 1. In contrast, however, the tobacco industry was successful in getting the federal Tobacco Products Act struck down as unconstitutional.[82] The Court accepted that the Act, which banned cigarette and tobacco advertisements, unjustifiably infringed section 2(b) of the Charter.[83]

Disadvantaged groups have also found out that expressive rights are not always given unlimited protection under the Charter. Gays and lesbians have successfully invoked expressive interests when seeking the right to hold Pride parades in the face of hostile municipalities or municipal officials.[84] The Aboriginal women of the Native Women's Association of Canada, partially succeeded at the Federal Court of Appeal in getting a declaration that the federal government had restricted the freedom of expression of Aboriginal women in a manner that violated sections 2(b) and 28 of the Charter. The federal government had "frozen them out" of government consultation and funding aimed at enabling Aboriginal organisations to participate in negotiations around constitutional renewal. However, this decision was overturned by the Supreme Court,[85] which held that section 2(b)

---

[79] *CBC v New Brunswick (AG)* [1996] 3 SCR 480.

[80] *Ford v Quebec (AG)* [1988] 2.SCR 1326.

[81] *Irwin Toy Ltd. v Quebec (AG)* [1989] 1 SCR 927.

[82] *RJR-MacDonald v Canada* [1995] 3 SCR 199.

[83] The court gave indications that had the legislation been more carefully directed at banning advertisements aimed at young people or non-smokers then it might have survived. See [1995] 3 SCR 199, paras 164, 191.

[84] Eg *Geller v Reimer* (1994) 21 CHRR D/156; *Hudler v London (City)* [1997] OHRBID No 23 (Ont Bd of Inq) discussed in Lahey, *Are We Persons Yet?*, n 76 above, 153; 404: nn 111,112.

[85] *Native Women's Assn of Canada v Canada* [1994] 3 SCR 627.

does not guarantee any particular means of expression or place a positive obligation upon the government to fund or consult anyone.[86]

PRIVACY VERSUS EXPRESSIVE INTERESTS—
CREATING A BALANCE

The recognition of the right to privacy initially arose from concerns about the use of images of private people by "public" media either without their permission or outside the terms of any permission given. While the right to sue for misappropriation of personality or unauthorised use of private images or information has become reasonably well established in Canadian law, the shift from pure private law principles to Charter discourse has raised the basic questions all over again: Is the right to privacy a fundamental right or freedom? And does freedom of expression give actions for invasion of privacy right less scope than they may have had at common law?

Overall, it appears that the growing judicial articulation of privacy interests in various provisions of the Charter reinforces the status of common law actions for invasion of privacy.[87] The reluctance of the Supreme Court of Canada to treat freedom of expression even as entrenched in the Charter as an unbounded right further suggests that expressive interests certainly will not spell the end of these private tort actions.

---

[86] For insight into some of the problems that have faced Aboriginal women, see Kathleen Jamieson, "Indian Women and the Law in Canada: Citizens Minus" (Advisory Council on the Status of Women, Ottawa, 1978).

[87] Eg *R. v Salituro* [1991] 3 SCR, a case concerning the common law rule prohibiting spouses from testifying against each other was found to be inconsistent with developing social values and with the values enshrined in the Charter. See Iacobucci J, at 675:

"Where the principles underlying a common law rule are out of step with the values enshrined in the Charter, the courts should scrutinize the rule closely. If it is possible to change the common law rule so as to make it consistent with Charter values . . . then the rule ought to be changed."

The courts can and should make incremental changes to the common law to bring legal rules into step with a changing society.

General Principles

There has been as yet no definitive ruling directly on the question, but several Supreme Court of Canada cases have considered how competing Charter values or rights are to be applied. *Big M Drug Mart*[88] was the first significant case to consider this issue.[89] In this case, the Supreme Court reached its decision not by "balancing" the competing Charter values, but through the more complex process of contextualising the rights involved and endeavouring to reach a conclusion based on underlying core values in the Charter rather than on the basis of a hierarchical assessment of rights.

This approach was emphasised in *Dagenais*,[90] where Chief Justice Lamer stated:

> The pre-Charter common law rule governing publication bans emphasized the right to a fair trial over the free expression interests of those affected by the ban. In my view, the balance this rule strikes is inconsistent with the principles of the Charter, and in particular, the equal status given by the Charter to ss.2(b) and 11(d). It would be inappropriate for the courts to continue to apply a common law rule that automatically favoured the rights protected by s.11(d) over those protected by s.2(b). A hierarchical approach to rights, which places some over others, must be avoided, both when interpreting the Charter and when developing the common law. When the protected rights of two individuals come into conflict, as can occur in the case of publication bans, Charter principles require a balance to be achieved that fully respects the importance of both sets of rights.
>
> It is open to this Court to "develop the principles of the common law in a manner consistent with the fundamental values enshrined in the Constitution": *Dolphin Delivery, supra*, at p. 603 (*per* McIntyre J). I am, therefore, of the view that it is necessary to reformulate the common law rule governing the issuance of publication bans in a manner that reflects the principles of the Charter. Given that publication bans, by their very

---

[88] [1985] 1 SCR 295.

[89] The most recent case where competing rights have been considered is *Trinity Western University v British Columbia College of Teachers* [2001] SCC 31 (File No 27168). The dissenting judgment of Madame Justice Claire L'Heureux-Dubé demonstrates a vision of the Charter's equality values that hopefully will be followed.

[90] See n 78, above at paras 72 and 73.

definition, curtail the freedom of expression of third parties, I believe that the common law rule must be adapted so as to require a consideration both of the objectives of a publication ban, and the proportionality of the ban to its effect on protected Charter rights.

A similar point was made in *Mills*,[91] in which the accused had sought access to confidential records of the complainant. The Supreme Court discussed in detail the problems inherent in rape shield laws and the right of an accused to a fair trial. The Supreme Court, having struck down a previous law, now emphasised "a posture of respect to Parliament" and went on to stress Parliament's role in protecting rights and freedoms. In a telling passage the Court set out the problem:

> In adopting Bill C–46, Parliament sought to recognize the prevalence of sexual violence against women and children and its disadvantageous impact on their rights, to encourage the reporting of incidents of sexual violence, to recognize the impact of the production of personal information on the efficacy of treatment, and to reconcile fairness to complainants with the rights of the accused. Parliament may also be understood to be recognizing "horizontal" equality concerns where women's inequality results from the acts of other individuals and groups rather than the state.

The Court went on to reiterate the way in which the problem of competing rights should be addressed:

> Two principles of fundamental justice seem to conflict: the right to full answer and defence and the right to privacy. Neither right may be defined in such a way as to negate the other and both sets of rights are informed by the equality rights at play in this context. No single principle is absolute and capable of trumping the others; they must all be defined in light of competing claims. A contextual approach to the interpretation of rights should be adopted as they often inform, and are informed by, other rights at issue in the circumstances.

In the final analysis, the Court decided that the accused's right to make full answer and defence had to be considered in light of other principles of fundamental justice, and accordingly ruled that the

---

[91]   *R v Mills* [1999] 3 SCR 668.

right to make full answer did not include the right to evidence that could distort the trial process.[92]

Privacy Versus Expression in the Charter

Only a few Charter cases have directly considered the interaction between privacy and expression rights in the context of the common law. Because the Charter applies only to government action, one might expect that when a party is employed by the government and acting in the course of that employment, it would be the Charter expression rights that would be seen as relevant to issues arising out of critical allegations concerning the official rather than a simple application of the common law of defamation.[93] This is because the Charter's freedom of expression provisions do not make exceptions for such statements. Thus the Charter right appears to conflict with the common law.[94]

In the US and Australia, this conflict had already been before the courts in the context of press freedom and criticism of public officials.[95] When the same underlying issue of the Charter right of freedom of expression and the common-law of defamation came before the Canadian Supreme Court in *Hill v Church of Scientology*,[96] the

[92] There are also two other Supreme Court cases involving related issues: In *R v Seaboyer* [1991] 2 SCR 577, the court held that the "rape-shield" provision under section 276 of the Criminal Code restricting the right of the defence to cross-examine and lead evidence of the complainant's previous sexual conduct did infringe s 7 or s 11(d) of the Charter. *R v O'Connor* [1995] 4 SCR 411, involved disclosure of third party records (medical, counselling and school records) where the Crown had not properly complied with a court order. The Court held that a stay of proceedings was inappropriate and upheld an appellate order for a retrial.

[93] Historically, the common law tort of defamation has provided a remedy for harm caused to a person's reputation by untrue statements.

[94] See Peter W Hogg, *Constitutional Law of Canada* Vol 2 (Carswell, Toronto, 1997) at para 40.10 for a fuller discussion of these issues.

[95] *New York Times v Sullivan* (1964) 376 US 254; *Theophanous v Herald & Weekly Times* (1994) 124 ALR 1 (HC of Aust).

[96] [1995] 2 SCR 1130. The appellant in this case was a lawyer who, when representing the Church of Scientology (the other appellant), had held a press conference, reading from and commenting upon allegations contained in a notice of motion. The Church intended to commence criminal contempt proceedings against the respondent, a Crown attorney. The allegations were that the respondent had misled a judge and had breached orders sealing certain documents belonging to the Church. The remedy sought was the imposition of a fine or his imprisonment. At the contempt proceedings, the allegations against the respondent were found to be untrue and without foundation. The Crown Attorney then sued for libel damages. Both appellants were found jointly liable for general damages in the amount of $300,000 and

Court, in a unanimous decision, upheld the common law position in its entirety. The Court began by holding that because the criticised official had sued in his own right (albeit this suit funded by his Ministry), his defamation suit was not "government action" within the meaning of section 32 of the Charter.[97] The Court then declined to follow either the US or Australian precedents. Instead the Court determined that in Canada, while the common law had to be interpreted in a way that was consistent with Charter principles, this was simply a manifestation of the inherent jurisdiction of the courts to modify or extend the common law in order to reflect with prevailing social conditions and values. When applying that principle to the facts, the Court held that the common law of defamation was consistent with the underlying values of the Charter. Thus the Court found that there was no need to amend or alter the common law, because it already struck an appropriate balance between the values of reputation and freedom of expression.[98] In his judgment, Cory J specifically dealt with the interface between freedom of expression, privacy, and the reputation aspect of libel:

> Further, reputation is intimately related to the right to privacy which has been accorded constitutional protection. As La Forest J wrote in *R. v Dyment*, [1988] 2 S.C.R. 417 at 427, privacy, including informational privacy, is "[g]rounded in man's physical and moral autonomy" and "is essential for the well-being of the individual". The publication of defamatory comments constitutes an invasion of the individual's personal privacy and is an affront to that person's dignity. The protection of a person's reputation is indeed worthy of protection in our democratic society and must be carefully balanced against the equally important right of freedom of expression . . . the individual represents and reflects

the Church alone was found liable for aggravated damages of $500,000 and punitive damages of $800,000. This judgment was affirmed by the Court of Appeal.

[97] Section 32 (1) This Charter applies—

(a) to the Parliament and government of Canada in respect of all matters within the authority of Parliament including all matters relating to the Yukon Territory and Northwest Territories; and

(b) to the legislature and government of each province in respect of all matters within the authority of the legislature of each province.

[98] The court found that for lawyers reputation had particular significance!

the innate dignity of the individual, a concept which underlies all the Charter rights.[99]

In the Quebec case of *Aubry v Éditions Vice-Versa*,[100] another recent decision of the Supreme Court of Canada, we can gain further insight into how the top court in Canada will apply the principles of *Big M* when giving effect to both privacy and expressive interests. The impact of *Aubry* is complicated by the fact that it arose under Quebec civil law and the Quebec Charter of Human Rights and Freedoms. This places this decision in a unique position in relation to both private law and human rights jurisprudence on the rights of the media to invade privacy.

Privacy interests are given comparatively progressive recognition under French civil law. Not surprisingly, the Quebec civil code thus has followed the French civil law tradition in protecting privacy as a civil right that can give rise to damages when liability for a "fault" has been established. In 1977, the protection thus given to privacy interests in civil law was further enhanced by several provisions of the Quebec Charter of Human Rights and Freedoms.[101] The meaning of this protection was tested in the *Aubry* case when an arts magazine published a photograph of a teenage girl that had been taken in a public place without her permission. When she complained that she was being singled out at school because of the picture, her parents brought a suit against the magazine for invasion of privacy, claiming that publication of the photograph infringed her right to her image and to privacy. The magazine countered with the claim that freedom of artistic expression or the public's right to information justifies publication of such photographs. In addition to having to assess the impact of the Quebec Charter on its civil code privacy provisions, the Court had to rule on the extent to which expressive interests may have to be balanced or otherwise reconciled with each other.

Even though this is not a Canadian Charter case, the fact that *Aubry* was decided in such detailed and careful reasons by the Supreme Court, and the way in which the Canadian Charter privacy and expressive provisions will likely operate in a similar common-law

---

[99] At para 121 *et seq.*

[100] *Aubry v Éditions Vice-Versa* [1998] 1 SCR 591 (SCC) *per* L'Heureux-Dubé and Bastarache JJ, writing for the majority, and Lamer CJ and Major J dissenting.

[101] RSQ, c C–12, ss 3, 5, 9.1, 49.

context, has meant that *Aubry* offers useful insight into whether com-mon-law jurisdictions in Canada will be able to continue to develop the right of action for invasion of privacy by the media. The modest award of damages ($2,000, upheld by the Supreme Court) belies the importance of this case for both common-law and civil code juris-dictions.

The majority judgment for the Court was written by Madame Justice Claire L'Heureux-Dubé. L'Heureux-Dubé J, herself a civilly-trained jurist, began by recognising that although the infringement of a right guaranteed by the Quebec Charter of Human Rights and Freedoms gives rise, under section 49, paragraph 1, to an action for moral and material prejudice, such an action is still subject to the civil law principles of recovery. As a result, she had to demonstrate first that the traditional elements of liability in civil law must be established, which she did by analysing the status of privacy claims in the civil code.

She then ruled that the right to one's image is an element of the right to privacy under section 5 of the Quebec Charter. From this, she reasoned that if the purpose of the right to privacy is to protect a sphere of individual autonomy, it must include the ability to control the use made of one's image. The element of fault was satisfied as soon as the image was published without the girl's consent in a way that enabled her to be identified, and at that moment, her right to her image was infringed.

L'Heureux-Dubé and Bastarache JJ concluded that the right to respect for private life comes into conflict with the right to freedom of expression, which is protected by section 3 of the Quebec Charter, because freedom of expression includes freedom of artistic expres-sion. (Interestingly, the Court refused to subdivide "expression" or to create special categories of expressive rights.) Looking to section 9.1 of the Quebec Charter as containing the over-arching principles by which all Charter protections are to be interpreted, the majority Justices concluded that the public's right to information, which is part of the meaning of "freedom of expression", does limit the right to respect for one's private life in certain circumstances.

Just where that dividing line is to be drawn remains elusive. The majority decision directs that any balancing of inconsistent or competing rights must depend on evaluating two factors in con-text: (a) the nature of the information and (b) the situation of those concerned. The Court rejected the notion that some types of information could be deprived of their private quality if they could be considered to fall into the category of "socially useful information", and instead asked whether the girl's right to protection of her image was more important than the magazine's right to publish it without having to obtain her permission first. It may be that the case does come down to this—if it is reasonable for the publisher to obtain permission at the time the image is taken, then that permission is a legal requirement. How the difficulty of asking for permission or how a degree of celebrity would affect that basic proposition is not clear.

What is clear from the *Aubry* case, however, is that the Court is willing to recognise only a limited right of artistic expression. As the Court stated, an artist's right to publish his or her work is not absolute and cannot include the right to infringe, without any justification, a fundamental right of the subject whose image appears in the work unless there is some further element of public interest.

In common-law terms, the significance of the *Aubry* decision is that it moves somewhat out of the realm of strictly civil liability and into the as-yet highly uncertain terrain of civil suits for violation of Charter rights. Although the Quebec Charter is considered to be quasi-constitutional, it is still in function more like an ordinary statute or an interpretation statute than it is like a constitutional document. Nonetheless, the entire notion of permitting private individuals to sue others for violations of rights still induces a fairly high level of anxiety among the legal establishment in Canada.

The Chief Justice of the Court, Antonio Lamer, agreed that privacy and expressive interests could be balanced. In his dissenting decision, he emphasised that the defendant's liability could not be grounded in the Quebec Charter alone, but must be established only by proving that a fault committed by the appellants caused her prejudice. He pointed out that although the law of civil liability is informed by the constitutional or quasi-constitutional rights protected by charters of rights, he urged his colleagues to be reluctant to view fault as stemming from a violation of rights alone. In his words, "mere infringement of a right or freedom does not necessarily constitute fault. It is unjustifiable infringements that constitute fault".

Lamer CJ also felt that section 9.1 of the Quebec Charter, which provides that rights and freedoms must be exercised in relation to each other, with proper regard for public order, democratic values and general well-being, should be given interpretative significance that would enable it to be used to render the law of civil liability consistent with the rights-bearing provisions of the Quebec Charter. While Lamer CJ did agree that expressive and privacy rights should be balanced, he was of the opinion that the two concepts of civil fault and public interest would suffice to protect both interests.

In the end, Lamer CJ's views do not seem to be too different from those of the majority: He also concluded that the nature of the information conveyed by the image should be balanced against the reasonable expectation of privacy, and he also concluded that the photographer had reasonable opportunity to obtain the girl's consent. The difference in outcome, however, he put down to the proof of prejudice said to result from the fault. In his view, the girl's simple statement that her classmates had laughed at her did not in itself constitute sufficient evidence of prejudice because it did not provide any information about how she felt. Major J dissented on the narrower basis that he felt there was no evidence of damage.

With the Supreme Courts endorsement of both the common law and "privacy" in the *Hill* case, it might have been anticipated that the lower courts would have a strong Charter framework in which to develop the rather limited jurisprudence concerning privacy. Yet when the case of *Gould Estate*,[102] which concerned the related "publicity right"[103] inherent in privacy concepts, came before the Ontario courts, the publisher's expressive interests were given primacy. The case arose when the Estate of a reclusive concert pianist tried to prevent publication of a book by a journalist who was using the record of an interview from some forty years previously and photographs of the pianist taken at that time. It was accepted that the journalist had copyright in the material, and at the lower level, the court agreed that the personality right had to be balanced against the interests of society in freedom of expression. On appeal, the Ontario Court of Appeal, although upholding the decision, retreated from the discussion of balancing rights, ie publicity rights as an aspect of privacy rights as opposed to expressive rights, and simply relied instead on freedom of expression.

---

[102] *Gould Estate v Stoddart Publishing* [1996] 15 Estates and Trusts Reports (2d); *Gould Estate v Stoddart Publishing* (1998) 321 DLR (4th) 161 (Ont CA).

[103] See n 12, above.

CONCLUSIONS

The context of the *Aubry* decision is limited to the Quebec Charter. The Court did not specifically evaluate the common law relating to personality rights in the rest of Canada. Thus the decision is not readily applicable to the common law provinces in Canada. In addition, the tort of appropriation of personality is still a relatively recent legal development in common-law jurisdictions, and will clearly need more time to evolve. It is still not clear whether the tort of misappropriation of personality incorporates privacy and proprietary protections against unauthorised merchandising, and how far beyond non-commercial appropriation the tort actually extends.

While these unresolved issues create considerable uncertainty in the law, the decision in *Aubry* has the potential to influence the evolution of this area of tort liability substantially. *Aubry* appears to contemplate that the scope of personality rights will continue to expand in the future. Whether this will be true of "private" personalities only remains to be seen. The decision in *Gould Estate* suggests that there will still be circumstances in which celebrities will be considered to have relinquished their right to privacy or to have failed to establish a right to "publicity" where media expressive interests are in the balance. However, *Hill v Church of Scientology* suggests that Charter expressive rights cannot completely alter the shape of common law doctrine when the common law has evolved consistent with contemporary social practices and realities.

The impact of these decisions is far from crystal clear. One commentator has concluded that the Supreme Court in *Aubry* has further complicated the issues by creating two contrasting levels of protection for publicity and privacy within Canada—one in the common law jurisdictions and a differing one in Quebec.[104] However, it is possible that the Supreme Court of Canada's analysis of the critical importance of protecting the right to privacy could also inspire other courts to adopt their reasoning in common law jurisdictions on the basis that the protection of privacy in common law was originally and continues to be reasoned soundly.

---

[104] Conrad Nest, "From 'Abba' to Gould: A Closer Look at the Development of Personality Rights in Canada", (1995) 5 *Appeal* 12–17.

6

Privacy and Freedom of Expression in New Zealand

Rosemary Tobin

INTRODUCTION

In New Zealand freedom of expression has emerged as a principle of the common law,[1] although it is fair to say that the principle remained largely unstated until the latter part of the twentieth century.[2] At about the same time it also attracted interest from the New Zealand legislature. Freedom of information, for example, became a political issue in New Zealand in the mid-1970s culminating in the Official Information Act 1982 and the enshrinement of the principle of availability of official information in section 5 of that Act.[3]

The enactment of section 14 of the New Zealand Bill of Rights Act 1990—"Everyone has the right to freedom of expression, including the freedom to seek, receive, and impart information and opinions of any kind in any form"—gave freedom of expression greater currency. The rights contained in the Bill of Rights, like those of the common law, are not absolute,[4] or to be applied each in isolation.[5] There are numerous instances when our New Zealand law restricts free speech—the Films, Videos and Publications Classification Act 1993 is but one example. The common law also restricts free speech

---

[1] See, for example *Bell Booth Group Ltd v AG* [1989] 3 NZLR 148 at 156, and see also Richardson J in *MOT v Noort* [1992] 3 NZLR 260 at 277 where His Honour confirms that the Act is declaratory of existing human rights.

[2] See the discussion in G Huscroft and P Rishworth, *Rights and Freedoms* (Brookers, Wellington, 1995) ch 5.

[3] For a legislative history of the Act see I Eagles, M Taggart and G Liddell, *Freedom of Information in New Zealand* (OUP, Auckland, 1992) ch 1.

[4] *MOT v Noort*, n 1, above at 283; *Solicitor General v Radio New Zealand* [1994] 1 NZLR 48 at 59.

[5] *Ibid.*

through the torts of invasion of privacy and defamation, although in both torts the public figure may be treated differently.

Privacy is not protected in the Bill of Rights,[6] although it does have statutory protection. The first privacy Bill to be brought before the New Zealand Parliament was the Preservation of Privacy Bill introduced in 1972, but it was not until the Privacy Act 1993 that comprehensive privacy legislation was enacted. Privacy of personal information receives statutory protection through the information privacy principles (IPPs)[7] in the Privacy Act.

There is an obvious tension between freedom of expression and privacy. Where, for example, a police officer shot a man in the course of his duty then sought to prevent publication of details of his identity the application for an interim injunction was dismissed.[8] There could be no breach of privacy in respect of an action by a public officer doing a public act in a public place.[9] The court would only intervene in respect of the recognised right of free expression given under section 14 if there was a likelihood of an interference with a probable trial.[10]

There are nonetheless several ways that an individual whose privacy has been invaded can seek redress. Where the complaint relates to personal information the injured party can complain to the Privacy Commissioner. This does not, however, assist where the invasion of privacy has been by the news media in its news gathering activities which are exempt from the Commissioner's jurisdiction. However the privacy principles developed by the Broadcasting Standards Authority (the BSA)[11] will provide a measure of protection for disaffected parties. The alternative is to bring an action in the common law tort of invasion of privacy which emerged in the late 1980s. The number of

---

[6] See the White Paper, *A Bill of Rights for New Zealand* (1985) para.10.145 where it was argued that it would be inappropriate to include a right that was not fully recognised and which was in the course of development and whose boundaries would be both uncertain and contentious.

[7] The Privacy Act has 12 Information Privacy Principles which apply to personal information held about individuals by an "agency" as defined in the Act.

[8] *A v Wilson & Horton* [2000] NZAR 428.

[9] *Ibid*, 431.

[10] *Ibid.*

[11] In 1992 the BSA provided an advisory opinion for broadcasters setting out the original five privacy principles which it used as a guide when hearing complaints. The number has now been increased to seven.

cases concerning the tort is limited, while there are now several hundred privacy decisions by the BSA, but the commonalities between the tort developed in the courts, and the privacy principles are unmistakable. This was inevitable as both took US case law, and the analysis of that case law by Prosser,[12] as their starting point. The Press Council is another body which has jurisdiction to hear complaints about privacy, but its jurisdiction is rather more limited, and the decisions are not as detailed, or the remedies as effective.[13] It is true that the third of the principles developed by the Press Council confirms the right to privacy, but not surprisingly the overriding commitment of the Press Council is to the freedom of the press.

THE PRIVACY ACT AND THE MEDIA EXCEPTION

The Privacy Act 1993, which is similar to UK data protection law, does not create a right of privacy as such, but it does give people a measure of control over personal information that agencies hold about them. The legislation was enacted in response to concerns about the increasingly intrusive nature of society, and the need to protect individual privacy.[14] Twelve IPPs are at the heart of the legislation. These cover the collection, storage, use and disclosure of personal information by agencies, and recognise a right of access to, and correction of, personal information by the individual concerned. The legislation also enables a particular industry to develop its own code of practice, approved by the Privacy Commissioner, where there may be specialist needs.[15]

---

[12] W Prosser, "Privacy" (1960) 48 *Cal LR* 383 as discussed further in WP Keeton, *Prosser and Keeton on the Law of Torts*, 5th edn (West, St Paul, Minn, 1984).

[13] The Press Council is a self-regulatory body that was established by Publishers and Journalists in 1972 to provide the public with a independent forum for resolution of complaints against the Press. It has no legally enforceable punitive powers, although newspapers subject to a complaint are expected to publish the decision. What is of more concern is that where the complainant may have a legal remedy she is required to undertake in writing that having referred the matter to the Press Council she will not continue or commence proceedings against the newspaper or the journalist.

[14] For a detailed discussion of the Privacy Act 1993 see E Longworth and T McBride, *The Privacy Act: A Guide* (GP Publications, Wellington, 1994).

[15] An important example is the code of practice developed by the health sector: The Health Information Privacy Code 1994.

As the IPPs are all expressed to apply to agencies it is important to note that the definition of "agency" excludes the "news media" in relation to their "news activities". Both terms are defined.[16]

News activity means—
(a) The gathering of news, or the preparation or compiling of articles or programmes of or concerning news, observations on news, or current affairs, for the purposes of dissemination to the public or any section of the public:
(b) The dissemination, to the public or any section of the public, of any article or programme of or concerning—
    (i) News:
    (ii) Observations on news:
    (iii) Current affairs:

News medium means any agency whose business, or part of whose business, consists of a news activity; but, in relation to *principles 6 and 7*, does not include [[Radio New Zealand Limited or]] Television New Zealand Limited.[17]

The news media exemption is important. It was supported by the Privacy Commissioner when the Bill was first introduced, and his experience during the first few years of the Act's operation did not cause him to change his mind.[18] He recognised that without it the media would find it difficult to function effectively.[19] Case note 18148 is a straightforward application of the exemption. The Department of Corrections allowed a television broadcaster to film a documentary inside a prison. The inmates had been advised they would not be identified, and the broadcaster agreed to pixelate any identifying features of any of the inmates before the documentary was broadcast. Unfortunately the television company failed to do so, and one of the inmates complained that he had been identified. The

---

[16] See Privacy Act 1993, s 2(1).

[17] IPPs 6 & 7 require agencies that hold personal information about an individual to allow that individual access to and a right to request the information to be corrected. The reason Radio NZ and TVNZ remain subject to IPPs 6 & 7 is historical. See Longworth and McBride, n 14 above, at 106–07.

[18] See *Necessary and Desirable: Privacy Act 1993 Review* (1998) paras 1.4.49 and 1.4.52.

[19] *Ibid* para 1.4.51. In particular he was aware that the press perceived a significant conflict between privacy law and the legitimate activities of the media. He hoped the exemption would ensure that concerns about constraints on the news media would not eventuate.

Privacy Commissioner accepted that the television company was a news medium and not subject to the information privacy principles while collecting and holding information for the current affairs documentary, nor was it subject to the IPPs while disseminating the documentary. The investigation was discontinued.

Of rather more interest is the decision of the Complaints Review Tribunal in *Talley Family v National Business Review*.[20] The defendant was a weekly business newspaper which published an annual edition called *The Rich List*. The plaintiff was included in the list in two editions of the paper. A complaint was lodged with the Privacy Commissioner about the personal details included in the biographical information. The Commissioner considered that the complaint was not within his jurisdiction as the defendant was an "agency" and the publication was a news activity by a news medium.

In making a determination as to whether a particular defendant is a news agency there are two possible approaches. The first is a narrow approach which requires an analysis of the content of the actual publication, while the second simply requires a determination of whether the particular activity concerned was part of an undertaking broadly described as a "news activity".

Before the Tribunal the plaintiff argued the real question was whether the defendant was acting in relation to a news activity when it published the list. This in turn depended on whether the contents of the list itself were news or current affairs. The central plank of the plaintiff's argument was that "news" should be interpreted narrowly, and based upon whether or not there was public interest in the material, in the sense of legitimate public concern. *The Rich List* was, the plaintiff said, based on private facts with no distinguishing characteristic to give the private facts therein the character of news and current affairs. More specifically the plaintiff's holdings were private, and if private facts were to be published there had to be something which gave the private facts the character of news and current affairs. Wealth, it was argued did not.

Both the defendant and the Privacy Commissioner, who also made submissions, argued for a broader interpretation. The defendant argued simply that publication of *The Rich List* was a news activity, as distinct from its non-news activities such as employment of staff,

[20] (1997) 4 HRNZ 72.

compilation of subscription lists, and marketing. The Privacy Commissioner argued that the words "news" and "current affairs" should be given their ordinary meaning, and that any attempt to do otherwise would place an unacceptable limitation on the freedom of the press. In turn he said "news activity" encompassed news, current affairs and articles both of and concerning news and observations on news.[21] It thus followed that the compilation and publication of *The Rich List* contained observations on news, and were of and concerning news, and in this way clearly fell within the definition of news activity.

Ultimately the Tribunal did not decide between the two approaches as on either approach it considered the result was the same.[22] On the broad approach the nature of the publication itself was clearly a news activity of the defendant. On the narrow approach what constituted public interest could include people who raise issues in which a community is interested or who are connected to those issues. As some people were more involved in the community than others it was a short step to accepting that[23]:

> dependent upon the extent of their influence or power in a community, the family history, details, finances, assets owned, business interests, job roles, personal characters, places of residence, occupation and views of those people may well be of public interest because of the way those characteristics affect the way in which they behave in that community. If the way they behave, or conduct their affairs, affects others in the community (perhaps because they are employers, perhaps because their activities have an effect on the physical environment, perhaps because of the way they affect the local economy) then otherwise personal details may well be of public interest. Businesses which are economically significant in New Zealand will fall within this definition as well as the people behind those businesses.

Information about prominent members of the community could be of legitimate public interest to those in the community. The corollary would be that personal details written about others in the

---

[21] (1997) 4 HRNZ, 76.

[22] See E Paton Simpson, "The News activity Exemption in the Privacy Act 1993" (1999) 6 *NZBLQ* 269, 272.

[23] N 20 above, 76.

community who were not in a position to influence affairs in the community would not be of public interest, and would not be "news" on the narrow interpretation for which the plaintiff contended.

Nor has the Tribunal subsequently clarified its position as to which approach should be taken. In *Wallingford v National Beekeepers Association of NZ*[24] the plaintiff unsuccessfully sought information from the defendant about the identity of the author of a series of letters in the *New Zealand Beekeeper* published by the defendant. The case is particularly useful as it demonstrates the width of the exemption. The arguments against the Tribunal's jurisdiction were twofold. First, the plaintiff said that the defendant was not a news medium because its activities in the collection of material for the journal bore little resemblance to the activities of a journalist working for news organisations. The Privacy Commissioner elaborated on this. He argued that the definition of news medium meant an agency, a substantial part of whose business consisted of a news activity, and whose activities were such that they deserved the special protections available to ensure the freedom of the news media in a democratic society. The second issue was whether the Letters to the Editor column could be considered a news activity. Both the defendant and the Privacy Commissioner argued that it was not as it was neither an article nor a programme.

The Tribunal struck out the proceedings applying its earlier comments in *Talley*. In its opinion a news activity encompassed not only publications like *The Rich List* which contained a number of articles and columns and other pieces of writing, but also publications which contained a single piece only.[25] The important point was that it was the publication as a whole that was under scrutiny, not the individual pieces contained within the publication.[26] Once again, on either of the two approaches discussed the defendant was carrying out a news activity.

The news medium definition also required that the publication was created for the purposes of dissemination to the public, or a section of the public. The journal itself although not available to the public by general subscription, was not limited to financial members

---

[24] [2001] NZAR 251.
[25] *Ibid*, 255.
[26] *Ibid.*

of the association, but was distributed to public libraries throughout New Zealand. It gave every appearance of being available to that section of the public, interested in beekeeping and who wished to read it either through subscription or in a public library.

The dissemination of news and current affairs is of paramount importance in a democracy, and the news media exemption in the Privacy Act confirms that. This is not to say that an individual whose privacy has been invaded by the news media will always be left without a remedy; the remedy may lie against the person who disclosed the personal information to the media. Where, for example, a police sergeant advised the media of his intention to obtain a temporary protection order without the knowledge of the person in respect of whom it was sought, the complainant was successful in obtaining damages for the humiliation, loss of dignity and injury to feelings she suffered upon the widespread publication the information received.[27] Although the complainant was not identified by name, her age, the occupation of her parents and the region they lived in, together with parts of a statement she had made to the police, including details of injuries she had suffered in past assaults, were disclosed. These details enabled a newspaper to identify her. The actions of the media in publishing the story were exempt from the Privacy Act, and any remedy in respect of the actions of the journalists concerned lay with the tort, or by virtue of a complaint to the Press Council or the BSA.[28]

It might be thought that where there is comprehensive legislation covering privacy interests that a common law tort could not survive, but an early attempt to argue that the Privacy Act had codified the law relating to privacy leaving no room for any common law right was unsuccessful.[29]

---

[27] *Proceedings Commissioner v Commissioner of Police* [2000] NZAR 277. The complainant was awarded $10,000.

[28] In fact a complaint was laid with the BSA, although not by the complainant, but the BSA declined to uphold the complaint under standard G5. See decision 1997–031.

[29] *Hobson v Harding* (1994) 1 HRNZ 342. The judge accepted that as the Act enacted a set of principles governing the collection, use and disclosure of personal information, enforceable by the machinery in the Act and which could lead to proceedings before a Complaints Review Tribunal this suggested that no common law remedy should be available. However he was reluctantly forced to reject this argument. Not only were common law rights not excluded by the Act, which was affirmative in nature, but section 115 enacted a specific exception to civil liability insofar as personal information was made available in good faith pursuant to principle 6.

The Common Law Tort of Invasion of Privacy

The common law tort of invasion of privacy, which emerged in New Zealand in 1986, is founded on an individual's right of autonomy, the right of any person to decide who will learn what about her.[30] Unfortunately the cases have almost all been ones where an injunction was sought to prevent publicity, and as most decisions had to be given fairly quickly, this has hampered a detailed analysis of the tort. The rationale for the tort has been expressed by Jeffries J as follows[31]:

> a person who lives an ordinary private life has a right to be left alone and to live the private aspects of his life without being subjected to unwarranted or undesired publicity or public disclosure.

It is important to acknowledge at the outset that both the privacy tort and the privacy principles developed by the BSA evolved from the privacy jurisprudence developed in the American courts. Not surprisingly, when freedom of expression came into conflict with privacy, the American courts accorded primacy to freedom of speech.[32] Two of the four separate torts identified by the great American jurist Prosser[33] have been influential in both the BSA's Privacy Principles and the New Zealand cases[34]: the intentional intrusion into the plaintiff's seclusion or solitude or into his or her private affairs, and the public disclosure of private facts about the plaintiff. In respect of the first of these, the New Zealand courts have adopted the requirement that the matter into which the defendant intruded had to be a private matter, and that the intrusion itself had to be highly offensive and objectionable to a reasonable person. The courts have also considered the means used to intrude, and the defendant's purpose in seeking the information, usually for the purpose of news or current

---

[30] See discussion in Laster, "Commonalities Between Breach of Confidence and Privacy" (1990) 14 *NZULR* 144.

[31] *Tucker v News Media Ownership Ltd* [1986] 2 NZLR 716 at 731.

[32] See for example *Florida Star v BJF*, 105 L Ed 2d 443 (1989).

[33] See Prosser, n 12, above. The other two torts, the false light tort and the tort of misappropriation of the plaintiff's name or likeness, have not been considered.

[34] See *Tucker v News Media Ownership Ltd*, n 31, above; *T v AG* (1988) 5 NZFLR 357; *Morgan v TVNZ* (HC Christchurch, 1 March 1990, CP 67/90); *Marris v TV3 Network Services Ltd* (HC Wellington, 14 October 1991, CP754/91); *Bradley v Wingnut Films* [1993] 1 NZLR 415; *P v D* [2000] 2 NZLR 591; *L v G* [2002] DCR 234.

affairs, in determining whether privacy has been invaded. In respect of the second tort, Prosser's three requirements[35] have also been applied:

(i)   the disclosure of private facts must be a public disclosure, and not a private one;

(ii) the facts disclosed must be private facts and not public ones; and

(iii) the matter made public must be one which would be highly offensive and objectionable to a reasonable person of ordinary sensibilities.

Public interest, that the matter is of legitimate concern to the public, can defeat an individual's claim to privacy. Truth, however, is not a defence to the tort.

Although *Tucker v News Media Ownership Ltd*[36] was the first case to recognise a potential cause of action for the tort of privacy, and in the course of the proceedings judges in the High Court and the Court of Appeal referred to the new tort with approval, very little analysis of its ambit was attempted. Two of the judges saw the tort as an adaptation or extension of the tort of intentional infliction of emotional distress,[37] but unfortunately there was no analysis of the extent to which intention might be an element of the tort, and if so what it was the defendant had to intend. The case did however confirm that a public fact, in *Tucker* a criminal conviction, could over time become a private fact. How this happened, how long it took, and whether all public facts could become private facts over time was left for subsequent determination. The case also raised, but did not decide, the extent to which those who sought publicity might lose a right to privacy. McGechan J considered that as Tucker had gone to the public for funds, although he did so reluctantly, this could mean some loss of his privacy interests.

In *Bradley v Wingnut Films*[38] the formulation of the tort used by the judge was that involving the public disclosure of private facts. His Honour accepted that the three requirements would need to be satisfied,[39] but the plaintiff's difficulty was twofold. Not only was the

---

[35] N 12, above.

[36] See n 31 above.

[37] As exemplified in *Wilkinson v Downtown* [1897] 2 QB 57.

[38] See n 34 above.

[39] *Ibid*, 423–24.

fact which he sought to suppress a public fact, and hence not within the ambit of the tort, but it was something which if disclosed would not be highly offensive or objectionable to the ordinary person. The judge also observed that in certain circumstances the fact that something existed or occurred in a public place did not necessarily mean that it should receive widespread publicity if it did not involve a matter of public concern.[40]

The more interesting aspect of *TV 3 Network Services Ltd v Fahey*[41] was that it involved the use of a hidden camera in a doctor's surgery. Dr Fahey was a public figure and medical professional, and the subject of a 20/20 programme which alleged sexual impropriety and professional misconduct with former patients. Not only did Dr Fahey issue defamation proceedings against TV3 the next day, he also strenuously denied the allegations made in the programme. However, as a result of the publicity accorded the first programme a former patient came forward who wanted to confront the doctor with her own allegations. She kept an appointment with him carrying a hidden camera, provided by TV3, to record the interview for a second programme. Although Fahey was initially able to obtain an *ex parte* interim injunction restraining the screening of the second programme, the injunction was overturned by the Court of Appeal.

First the Court emphasised that the application had to be seen in the context of the existing defamation proceedings, and any which might follow should the second programme screen. This immediately presented Fahey with a difficulty, because a court will only restrain the publication of defamatory matter where there are clear and compelling reasons. This is particularly so where the defendant indicates that it intends to rely upon the defence of truth.

Fahey advanced three grounds for sustaining the injunction, the third of which was that the confrontation in the surgery and the taping of the interview amounted to trespass or unlawful invasion of his privacy. As to this the court clearly agreed that concealing a camera and recording what was said and done did not come within the terms

---

[40] *Ibid*, 424. A tombstone in a public cemetery containing information directed at the public could not be said to be a private aspect of the plaintiff's life. Nor, taking into account the limited extent to which it appeared in the film, was it subjected to unwarranted publicity or public disclosure.

[41] [1999] 2 NZLR 129.

of the normal implied licence to attend at a doctor's surgery. Once the court had determined there had been a breach of the licence it had to balance the competing rights and values at stake. This meant evaluating the circumstances in which the impugned methods were used, public interest considerations and the adequacy of damages. Fahey had been accused of serious criminal offences, which he had strenuously denied in the media; there was therefore a legitimate public interest in exposing his misconduct.[42] On the one hand TV3 might have mixed motives for encouraging and assisting the former patient, but on the other its credibility had been put into question by the doctor's actions. Not only that, but during the confrontation in the surgery Fahey had come very close to acknowledging his crimes. The interim injunction was set aside, but in doing so the court was careful to deny any suggestion that the decision could be seen as supporting a general proposition that the ends of news gathering justified the means.

P v D & Independent News Ltd[43] raised, but did not decide the extent of privacy accorded a public figure plaintiff. A journalist was planning a profile article on the plaintiff P, who the judge referred to at as a "public figure".[44] During his initial investigations the journalist became aware of a suggestion that P had suffered some psychological or psychiatric problem, had previously spent some time in a psychiatric hospital, and that the police had attended an incident involving P. The journalist considered that if he could get some verification this would provide added depth to the article by showing that P was someone who had experienced, and overcome, personal difficulties. The journalist made further cautious inquiries, but found it difficult to get any verifiable information, and approached P directly with some written questions. P, through solicitors, advised the journalist's editor that unless confirmation was received that any article would contain no such information, an interim injunction preventing publication would be sought. No such confirmation was given. P argued two causes of action: breach of confidence and privacy. As no information had been imparted in confidence the first could not succeed. This left the allegation of breach of privacy.

---

[42] In New Zealand an inequity defence or justification is available in the appropriate case where information has been obtained unlawfully. *Ibid*, 136.

[43] See n 34, above.

[44] *Ibid*.

The defendants argued that a number of factors told against the exercise of the discretion to award an injunction, the principal of which was the guarantee of freedom of expression under section 14 of the NZ Bill of Rights Act, and the right of the press to make inquiry in respect of matters of interest to its readers. Other factors argued by the defendant against the injunction placed some emphasis on the lack of any evidence that publication was likely. These included the undesirability of imposing prior restraint in the absence of reliable evidence that a breach of any clearly defined obligation was likely, the presumption that individuals and organisations must be expected to act lawfully unless there was clear evidence otherwise, and that individuals should not be required to give undertakings where there was no substantial evidence that they intended to act in flagrant disregard of the rights of another. Somewhat surprisingly counsel also attempted to argue that it was far from settled whether there was a tort of privacy in New Zealand law. In light of the many expressions, both judicial[45] and academic,[46] in support of the defence this argument was never going to succeed, and the judge dealt with it by citing extensively from the New Zealand case law. He also added that he took account of the English Court of Appeal decision in *Kaye v Robinson* and the provisions of section 14 of the Bill of Rights. Most unfortunately this is the only reference in the entire judgment to the New Zealand Bill of Rights Act, and constitutes a serious deficiency in the decision.

The judge concluded that there was a tort of privacy in New Zealand that encompassed the public disclosure of private facts. He added that the three factors propounded by Prosser and adopted by Gallen J in *Bradley,* were sufficient to provide the appropriate balance between the right to freedom of expression and the right of privacy in such cases. He supplemented the three factors by a fourth which required the court to have regard to: "the nature and extent of legitimate public interest in

---

[45] Quite apart from the comments made in the cases cited at n 34 and discussed above see also P Cooke in *Sharma v ANZ Banking group (New Zealand) Ltd* (1992) 3 NZBORR 183, 189 (CA).

[46] See for example S Todd, "Protection of Privacy" in N Mullany (ed) *Torts in the Nineties* (Sweet & Maxwell, London, 1997) 174; R Tobin, "Invasion of Privacy" [2000] NZLJ 216; R Tobin, "The New Zealand Tort of Invasion of Privacy" (2000) 5 *Comms L* 129: J Burrows, "Media Law [2000] *NZ Law Review* 193, 206. See also J Burrows and U Cheer, *News Media Law in New Zealand,* 4th edn (Oxford University Press, Auckland, 1999) ch 6.

having the matter disclosed." Whether the fourth factor is an element of the tort, or a defence to it, remains to be decided by subsequent cases.

Applying those factors to the case before him the judge decided that the information that a person had been treated in a psychiatric hospital fell into the category of a private fact. Clearly any disclosure of the information in the news media would be a public disclosure. The real question was, however, whether that disclosure would be highly offensive and objectionable to a reasonable person of ordinary sensibilities. A decision on that was not clear cut. On the one hand an increasingly enlightened public attitude that disabilities such as mental illness were not a cause for exclusion or scorn tended to suggest it would not. That however was an idealistic view and took no account of the actual value which people placed on having what they saw as intimate personal information such as their medical treatment kept private. P's affidavit stated that P would be "devastated" if the information was published, and added that such was the value P placed on privacy that P was prepared to cease work if publication of the information was permitted. The judge accepted P's stated feelings and was persuaded that a reasonable person of ordinary sensibilities would in the circumstances, also find publication of the information that they had been a patient in a psychiatric hospital highly offensive and objectionable. He did not consider that the reasonable person would react the same way to publication that the police had come to their aid. On its own that statement could relate to many situations.

On the material before him there was no basis for concern that P's past or present mental health meant that P was unfit to carry out his or her occupation to an appropriate standard. Nor was disclosure of the information in the public interest insofar as an assessment of P's character, credibility or competence was concerned. Thus, in respect of the fourth factor judge considered that legitimate public interest in having the information disclosed was minimal. He concluded that publication of the information that P had been treated at a psychiatric hospital, or information to that effect, would be a breach of the tort of privacy. The judge was also satisfied that there was a sufficient risk that the defendants would publish the information if, and when, they got verification of its accuracy.

An injunction prohibiting D from printing, publishing or distributing any information that P had been treated at a psychiatric hospital was issued. The judge accepted that the principle of freedom of information was an important principle that the defendants strove to uphold, but he thought there would be no hardship if the order granted them leave to apply for its revocation or amendment if there was a significant change of circumstances. The order issued, but the defendants must give the plaintiff seven days notice of any application to amend or revoke the order. The judge also ordered that the identity of the plaintiff, the journalist and the contents of the Court file not be disclosed without a further order of the Court.

There are a number of factors about the decision which are disquieting. First on the facts the decision would be seem to be correct, but it is disappointing that the judge should refer to the importance of freedom of expression, but only refer briefly to section 14 of the New Zealand Bill of Rights Act. Privacy, like contempt of court, is an abrogation of the right to freedom of expression. It was axiomatic that the judge should have considered the extent to which it was a reasonable limitation on the right to freedom of expression.[47] It was also disappointing that the judge did not adequately discuss the extent to which a public figure's privacy might be limited by virtue that he or she is a public figure. The judge must have been aware of the perceptible shift in protection of the politician plaintiff's reputation occasioned by recent high profile defamation cases.[48] The judge also spoke of the objective test for matter which is highly offensive and objectionable to a reasonable person, but he appeared to give the test a subjective element. This too needed careful consideration.

L v G,[49] the latest case to discuss the tort of invasion of privacy was in the District Court, but the case is notable for its rather more careful analysis of the tort. It is also the first case which was a claim for injunction relief. The judge confirmed that the right to freedom of expression as enshrined in the Bill of Rights Act and the corresponding right of the media to publish information must be given due recognition in this context. However, the right to freedom of

---

[47] S 5 of the New Zealand Bill of Rights Act discussed below.

[48] See *Lange v Atkinson* [1998] 3 NZLR 424. The case confirmed the common law qualified privilege could be extended to discussion about past, present and future politicians. It did confirm that the subject matter should relate to what was of public concern, but the case recognised that the politician plaintiff could expect to be the legitimate subject of greater publicity about their lives than other persons.

[49] See n 34 above.

expression was not absolute but subject to reasonable limits as described in section 5, and the fact that the common law was in the process of development did not mean that this section did not apply. The judge summarised the preconditions for the tort as follows:

(1) The facts disclosed must be private facts as distinct from public ones.
(2) The disclosure of the private facts must be a public disclosure, as distinct from a private disclosure.
(3) The facts which are disclosed must be highly offensive and objectionable to a reasonable person of ordinary sensibilities.
(4) Any legitimate public interest in the disclosure of the facts would be insufficient to override the right to privacy in respect of them.

Although the sequence differs from that usually used when the elements of the tort are identified, he considered this sequence more logical. He also expressed reservations as to whether the fourth was an element of the tort or a defence to it, but was bound to follow the approach adopted by the High Court in *P v D*.

Ms L and Mr G were in a sexual relationship during the course of which a number of sexually explicit photographs of L were taken, one of which was published in an adult magazine by G. She consented to the taking of the photos; she did not consent to the publication in the magazine. The plaintiff conceded that, apart from the distinctive patterned blue top that some who knew her might recognise, and part of which was visible, she would not be identified from the photograph. One of the issues the judge therefore discussed was whether the public disclosure of private facts must result in the identification of the person to whom the facts relate.

The judge identified privacy as a value which was peculiarly personal in the sense that it reinforced a psychological need of the person to preserve an intrusion-free zone of personality and family, with the result that there was always anguish when that zone was violated. If this was so, then the rights protected by the tort related to the loss of the personal shield of privacy, rather than issues of perception and identification.[50]

---

[50] *Ibid*, 246. The judge saw implicit support for this proposition in *Bathurst City Council v Saban* [1985] 2 NSWLR 704.

The rights which are protected by the tort of breach of privacy relate not to the issues of perception and identification by those members of the public to whom the information is disclosed but to the loos of the personal shield of privacy of the person to whom the information relates.

The fact that L could not be identified did not prevent her from recovering for any breach of her privacy, but could be reflected in any assessment of damages.

The judge also briefly discussed the issue of publication. Although publication was not to the public at large, it was to that section of the adult public who purchased a copy of the magazine. The disclosure was certainly not a private disclosure as in the context of the initial sharing of the photographs, but was to a limited, but nevertheless identifiable, public audience. Damages of $2,500 were awarded.

The boundaries of the new tort are not yet certain. An analysis of the cases discloses essentially two forms of the tort, public disclosure of private facts and intentional intrusion into the plaintiff's solitude, but this does not preclude further development of the tort when an appropriate case arises. Other issues that require further elucidation include: an analysis of what is a "public disclosure", a proper analysis of what is a private fact and what is a public fact, more guidance on when the latter can become the former, and the extent of the privacy to which a public person is entitled.

THE BROADCASTING ACT 1989

The power of the BSA to hear complaints about privacy comes pursuant to section 4 of the Broadcasting Act 1989. Initially there were five privacy principles although these were later renumbered and increased to seven as the number and variety of complaints increased. After the broadcasts of two programmes which invaded the privacy of the subject children in a particularly invasive manner[51] the principles were amended to reflect the concerns raised by a number of people including the Commissioner for Children. The principles are:

---

[51] See Decisions 1999–087 to 1999–098 (Item on *Holmes* programme examined the situation of a woman coping with the behavioural problems of her child who had Attention Deficit Syndrome. The child became distressed at the presence of the camera, but filming continued.) and Decisions 1999–93 to 1999–101 (results of a paternity test disclosed to child on a *You be the Judge* programme).

(i) The protection of privacy includes protection against the public disclosure of private facts where the facts disclosed are highly offensive and objectionable to a reasonable person of ordinary sensibilities.

(ii) The protection of privacy also protects against the public disclosure of some kinds of public facts. The "public" facts contemplated concern events (such as criminal behaviour) which have, in effect, become private again, for example through the passage of time. Nevertheless, the public disclosure of public facts will have to be highly offensive to a reasonable person.

(iii) There is a separate ground for a complaint, in addition to a complaint for the public disclosure of private and public facts, in factual situations involving the intentional interference (in the nature of prying) with an individual's interest in solitude or seclusion. The intrusion must be offensive to the ordinary person but an individual's interest in solitude or seclusion does not provide the basis for a privacy action for an individual to complain about being observed or followed or photographed in a public place.

(iv) The protection of privacy also protects against the disclosure of private facts to abuse, denigrate or ridicule personally an identifiable person. This principle is of particular relevance should a broadcaster use the airwaves to deal with a private dispute. However, the existence of a prior relationship between the broadcaster and the named individual is not an essential criterion.

(v) The protection of privacy includes the protection against the disclosure by the broadcaster, without consent, of the name and/or address and/or telephone number of an identifiable person. This principle does not apply to details which are public information, or to news and current affairs reporting, and is subject to the "public interest" defence in principle (vi).

(vi) Discussing the matter in the "public interest", defined as of legitimate concern or interest to the public, is a defence to an individual's claim for privacy.

(vii) An individual who consents to the invasion of his or her privacy, cannot later succeed in a claim for a breach of privacy. Children's vulnerability must be a prime concern to broadcasters. When consent is given by the child, or by a parent or someone in loco parentis, broadcasters shall satisfy themselves that the broadcast is in the best interest of the child.

Re McAllister,[52] the first privacy complaint determined by the BSA preceded the privacy principles, but the decision indicates the way the BSA saw issues of privacy. It could not rely solely on everyday notions of privacy to determine complaints, as the tort was at the time in its infancy, so BSA turned to United States jurisprudence where the most developed ideas on the concept could be found. Once again Prosser's torts can be seen reflected in the privacy principles.

The High Court approved the approach the BSA took to the concept of privacy in *TV3 Network Services Ltd v BSA*.[53] The complainant had alleged that her privacy had been invaded (a) in an interview which had been filmed and recorded surreptitiously and (b) by the voice over comment in the programme which revealed that she had been an incest victim. The BSA upheld her complaint on the basis that there had been breaches of privacy principles (i), (ii) and (iii). The majority thought there had been a disclosure of a highly offensive fact and that the surreptitious filming of an interview which had included questions about sensitive matters, was in the nature of prying. The complainant had thought that all she was being asked to do was take part in interview and its subsequent publication would have been offensive to the ordinary person. The BSA also added that for the public place exception of privacy principle (iii) to apply that it was the person who was the subject who had to be in a public place not the person filming. TV3 appealed to the High Court.

The High Court judge thought that the BSA could properly decide that the protection provided by section 4(i)(c) of the Broadcasting Act could include relief where individuals were harassed with disclosure of past events insufficiently connected with anything of present public interest. He saw no error in principle in the BSA's decision to regard prying as one potential form of breach of privacy.

The judge also looked at whether the information could properly be said to be in the public domain. The fact that Mrs S was an incest victim had been given in open court and, but for the relevant legislation, she could have been named. However, it was only to a limited

---

[52] [1990] NZAR 324.

[53] [1995] 2 NZLR 720.

extent that the facts had become public and Mrs S's identification with them had been slight. His Honour thought that in determining whether information had lost its "private" character it would be appropriate to look realistically at the nature, scale and timing of previous publications.[54]

The judge was also prepared to infer that Mrs S would not in the circumstances have agreed to an interview, and that TV3 knew this. This meant that the reporter's action in filming and interviewing her did not fall within the terms of any implied licence to enter the property[55] and therefore she was a trespasser from the outset. However, even had the reporter not been a trespasser, TV3 could still have been liable for breaching broadcasting standards. His Honour agreed with the BSA that the actions of the mother 20 years earlier were not a matter properly within the public interest defence. Nor did he consider the covert approach to the mother necessary to give balance to the programme.

In confirming the approach of the BSA the judge considered that in reaching any decision the BSA could properly take into account the actions of the reporter and camera crew in obtaining any material later broadcast. Thus in most cases where a reporter enters private property knowing that the interviewee is likely to refuse an on-camera interview that reporter will be a trespasser from the outset. The fact that any camera crew might be lawfully situated on public property might not prevent its activities being something in the nature of prying. This does not mean that such as approach can never be justified. On occasions privacy must give way to a public interest defence, but this was not such a case. But in determining what is in the public interest the court will distinguish between matters of genuine public concern and those matters which the public might find interesting.[56] Although the judge drew a distinction between the concept of privacy as used in the Broadcasting Act and interpreted by the BSA, and the concept as it was slowly emerging in the tort of invasion of privacy, there are nonetheless strong links between the two.

---

[54] [1995] 2 NZLR 731.

[55] See *Robson v Hallet* [1967] 2 QB 939.

[56] This aspect has received detailed consideration in respect of an action for breach of confidence and also in the context of an action for defamation where the honest opinion defence is in issue.

Although *Fahey* is the only case where the Court of Appeal has considered the use of hidden cameras, the same cannot be said of the BSA, where some form of surreptitious filming has frequently been the subject of complaints. The Fahey programme itself was the subject of one of these. Notwithstanding the comments of the Court of Appeal several viewers argued that the doctor's privacy had been unfairly invaded by one or other of the two programmes. The main concern of one of the complainants was the danger of trial by media.[57] The BSA confirmed that use of a hidden camera was an extreme measure and one that could only be justified by exceptional circumstances. This was because the broadcast inevitably overrode the right of the person who was being filmed to withhold comment. Not only had there to be a legitimate and strong public interest in the broadcast, but the broadcaster had to believe that there was no other reasonable way to get the information. "Public interest must clearly outweigh competing individual rights if hidden camera footage is to be considered warranted".[58] The BSA added[59]:

> On of the established roles for the media in a democratic society is to investigate candidates for public office and otherwise to report on issues of public importance. Allegations about serious misconduct on the part of a candidate for public office, and a practising general practitioner, are matters about which there is high public interest. Furthermore, the fact that some of the alleged misconduct was said to have taken place 30 years ago does not, in the Authorities view, diminish the seriousness of relevance of the matter, particularly as Dr Fahey was then seeking high public office, and continuing to treat female patients.

The BSA considered that the public interest was sufficient to justify the use of a hidden camera.

For those whose privacy had been invaded by the media there are advantages in pursuing a complaint to the BSA. The process is cheap, the decisions are made on the papers, the BSA has been careful to take legal principles into account in reaching its decisions, and an award of

[57] See BSA decisions 200–108 to 2000–113. In reaching its decision the BSA referred to the *BBC Producers' Guidelines* (BBC 1993) and the British broadcasting Standards Commission's Code on fairness and Privacy.

[58] See BSA decisions 200–108 to 2000–113. In reaching its decision the BSA referred to the *BBC Producers' Guidelines* (BBC 1993) and the British broadcasting Standards Commission's Code on fairness and Privacy, and see also decision 1992–094 and 1996–130.

[59] *Ibid, Hidden Camera.*

up to $5000 can be made.[60] In more recent decisions, the BSA[61] has been careful to adopt a *Moonen* analysis[62] to the cases it decides in order to dispel fears that proper attention was not being paid to section 14 of the Bill of Rights.[63] This suggests that in future decisions the BSA will consider more explicitly the importance of freedom of speech.

SECTION 14 NEW ZEALAND BILL OF RIGHTS ACT

The New Zealand Act is not an entrenched Bill of Rights like the United States Constitution, but nonetheless it affirms in a positive way the public's right to freedom of expression[64];

> The freedom now permeates and shapes the substantive law. The enactment of section 14 in the Bill of Rights now emphatically confirms the public interest in protecting free expression; the media's right to seek and impart information and the public's right to receive that information.

The Bill of Rights applies only to actions of the executive, judiciary and legislative branches of government.[65] It requires development of the law where necessary and must be given practical effect irrespective of the state of New Zealand law before it was enacted.[66]

In *R v H* Cooke P saw "considerable force" in the view that the protections afforded by the Bill of Rights should be recognised as and where appropriate in evolving the common law.[67] Likewise in *TVNZ v Newsmonitor Services Limited*[68] Blanchard J observed that it would be undesirable for a court to make a decision inconsistent with the rights and freedoms guaranteed by the Bill of Rights. It was in this indirect way that his Honour thought the Bill of Rights was always present in the background to judicial decision making.

Although what is guaranteed is the right to express unwanted, unpopular and distasteful opinion some forms of expression are not

[60] There is no other type of complaint where the BSA has this power.
[61] Decisions 2001–071 to 2001–084.
[62] Discussed below.
[63] In the decisions above n 61, the BSA considered *de novo* the original complaints against the Radio Code of Broadcasting Practice. As a result it reversed its decision on two of the complaints.
[64] *O'Connor v Police* (1991) 1 NZBORR 259.
[65] New Zealand Bill of Rights Act 1990, s 3.
[66] *MOT v Noort*, n 1, above, 270 *per* Cooke P.
[67] [1993] 2 NZLR 143 at 147.

within the guarantee.[69] Freedom of expression can be subordinated to other legislation[70] such as the public policy behind section 139(2) of the Criminal Justice Act 1985[71] and the censorship of objectionable publications.[72] It must be balanced against all other affirmed freedoms and rights,[73] not only those in the Bill of Rights Act itself such as minimum standards of criminal procedure,[74] but fundamental principles of law outside the Act such as the protection and promotion of the free and impartial administration of justice.[75] Freedom of expression, a right as wide as human thought and imagination,[76] ought to be restricted only so far as necessary to protect a countervailing right or interest.[77] Section 5 of the Bill of Rights confirms that the freedom is subject only to such reasonable limitations as are prescribed by law and demonstrably justifiable in a democratic society.

As freedom of expression can be abrogated by both statute and the common law the application of, and the relationship between, section 4 (inconsistent provisions),[78] section 5 (reasonable

---

[68] [1994] 2 NZLR 91, 95 *per* Blanchard J.

[69] See for example *Solicitor General v Radio NZ*, n 4 above; *Jeffrey v Police* (1994) 11 CRNZ 507, 515 (obscene words not within the guarantee) but see *Re Penthouse (US) Vol 19 No 5* [1990–1992] 1 NZBORR 429.

[70] S 4, which provides that where an enactment is inconsistent with the Bill of Rights the enactment prevails.

[71] *TV3 Network Services Ltd v R* [1993] 3 NZLR 421, 423.

[72] *Moonen v Film and Literature Board of Review* [2000] 2 NZLR 9. For comment thereon see P Rishworth, "Human Rights" [1999] *NZ Law Review* 457, 467–70; A Butler, "Judicial Indications of Inconsistency—A New Weapon in the Bill of Rights Armoury?" [2000] *NZ Law Review* 43.

[73] *Solicitor General v Radio NZ*, n 4 above, 59, and see comments in *R v Chignall & Walker* [1990–1992] 1 NZBORR 179.

[74] *Solicitor General v Radio NZ*, n 4 above, 64; and see discussion in *O'Connor v Police*, n 64 above, 274–75.

[75] *Solicitor General v Radio NZ*, n 4 above; *Duff v Communicado Ltd* [1996] 2 NZLR 89 (HC).

[76] *Moonen v Film and Literature Board of Review*, n 72 above, 15.

[77] *O'Connor v Police*, n 64 above, 275 *per* Thomas J.

[78] **4. Other enactments not affected**

No court shall, in relation to any enactment (whether passed or made before or after the commencement of this Bill of Rights),—

(a) Hold any provision of the enactment to be impliedly repealed or revoked, or to be in any way invalid or ineffective; or

(ii) Decline to apply any provision of the enactment—

by reason only that the provision is inconsistent with any provision of this Bill of Rights

limitations)[79] and section 6 (consistent interpretation)[80] of the Bill
of Rights must be understood. The first Court of Appeal decision
to consider whether the provisions of another statute abrogated or
limited the scope of a right or freedom was *Ministry of Transport v
Noort*,[81] but although there was unanimity as to the result, the same
could not be said of the reasoning, and in particular the judicial
approach to the role of section 5 was not consistent. A more helpful
approach is to be found in *Moonen v Film and Literature Board of
Review*,[82] where the court rejected the approach that an inconsistent
statute overrode the provisions of section 14 to such an extent that it
was not even considered.[83] *Moonen* concerned the relationship
between freedom of expression and censorship of objectionable publications under the Films, Videos, and Publications Classification Act
1993. The Court of Appeal decision confirmed that the censorship
provisions must be interpreted so as to adopt such tenable construction as constitutes the least possible limitation on freedom of expression. The Court then suggest an appropriate methodology to be
adopted in the future. Once the scope of the relevant right or
freedom has been determined the Court should follow five steps.
First, it should identify the different interpretations of the words of
the statute. Secondly, where there is more than one possible interpretation it must identify that meaning which least infringes the
right, as it is this meaning that section 6 aided by section 5 requires
the court to adopt. Thirdly, it must then identify the extent to which
that meaning limits freedom of expression. In doing so the court
must give careful consideration to the extent to which that limitation
can be demonstrably justified in a free and democratic society in

---

[79] **5. Justified limitations**

Subject to section 4 of this Bill of Rights, the rights and freedoms contained in this Bill
of Rights may be subject only to such reasonable limits prescribed by law as can be
demonstrably justified in a free and democratic society.

[80] **6. Interpretation consistent with Bill of Rights to be preferred**

Wherever an enactment can be given a meaning that is consistent with the rights and
freedoms contained in this Bill of Rights, that meaning shall be preferred to any other
meaning.

[81] For comment thereon see P Rishworth and O Optican, "Two Comments on *Ministry of
Transport v Noort*" [1992] *NZ Recent Law Review* 189.

[82] See n 72 above.

[83] See the approach articulated by the Full Court in *News Media v Film and Literature
Board of Review* (1997) 4 HRNZ 410.

terms of section 5. The final step arises after the Court has made the necessary determination under section 5. The Court must indicate whether the limitation is justified. If the limitation is not justified there is an inconsistency with section 5 and the Court must declare this to be so, but it is nonetheless bound to give effect to the limitation by virtue of section 4.

The final step envisages a judicial declaration of inconsistency.[84] The Court explained that although section 4 required that the inconsistent enactment by given effect this would not make a court's declaration that a provision is inconsistent with the Bill of Rights a futile exercise. It could, for example, be useful if the matter came to be examined by the Human Rights Commission. It could also be of assistance to Parliament if the subject arose in that forum.[85]

Section 5 requires that Any limit on a guaranteed right or freedom must be:

(i)   reasonable
(ii) prescribed by law; and
(iii) demonstrably justified in a free and democratic society.

The requirement that the limit be prescribed by law is important. It means that the limit should be identifiable, adequately accessible and sufficiently precise.[86] The common law is always evolving, and is not as precise as a statute, so whether the limit is so will be a question to be decided in each case. The tests propounded by European Court of Human Rights could be inappropriate in an independent common law jurisdiction where either novel situations might emerge requiring some reasonable limits to be imposed, as a matter of common law, on one of the guaranteed rights and freedoms, or where the common law was in the process of development.[87]

Whether a limit is "reasonable" or "demonstrably justified in a free and democratic society" tends to be considered together. In doing so the courts have identified the following factors as ones that need to be carefully weighed: the significance in the particular case of the values underlying the Bill of Rights Act, the importance in the public

---

[84] This had been mooted earlier. See FM Brookfield, "Constitutional Law" [1992] *NZ Recent Law* 231, 239.

[85] See n 72 above, 17.

[86] *Solicitor-General v Radio NZ*, see n 4 above, 63.

[87] *Duff v Communicado Ltd*, see n 75 above, 100.

interest of the intrusion on the particular right there protected, the limits sought to be placed on the application of the common law in the particular case and the effectiveness of the intrusion in protecting the interests put forward to justify those limits.[88]

Although Blanchard J's comments were made in the context of contempt of court in *Duff v Communicado Ltd*[89] they illustrates the proper approach to be adopted when the Bill of Rights and the common law conflict. Essentially a modified *Moonen* approach should be adopted. The rationale for any abrogation of freedom of speech is that other values predominate. But the extent of the abrogation must in terms of section 5 of the Bill of Rights constitute only such reasonable limitation on freedom of expression as can be demonstrably justified in a free and democratic society. As each case must be considered individually, a balancing exercise must be carried out between the individual litigant's right to freedom of expression and society's interest in protecting the administration of justice. The balancing exercise involves weighing the significance in the particular case of the values underling the Bill of Rights, the importance, in the public interest, of the intrusion on the particular right the Bill of Rights protected, the limits which it was sought to place on the application of the common law in that case and the effectiveness of the intrusion in protecting the interests put forward to justify the limits.[90]

Blanchard J identified the true nature of the decision in each case of contempt of court as whether the particular interference with the administration of justice was so serious as to override freedom of expression.[91] The objective of the law of contempt in general was sufficiently important to warrant limiting freedom of expression,[92] but the limit imposed must impair the freedom as little as possible. It must also be sufficiently serious to justify any order before any punishment was imposed. The judge concluded that fair and temperate criticism was protected, and only expression which would have a real likelihood of preventing a litigant from availing itself of its constitutional right of resort to the judgment of the Court was limited. In the same way where there is a real risk that publication of an article

---

[88] *Ministry of Transport v Noort*, see n 1 above, 284, as reworded by Blanchard J, *ibid*, 101.

[89] See n 75 above.

[90] *Ibid.*

[91] *Ibid*, 100.

[92] *Solicitor General v Radio NZ*, n 4 above.

would prejudice a fair trial, both the importance of free speech and the administration of justice can be accommodated by deferring publication of the article until after the trial.[93] This curtails freedom of speech, but only temporarily, and in order to guarantee a fair trial.[94]

R V MAHANGA

A brief note on *R v Mahanga*[95] further illustrates the balancing process between freedom of speech and privacy the Courts may be asked to undertake. The media argument in this appeal was underpinned by the proposition that open justice and freedom of expression were denied when the trial judge refused to allow a television company access to a videotaped interview played during the course of a trial. The television company had been given permission to film the trial and hoped to use the evidentiary exhibit in a documentary it was making. The trial judge was persuaded that the privacy rights of the convicted person and the police interviewer, together with the absence of informed consent were against the exercise of his discretion under the Rules to allow the tape to be copied. Counsel for the media appellant argued that both section 14 and recognition of the principle of open justice under section 25(a) of the Bill of Rights should enable the media to report the reality of what had taken place in Court. Mahanga's privacy interests did not, he said, meet the section 5 test as he had been warned that the interview could be used against him, and further that any private character that the tape did have had been lost once played in court.

The Court of Appeal did not accept the argument and in the course of its judgment had some useful observations to make. First, the Court accepted that the press had a critical, indeed a constitutional role, of reporting proceedings before courts of justice.[96] Judges however also had the power and the responsibility of regulating their courts, and although the principles of open justice and freedom of speech were relevant to the exercise of the judge's supervisory power when requests such as the one before it were made, the principles did

---

[93] *Gisborne Herald Co Ltd v Solicitor General* [1995] 3 NZLR 566 (CA).

[94] *Ibid*, 575.

[95] [2001] 1 NZLR 641 (CA).

[96] [2001] 1 NZLR 643.

not directly govern its exercise. The various competing interests had to be weighed in the exercise of the discretion.

Secondly, the privacy interests of the convicted person were a legitimate factor to include in the balancing process.[97] Clearly the privacy interests of the accused person were displaced by the need for the open judicial process, but only while that process ran its course. Even during the process *The Guidelines for Expanded Media Coverage of Court Proceedings* recognised the sensitivity of filming the accused at the time evidence was given, and trial judges might allow an accused who objects not to be filmed at all. Once the criminal trial was concluded there was more room to recognise individual privacy interests. In the context of this case there was a considerable difference in playing an interview in open court during the course of a trial, and playing the same interview on national television. Ultimately the Court was not persuaded that the trial judge had exercised his discretion wrongly. It confirmed that the interests of open justice, and freedom of speech, had been fulfilled during the course of the trial by the opportunity to be present and to witness the interview played in court. Granting further access would not add to the substance of publicly available information.

CONCLUSION

Section 14 of the New Zealand Bill of Rights Act 1990 is now having a greater impact on media law in New Zealand. Although the importance of the Bill of Rights Act was immediately recognised in criminal cases it took longer for the potential of section 14 to be recognised in civil law cases. The judges are now more careful to consider its impact in cases involving contempt of court and defamation. Unfortunately, notwithstanding the prominence the section has otherwise achieved, in the most recent High Court case on privacy the judge did not properly take the section into account in reaching his decision. Given the media exemption from the privacy principles in the Privacy Act 1993 when undertaking news activities it is axiomatic that the section must be considered when a plaintiff wishes to pursue an action in privacy against a media defendant.

---

[97] [2001] 1 NZLR, 651.

This is not to say that an individual's privacy is not important. It is a factor which must be considered when an individual complains that his or her privacy is being invaded by the media. The BSA regularly makes decisions on media invasion of privacy. Indeed, the BSA is in many ways perhaps more familiar with the concept than the Court, and it is likely its jurisprudence will continue to be referred to as the tort develops. However, care must be taken to define the boundaries of the tort so that it does not expand to place unacceptable fetters on freedom of expression.

7

Freedom of Expression, Privacy and the Media in Australia

David Lindsay

INTRODUCTION

Australia, alone among contemporary Western democracies, does not have a bill of rights.[1] The absence of an over-arching legal statement of individual rights means that the relationship between privacy and freedom of expression is unsystematic and complex. To a certain extent, this is an inevitable reflection of difficulties inherent in the concepts of free speech and privacy.[2] In Australia, as in any complex, pluralistic society, the concepts of free speech and privacy are highly contestable and far from internally coherent.

The unsystematic nature of current Australian media law is, nevertheless, also a reflection of a customary Australian reticence to approach legal issues from the perspective of fundamental rights and freedoms.[3] Although there is an underlying social commitment to the values of free speech and privacy, the substantive content of these social values is rarely explored in detail in public debates outside academia.[4] Instead,

---

[1] For recent arguments in favour of an Australian bill of rights see: George Williams, *A Bill of Rights for Australia* (University of NSW Press, Sydney, 2000); Murray Wilcox, *An Australian Charter of Rights?* (Law Book Company, Sydney, 1993). For the argument against a constitutional bill of rights see: Frank Brennan, *Legislating Liberty: A Bill of Rights for Australia?* (University of Queensland Press, St Lucia, 1998).

[2] Influential treatments of the complexities include: Alan F Westin, *Privacy and Freedom* (Atheneum, New York, 1967); Frederick Schauer, *Free Speech: A Philosophical Enquiry* (Cambridge University Press, New York, 1982); Raymond Wacks, "Defining Privacy" in Raymond Wacks (ed) *Privacy: Volume 1* (Dartmouth, Aldershot, 1993); Raymond Wacks, *Privacy and Press Freedom* (Blackstone Press, London, 1995).

[3] See, for example, Hilary Charlesworth, "The Australian Reluctance About Rights" (1993) 31 *Osgoode Hall Law Journal* 195.

[4] The academic literature is voluminous, including: Peter H Bailey, *Human Rights: Australia in an International Context* (Butterworths, Sydney, 1990); Timothy H Jones, "Legal

there is a tendency to resolve conflicts that arise in relation to basic rights primarily through pragmatic compromise, and on a case by case basis. Unsurprisingly, this approach has not resulted in a consistent Australian jurisprudence in relation to individual rights and freedoms. Accordingly, the Australian law relating to free speech and privacy consists of a patchwork of constitutional principles, statutes (Commonwealth, State and Territory), common law principles and causes of action, and co-regulatory and self-regulatory media codes of conduct.

The conflicts that arise between freedom of speech and privacy are much like those that arise in all societies with active, commercially-driven media enterprises. A recent example to reach the courts concerned wedding photographs of the well-known Australian cricketer, Shane Warne, which appeared in an Australian women's magazine in September 1995. The media were prohibited from attending the wedding. The photographs were taken by a wedding guest and apparently supplied to the magazine by the manager of a photograph processing outlet. In this case, legal action was brought against the photograph processing company, not the magazine company. Warne relied on a number of causes of action, including breach of contract, breach of confidence, copyright infringement and a claim in relation to a "right to maintain and enforce the privacy" of the wedding. In an application for summary dismissal of the proceedings, Heerey J held that the privacy claim was the only cause of action "whose existence might be debatable as a matter of law".[5]

FREEDOM OF EXPRESSION IN AUSTRALIA

The most significant feature of Australian media law is the absence of an express legal guarantee of freedom of expression in the form of a

---

Protection for Fundamental Rights and Freedoms: European Lessons for Australia?" (1994) 22 *Federal Law Review* 57; Penelope Mathew, "International Law and the Protection of Human Rights in Australia" (1995) 17 *Sydney Law Review* 1777; Paul Chadwick and Jennifer Mullaly, *Privacy and the Media*, Communications Law Centre Research Paper No 4 (CLC, Sydney, 1997).

[5] *Warne v Genex Corporation Pty Ltd* (Unreported judgment of Heerey J, Federal Court of Australia, 4 July 1996).

bill of rights. This is despite sporadic attempts to either amend the Constitution to provide for a bill of rights, or to introduce a statutory bill of rights.[6]

This does not mean that freedom of expression is not protected under Australian law. On the contrary, freedom of expression is recognised in at least three distinct ways:

—There is an implied constitutional freedom of political commun-ication, derived from the system of representative democracy established by the Australian Constitution.[7]

—An important principle of the common law is the assumption of freedom of expression, unless there is a clear legal exception. Thus, legislation that restricts freedom of expression must do so in unmistakable and unambiguous language.

—Australia is a party to a number of international instruments that recognise freedom of expression, including Article 19 of the International Covenant on Civil and Political Rights (ICCPR) which provides for the protection of freedom of expression, sub-ject to certain restrictions.[8] These provisions are not part of Australian domestic law, but a rule of statutory construction pro-vides for legislation to be interpreted as consistent with inter-national law, wherever possible.[9]

In addition to the above, freedom of speech is often taken into account in the drafting of legislation and in recommendations for law reform.[10]

---

[6] For example, in anticipation of ratifying the ICCPR, the Human Rights Bill 1973 (Cth) was introduced in 1972 and later the Australian Human Rights Bill 1985 (Cth). A 1985 Commission reviewing the Commonwealth *Constitution* recommended a bill or rights in its final report: *Final Report of the Constitutional Commission* (AGPS, Canberra 1988). See Williams, n 1 above, 32–33. Although further constitutional changes were the subject of a Convention held in 1998, the focus was on proposals for Australia to become a republic.

[7] See page 162 below.

[8] Australia ratified the ICCPR in 1980 and acceded to the First Optional Protocol in 1991 which allows for individual communication to the Human Rights Committee.

[9] See dicta of Kirby J in *Young v Registar, Court of Appeal* (1993) 32 NSWLR 262 at 276.

[10] For examples, see Sally Walker, *Media Law: Commentary and Materials* (LBC Information Services, Sydney, 2000) 13–14.

The Implied Freedom of Political Communication

Prior to 1992, freedom of expression in Australia was a "residual liberty".[11] The legal position was expressed in the following terms by Dawson J in a dissenting judgment in *Australian Capital Television Pty Ltd v The Commonwealth* (the *ACTV case):*

> the Australian Constitution, unlike the Constitution of the United States, does little to confer upon individuals by way of positive rights those basic freedoms which exist in a free and democratic society. They exist, not because they are provided for, but in the absence of any curtailment of them . . . The right to freedom of speech exists here because there is nothing to prevent its exercise and because governments recognize that if they attempt to limit it, save in accepted areas such as defamation or sedition, they must do so at their peril.[12]

The *ACTV* case was one of two 1992 cases—the other being *Nationwide News Pty Ltd v Wills*[13] (the *Nationwide News* case)—in which the majority of the High Court re-cast the Australian law relating to freedom of expression. In these cases, the majority held that the ability of the Commonwealth to legislate was limited by a freedom of political discussion necessarily implied by the recognition of representative democracy in the provisions and structure of the Commonwealth Constitution. The two decisions were handed down simultaneously, and must be read together.[14] The origins and development of the doctrine explain the unique status of freedom of speech under Australian constitutional law.

The *Nationwide News* case concerned the constitutionality of a provision that prohibited criticism of a Commonwealth Commission.[15] In finding the provision unconstitutional, four of the seven judges recognised an implied freedom of communication regarding political

---

[11] On freedom of speech as a residual liberty under English law see Eric Barendt, *Freedom of Speech* (Clarendon Press, Oxford, 1985) 29; A Boyle, "Freedom of Expression as a Public Interest in English Law" [1982] *PL* 574.

[12] (1992) 177 CLR 106 at 182–83.

[13] (1992) 177 CLR 1.

[14] See Leighton McDonald, "The Denizens of Democracy: The High Court and the 'Free Speech' Cases" (1994) 5 *Public Law Review* 160.

[15] Section 299(1)(d)(ii) of the Industrial Relations Act 1988 (Cth) made it an offence to bring a member of the Industrial relations Commission, or the Commission, into disrepute.

matters.[16] The majority essentially held that Constitutional recognition of representative democracy necessarily implied a freedom to communicate in relation to political matters, or at least matters relating to the government of the Commonwealth.[17]

In *ACTV,* the implied constitutional freedom was recognised by six of the seven High Court judges, with more detailed analyses of the theoretical underpinnings of the implied freedom than in *Nationwide News.* The legal issue in *ACTV* was the constitutionality of Commonwealth legislation that prohibited radio and television election advertising.[18] The decision was characterised by important differences within the majority. Mason CJ, for example, gave considerable weight to representative government as a means for ensuring popular sovereignty, in the sense that representatives must be accountable to the people and have a responsibility to take into account the views of the people.[19] Brennan J, on the other hand, added the important rider that, unlike freedoms conferred by a bill of rights, the implication was a limitation of legislative power, not a positive source of personal rights.[20] The majority concluded that the prohibition on election advertising infringed the implied freedom.

However, the history of failed attempts to introduce a bill of rights meant that the High Court had to tread a fine line between entrenching the legal protection of free speech, while avoiding a full-blown judicial bill of rights. Together with differing emphases in the majority decisions, this juggling act explains the issues left unresolved by the cases, particularly the extent of the implied freedom, and whether it constrained State legislative powers or affected the operation of the common law.

---

[16] The other judges found the provision invalid on the ground that it exceeded Commonwealth legislative power. In a number of dissenting decisions, Murphy J had previously championed a number of implied freedoms derived from the structure and context of the Constitution: see Leslie Zines, "A Judicially Created Bill of Rights?" (1994) 16 *Sydney Law Review* 166 at 166–67.

[17] (1992) 177 CLR 1 at 48 *per* Brennan J; at 72–73 *per* Deane and Toohey JJ.

[18] Broadcasting Act 1942 (Cth) Pt IIID.

[19] See (1992) 177 CLR 106 at 139.

[20] (1992) 177 CLR 106 at 150. There is controversy concerning the practical significance of this distinction: see GJ Lindell, "Expansion or Contraction? Some Reflections about the Recent Judicial Developments on Representative Democracy" (1998) 20 *Adelaide Law Review* 111; Anne Twomey, " 'Expansion or Contraction?': A Comment" (1998) 20 *Adelaide Law Review* 147.

The next High Court decisions to consider the implied freedom of speech directly raised these unresolved issues. In two 1994 cases, *Theophanous v Herald & Weekly Times Ltd*[21] and *Stephens v West Australian Newspapers Ltd*,[22] the High Court held that the implied freedom applied to State and Territory defamation laws[23] and that it "shapes and controls" the common law. These decisions effectively "constitutionalised" Australian defamation laws, establishing a new defence to defamation actions in relation to "political discussion".

These cases therefore held that the implied freedom operates both "vertically", in that it protects freedom of speech against legislative and executive actions, as well as "horizontally", in that it may affect private law actions, such as civil defamation actions.[24] The authority of the 1994 decisions was, however, undermined by the narrowness of the majority. Following changes to the make-up of the High Court, it was unsurprising when, in 1997, the nature and scope of the implied freedom again came before the court in the most significant Australian free speech case to date, *Lange v Australian Broadcasting Corporation*.[25] In that case, a defamation action brought by a former New Zealand Prime Minister, a unanimous High Court substantially modified aspects of the constitutional implied freedom.

First, the *Lange* court confirmed the existence of the implied freedom, which it held was an "indispensable incident" of the system of representative government provided for by the Commonwealth Constitution.[26] Secondly, the court confirmed that the implied freedom operated as a limitation or restriction on laws, and not as a source of personal rights.[27] Thirdly, the court characterised the implication as a freedom of communication concerning "political or government matters", but held that the freedom was confined to that which is "necessary for the effective operation of the system of

[21] (1994) 182 CLR 104.

[22] (1994) 182 CLR 211.

[23] The High Court concluded that State and Territory defamation laws required modification in order to comply with the implied freedom.

[24] In this respect, Australian free speech law differs from some jurisdictions with an express bill of rights, such as Canada and South Africa: see Walker, n 10 above, 54–55. On the distinction between "vertical" and "horizontal" rights see, for example, Murray Hunt, "The 'Horizontal Effect' of the Human Rights Act" [1998] *Public Law* 423.

[25] (1997) 189 CLR 520.

[26] (1997) 189 CLR 520, 559.

[27] (1997) 189 CLR 520, 560.

representative and responsible government provided for by the Constitution".[28] Fourthly, the court held that, as Australian common law must conform with the federal Constitution, it must necessarily conform with the implied freedom.[29] Fifthly, the court established a two-stage test for determining whether a law infringed the implied freedom. [30] Under this test, known as the "*Lange* test", the following two questions must be asked:

—Does the law effectively burden freedom of communication about government or political matters either in its terms, operation or effect?
—Is the law reasonably appropriate and adapted to serve a legitimate end the fulfillment of which is compatible with the maintenance of the constitutionally prescribed system of representative and responsible government?

If the law is found to burden freedom of political communication and it is not "reasonably appropriate and adapted" to serve a legitimate end compatible with the maintenance of representative government, then it will infringe the implied freedom.

In applying the *Lange* test to State defamation laws, the court held that the established defences to defamation actions failed to satisfy the test. The court, nevertheless, rejected the approach taken in 1994, instead introducing a new expanded form of qualified privilege that applies to published material concerning political or government matters. The *Lange* form of qualified privilege applies if a defendant can establish that publication of the material was reasonable in all the circumstances, but is unavailable if the plaintiff can establish that the publication was actuated by malice.[31]

Although the free speech cases of the 1990s have resulted in a constitutional recognition of freedom of communication, the recognition differs from that in jurisdictions with a bill of rights. The most significant difference is that it applies only to the category of speech characterised in *Lange* as communication "concerning government and

---

[28] (1997) 189 CLR 520, 561.
[29] (1997) 189 CLR 520, 565.
[30] (1997) 189 CLR 520, 567.
[31] (1997) 189 CLR 520, 573–74. The court interpreted the concept of malice to mean that a publication was made otherwise than for the purpose of communicating government or political information or ideas.

political matters".[32] Some examples of decisions handed down following *Lange* illustrate the point. To begin with, it is clear that it is the nature of the discussion that is important, not the office or function of the publisher.[33] For example, in *Nationwide News Pty Ltd v International Financing & Investment Pty Ltd*[34] it was held that a newspaper report carrying allegations by the manager of one bank concerning the activities of another bank did not concern a government or political matter. In another case, a majority of the full Federal Court held that an article published in a student newspaper, which provided a guide to "shop-lifting", was not a communication concerning a "political or government matter".[35] The court concluded that the implied freedom could not apply to advocacy of law breaking,[36] and that the article was not "political" in the required sense of that term.[37]

Legal Assumption of Freedom of Expression

In construing legislation, Australian courts apply legal assumptions derived, in part, from an underlying conviction that Parliament will not abrogate individual rights and freedoms. The assumptions are a guide to the interpretation of legislation, but may be over-turned by clear expressions of a legislative intention to do so. The approach adopted by the courts was explained in the following terms by the High Court in *Coco v R:*

> The courts should not impute to the legislature an intention to interfere with fundamental rights. Such an intention must be clearly manifested by unmistakable and unambiguous language.[38]

Where possible, therefore, the courts will interpret legislation so as not to interfere with freedom of expression. As Brennan J put it in *Re Bolton, Ex parte Beane:*

---

[32] (1997) 189 CLR 520, 560.

[33] See Sally Walker, "*Lange v ABC:* The High Court Rethinks the 'Constitutionalisation' of Defamation Law" (1998) 6 *Torts Law Journal* 9.

[34] Unreported judgment of Full Court of the Supreme Court of Western Australia, 23 July 1999.

[35] *Brown v Members of the Classification Review Board of the Office of Film and Literature Classification* (1997) 154 ALR 67.

[36] *Per* Heerey J.

[37] *Per* Sundberg J.

[38] (1994) 179 CLR 427 at 437 *per* Mason CJ, Brennan, Gaudron and McHugh JJ.

The Constitution of the Australian Commonwealth does not contain broad declarations of individual rights and freedoms which deny legislative power to the Parliament, but the courts nevertheless endeavour so to construe the enactments of the Parliament as to maintain the fundamental freedoms which are part of our constitutional framework.[39]

The importance of freedom of speech has also been recognised by the courts in the development of legal principles, such as the "newspaper rule" which, in certain limited circumstances, protects journalists from contempt proceedings for refusing to reveal sources.[40]

Australian Privacy Laws

There is no general statutory or common law right to privacy under Australian law.[41] Although, as in the UK, there have been several initiatives since the 1970s to introduce such a law,[42] success has only been achieved in the area of data protection with the introduction of the Privacy Act 1988 (Cth) and the more recent Privacy Amendment (Private Sector) Act 2000 (Cth).[43] This means that an individual seeking redress for a perceived invasion of privacy not involving data protection has to seek redress through other forms of action not specifically designed to protect privacy, such as the torts of trespass and defamation or an action for breach of confidence.[44]

The importance of privacy as a fundamental right is, however, given limited direct legal recognition by two mechanisms, referred to above in the discussion of the common law recognition of freedom of expression. First, the principle of statutory interpretation that legislation will be assumed not to infringe fundamental rights and freedoms applies to privacy, as it does to freedom of expression. In

---

[39] (1987) 162 CLR 514, 523.

[40] See, for example, *McGuinness v Attorney-General (Victoria)* (1940) 63 CLR 73; *John Fairfax & Sons Limited v Cojuangco* (1988) 165 CLR 346. See also the "public interest" defence to actions for breach of confidence discussed at page xx below.

[41] The lack of a common law right to privacy was established by the High Court in *Victoria Park Racing And Recreation Grounds Co Ltd v Taylor* (1937) 58 CLR 479.

[42] For an overview see the website of the Australian Privacy Foundation: <http://www.privacy.org.au/>.

[43] See page 183 below.

[44] See page 173 below.

Coco v R,[45] the High Court had to decide whether State legislation could be interpreted to authorise an invasion of privacy. In that case, legislation allowed for police to use a listening device following written approval from a Supreme Court judge which purported to authorise unlawful entry onto premises to install a device. The High Court held that, absent an unmistakable and unambiguous legislative intention, the law could not be interpreted as permitting unlawful entry onto premises. In authorising a trespass, the judge exceeded the scope of the power conferred by the legislation.[46]

Secondly, as mentioned above, Australia is a party to a number of international instruments that recognise privacy interests including Article 17 of the ICCPR which provides for protection against arbitrary or unlawful interference with privacy.

Legal Protection Against Intrusion

Territorial privacy is protected mainly by common law torts. Electronic privacy, on the other hand, is protected by legislation regulating the interception of telecommunications, and the use of listening and surveillance devices.

Territorial Intrusions

Unlawful intrusions onto a person's land are dealt with by the torts of trespass to land and private nuisance. In addition, harassment may possibly give rise to an action for intentional infliction of emotional harm.

In actions for trespass, it is important to determine whether the intruder is a trespasser, or has a licence to enter onto or remain on land. For example, the High Court has held that there is an implied licence for a person to enter land to lawfully communicate with a householder.[47] In the leading case of *Lincoln Hunt Australia Pty Ltd v Willesee*,[48] a TV film crew, accompanied by a dissatisfied customer,

---

[45] (1994) 179 CLR 427.

[46] The result in *Coco* is notable in that courts in the United States, which accord constitutional protection to the right to privacy, have interpreted listening device legislation as authorising a right of entry to install such devices: see *Dalia v United States* (1979) 441 US 238.

[47] *Halliday v Nevill* (1984) 155 CLR 1. See also *Barker v The Queen* (1983) 153 CLR 338.

[48] (1986) 4 NSWLR 457.

entered the premises of a business that carried on an investment scheme. The court held that, although there was an implied invitation to the public to visit the business premises, this was limited to members of the public *bona fide* seeking information or business.[49] The invitation was held not to extend to those entering the premises with video cameras, or reporters seeking to harass the occupiers. In these circumstances, it was found that a trespass occurred from the time of entry onto the premises. It has, however, been contended that a journalist may lawfully enter premises to seek permission to conduct an interview.[50] In any event, any licence to enter will be revoked by a request to intruders to leave the premises.[51]

Damages may be awarded for the affront and indignity caused by an invasion of privacy resulting, for example, from a trespass to install a microphone to overhear private conversations.[52] In relation to media intrusions, however, the harm to the plaintiff is more likely to result from publication of material obtained by means of the trespass, not by the physical intrusion. In such cases, an injunction to prevent publication will usually be more desirable. In *Lincoln Hunt,* it was held that an injunction could be granted to prevent publication of film or a photograph obtained by a trespasser if, in the circumstances, publication is unconscionable.[53] An injunction will only be awarded on this basis, however, if it can be established that the plaintiff will suffer irreparable damage if an injunction is not given.[54] In *Lincoln Hunt,* the court concluded that damages, including punitive damages, were an adequate remedy and refused an injunction.[55] On the other hand, in *Emcorp Pty Ltd v Australian Broadcasting Corporation,*[56] a court held that publication of television material obtained following a request to leave premises would be unconscionable, and awarded an interlocutory injunction. Considerations taken into account in granting the injunction included the serious nature of allegations against the plaintiff, the limited opportunity

[49] (1986) 4 NSWLR 457, 460.
[50] James McLachlan and Paul Mallam, *Media Law and Practice* (Law Book Co, Sydney, 1995–) para [12.1110].
[51] See *Emcorp Pty Ltd v Australian Broadcasting Corporation* [1988] 2 Qd R 169.
[52] *Greig v Greig* [1966] VR 376.
[53] (1986) 4 NSWLR 457, 463.
[54] (1986) 4 NSWLR 457, 464.
[55] See also *Church of Scientology Inc v Transmedia Productions Pty Ltd* (1987) ART 80–101.
[56] [1988] 2 Qd R 169.

given to reply to the allegations, and the potential effect of publica-tion on the business of the plaintiff.[57] In these circumstances, the court held that damages would not be an adequate remedy.

Whether an injunction can be awarded to restrain the publication of material obtained by a trespass committed by another is contro-versial. In *Lenah Game Meats Pty Ltd v Australian Broadcasting Corporation*[58] an animal rights group provided video footage to the ABC that had been obtained from a plant for processing possum meat. Although there was no cause of action in trespass against the ABC, the operators of the plant sought an injunction to prevent the material being broadcast. The Tasmanian Supreme Court held that it had the power to grant an injunction to prevent the publication of material resulting from a trespass, even if the publisher was not a tres-passer, provided publication would be unconscionable. The court concluded that it would be unconscionable for the ABC to know-ingly use the fruits of an unlawful trespass and that the balance of convenience favoured the award of an injunction to prevent the material being broadcast.[59]

Intrusions from outside a person's property do not amount to tres-pass. For example, taking aerial photographs,[60] or taking photographs from a public street or adjoining property,[61] is not a trespass. An unreasonable interference with the use or enjoyment of land may, however, give rise to an action for private nuisance, provided actual harm can be established.[62] Nevertheless, merely overlooking land is not enough to constitute an action for nuisance.[63] In the *Victoria Park* case, for example, it was held that the broadcasting of races from a tower erected on neighbouring property to a race course did not inter-fere with the use or enjoyment of the land, but merely made the

---

[57] [1988] 2 Qd R 169 at 177–78.

[58] Unreported decision of full court of the Supreme Court of Tasmania, [1999] TASSC 114 (2 November 1999).

[59] The High Court has granted special leave to appeal the decision of the Tasmanian Supreme Court: see *High Court Bulletin*, No 2 2001, 19 March 2001.

[60] *Bernstein of Leigh (Baron) v Skyviews & General Ltd* [1978] QB 479.

[61] *Bathurst City Council v Saban* (1985) 2 NSWLR 704.

[62] The harm may consist of physical discomfort and inconvenience, damage to property or injury to health: see JG Fleming, *The Law of Torts*, 9th edn (Carswell, Toronto, 1998) 468.

[63] It is clearly established that there are no property rights in a "spectacle": *Victoria Park Racing and Recreation Grounds Co Ltd v Taylor* (1937) 58 CLR 479; *Sports and General Press Agency Ltd v "Our Dogs" Publishing Co Ltd* [1916] 2 KB 880.

racing less profitable.[64] On the other hand, an English case has suggested that constant surveillance, as opposed to taking a single photograph, may be an actionable nuisance.[65] It also appears that persistent telephone harassment may, depending on the circumstances, amount to an actionable nuisance.[66] Like trespass, an action for private nuisance is available only to a person entitled to exclusive possession and, thus, cannot assist licensees.[67]

In *Wilkinson v Downton*[68] it was established that an action in tort may lie if a person intentionally does an act calculated to cause physical harm and physical harm results. It has been argued that, in addition to harassment, the tort may be extended to apply to the publication of distressing personal material by the media, such as unauthorised photographs of a disaster.[69] In *Church of Scientology Inc v Transmedia Productions Ltd*,[70] however, Needham J questioned the application of the tort to the showing of "distressing" television film, maintaining that to do so would effectively deter freedom of speech.

Electronic Intrusions

The unlawful interception of telephone communications is regulated by the federal Telecommunications (Interception) Act 1979 (Cth) which also prohibits unlawful dealing with intercepted information.[71] As with similar legislation in the UK and elsewhere, the Act generally prohibits interceptions unless they are authorised under a judicial warrant scheme principally for policing or national security purposes.[72] In addition, each Australian jurisdiction has "listening

---

[64] (1937) 58 CLR 479 at 493 *per* Latham CJ.

[65] *Bernstein of Leigh (Baron) v Skyviews & General Ltd* [1978] QB 479 at 489 *per* Griffiths J.

[66] *Alma v Nakir* [1966] 2 NSWR 396; *Khorasandjian v Bush* [1993] 3 WLR 476.

[67] Some English decisions have suggested that the tort may protect all occupants of a property: *Khorasandjian v Bush* [1993] 3 WLR 476; *Hunter v Canary Wharf Ltd* [1996] 2 WLR 348.

[68] [1897] 2 QB 57.

[69] Raymond Wacks, *Privacy and Press Freedom* (Blackstone Press Limited, London, 1995) 87–89.

[70] [1987] ATR 80–101, 68, 643.

[71] See Telecommunications (Interception) Act 1979 (Cth), ss 7 (unlawful interception) and 63 (unlawful dealing with intercepted information).

[72] For analysis of the interception regime see Roger Magnusson, "Privacy, Surveillance and Interception in Australia's Changing Telecommunications Environment" (1999) 27 *Federal Law Review* 33.

devices" legislation.[73] The legislation generally defines a "listening device" to mean any device or equipment that is capable of being used to record or listen to a private conversation.[74] Although, the State and Territory laws are far from consistent,[75] they all prohibit the communication or publication of private conversations that have been unlawfully recorded, without the consent of the parties concerned.[76] There are also important exceptions, including the use of listening devices authorised by warrants.

In Victoria and Western Australia, the legislation has been extended to apply to the unlawful use of optical surveillance devices,[77] which are defined as devices capable of being used to visually record or observe a private activity.[78] However, the application of the surveillance legislation to media activities, such as news-gathering, is limited as the prohibition applies only to the surveillance of a "private activity". Under the Western Australian legislation, this means:

> any activity carried on in circumstances that may reasonably be taken to indicate that any of the parties to the activity desires it to be observed only by themselves, but does not include an activity carried on in circumstances in which the parties to the activity ought reasonably to expect that the activity may be observed.[79]

[73] Listening Devices Act 1992 (ACT) s 2; Listening Devices Act 1990 (NT) s 3(1); Listening Devices Act 1984 (NSW) s 3(1); Invasion of Privacy Act 1971 (Qld) s 42(1); Listening Devices Act 1972 (SA) s 3; Listening Devices Act 1991 (Tas) s 3(1); Surveillance Devices Act 1999 (Vic) s 3(1); Surveillance Devices Act 1998 (WA) s 3(1).

[74] Listening Devices Act 1992 (ACT); Listening Devices Act 1990 (NT); Listening Devices Act 1984 (NSW); Invasion of Privacy Act 1971 (Qld); Listening Devices Act 1972 (SA); Listening Devices Act 1991 (Tas); Surveillance Devices Act 1999 (Vic); Surveillance Devices Act 1998 (WA).

[75] For example, in some jurisdictions an offence is committed only where the person recording a conversation is not a party, while in other jurisdictions an offence may be committed by a person recording a conversation to which he or she is a party provided the other parties have not consented to the recording.

[76] Listening Devices Act 1992 (ACT) ss 5, 6; Listening Devices Act 1990 (NT) s 9; Listening Devices Act 1984 (NSW) ss 6,7; Invasion of Privacy Act 1971 (Qld) ss 44, 45; Listening Devices Act 1972 (SA) s 5; Listening Devices Act 1991 (Tas) ss 9, 10; Surveillance Devices Act 1999 (Vic) s 11; Surveillance Devices Act 1998 (WA) s 9.

[77] Surveillance Devices Act 1998 (WA); Surveillance Devices Act 1999 (Vic). Note that the prohibition on the use of such devices is subject to exceptions, including the use under warrants or for emergencies.

[78] Surveillance Devices Act 1998 (WA) s 3(1); Surveillance Devices Act 1999 (Vic) s 3(1).

[79] Surveillance Devices Act 1998 (WA) s 3(1).

The Victorian definition is similar, but also excludes "an activity carried on outside a building".[80] It would therefore seem that the legislation limits the extent to which television media can engage in unannounced "walk-ins" onto private premises.[81] In addition, the legislation prohibits the unauthorised publication of records of a private activity made by the use of a device,[82] although under the Victorian legislation publication is allowed "in the public interest".[83]

Disclosure of Private Facts

The two main actions relied upon to protect private facts are the action for breach of confidence and the tort of defamation. The tort of malicious falsehood may possibly be relied upon in limited circumstances.[84]

Breach of Confidence

A duty to keep material confidential may be imposed by contract or arise from an equitable obligation. To maintain an action for breach of confidence the following elements must be satisfied:

—The information must have the necessary quality of confidence;
—The information must have been imparted in circumstances importing an obligation of confidence; and
—There must be an unauthorised use of the information by the person to whom it has been imparted, to the detriment of the confider.[85]

While the action for breach of confidence has been used mainly to protect trade secrets, it has also been relied upon to protect personal information about a plaintiff. For example, the action has been applied to prevent publication of information identifying a health worker as suffering from hepatitis B[86] and information identifying police informants.[87]

---

[80] Surveillance Devices Act 1999 (Vic) s 3(1).

[81] See Walker, n 10 above, 896.

[82] Surveillance Devices Act 1998 (WA) s 9(1); Surveillance Devices Act 1999 (Vic) s 11(1).

[83] Surveillance Devices Act 1999 (Vic) s 11(2)(b)(i).

[84] See *Ratcliffe v Evans* [1892] 2 QB 524 and *Kaye v Robertson* [1991] FSR 62.

[85] *Coco v AN Clark (Engineers) Ltd* [1969] RPC 41, 47 *per* Megarry J.

[86] *Y v TVW Enterprises Ltd* (Unreported, Supreme Court of Western Australia, 2 February 1990).

[87] *G v Day* [1982] 1 NSWLR 24; *Falconer v Australian Broadcasting Corporation* (1991) 22 IPR 205.

Information is not confidential once it has become public or common knowledge.[88] There are, however, degrees of secrecy, so that limited publication does not necessarily result in private information losing the quality of confidence.[89] Thus, in *G v Day*,[90] transitory broadcasts of an informant's name did not result in the identity of the informant losing the quality of confidentiality.

For an obligation of confidence to arise, the circumstances in which the information is communicated must be such that a reasonable person would realise that the information was communicated in confidence.[91] A third party who obtains information, such as a journalist, is under an obligation of confidence if the circumstances under which the information is obtained indicate that he or she knew, or ought to have known, that the information was confidential.[92] Moreover, a third party who is initially unaware that the information is confidential, will be under an obligation of confidentiality on having actual or constructive notice of the breach.[93]

There is continuing uncertainty concerning whether an obligation arises where confidential information has not been communicated, but has been acquired surreptitiously, for example by eavesdropping or theft, or accidentally.[94] In *Franklin v Giddens*[95] it was held that an action for breach of confidence could apply to protect secret information that was stolen with the intention of it being used in competi-

---

[88] *O Mustad & Son v Dosen* [1963] RPC 41; *Saltman Engineering Co Ltd v Campbell Engineering Co Ltd* (1948) 65 RPC 203 at 215 *per* Lord Greene MR; *Lennon v News Group Newspapers Ltd* [1978] FSR 573.

[89] Thus, in *Franchi v Franchi* [1967] RPC 149 it was pointed out that: "if relative secrecy remains, the plaintiff can succeed" (153).

[90] [1984] 1 NSWLR 24.

[91] *Coco v AN Clark (Engineers) Ltd* [1969] RPC 41, 47 *per* Megarry J.

[92] See *Commonwealth v John Fairfax & Sons Limited* (1980) 147 CLR 39; *Attorney-General (United Kingdom) v Heinemann Publishers Australia Pty Ltd* (1988) 165 CLR 30.

[93] *Fraser v Evans* [1969] 1 QB 349; *Malone v Commissioner of Police of the Metropolis [No 2]* [1979] 1 ch 344.

[94] For a discussion of this issue see: Megan Richardson, "Breach of Confidence, Surreptitiously or Accidentally Obtained Information and Privacy: Theory Versus Law" (1994) 19 *Melbourne University Law Review* 673. In the United Kingdom there is a well-known controversy concerning whether information obtained from telephone tapping may give rise to an action for breach of confidence: *Malone v Metropolitan Police Commissioner (No 2)* [1979] 2 All ER 620; cf *Francome v Mirror Group Newspapers Ltd* [1984] 1 WLR 892.

[95] [1978] Qd R 72.

tion with the owner. Nevertheless, the application of *Franklin* to personal information should be treated with caution, as the case was concerned with commercial information that had been obtained unlawfully.[96] On the other hand, there are indications in some Australian cases that suggest that an obligation of confidence may arise in the absence of a confidential relationship, and even if information is obtained accidentally.[97] If an action for breach of confidence can be maintained without there being a relationship of confidence, then the action, in its application to personal information, functions much like a right to privacy.[98]

The desirability of balancing the protection of confidentiality with the public interest in disclosure of information is recognised by a public interest defence. However, an extended "public interest" defence as developed under United Kingdom jurisprudence[99] has had an indifferent reception in Australia, with most courts being concerned to keep the defence within limits. For example, in *obiter* comments in *Commonwealth v John Fairfax & Sons Ltd*,[100] Mason J maintained that the defence exists to protect the community from destruction, damage or harm, applying to disclosures of breaches of national security, breaches of the law or matters endangering the public. Similarly, in *Castrol Australia Pty Ltd v Emtech Associates Pty Ltd*,[101] Rath J held that, to establish a "just cause" for breaking a confidence it is necessary to show something more weighty than a "public interest" in the truth being told. Furthermore, in the initial Australian *Spycatcher* decision, Powell J conflated the "iniquity" and "public interest" approaches, holding that "publication will be permitted in those cases

---

[96] See Raymond Wacks, *Privacy and Press Freedom* (Blackstone Press, London, 1995) 61; Jennifer Stuckey, "The Liability of Innocent Third Parties Implicated in Another's Breach of Confidence" (1981) 4 *University of NSW Law Journal* 73.

[97] See, for example, *Shaw v Harris (No 1)* (1991) 3 *TasR* 153 and cases cited by Walker, n 10 above, 959–60.

[98] This development appears to have been accepted in *obiter* comments made by Laws J in *Hellewell v Chief Constable* [1995] 1 WLR 806, 807. Richardson suggests that the extended operation of the action is properly based on the equitable doctrine of unconscionability: Richardson, n 94 above, 695–97.

[99] See for example *Initial Services Ltd v Putterill* [1968] 1 QB 396; *Woodward v Hutchins* [1977] 1 WLR 760; *Lion Laboratories Ltd v Evans* [1985] 1 QB 526.

[100] (1980) 147 CLR 39, 57.

[101] (1980) 33 ALR 31, 56.

in which there is shown to have been some impropriety which is of such a nature that it ought, in the public interest, be exposed".[102]

In one decision, Gummow J went so far as to cast doubt on the authority for even a limited "public interest" defence.[103] Instead of a defence, he maintained that any general doctrine was limited to the principle that information will lack the attribute of confidence if it concerns the existence or likelihood of "iniquity", meaning "a crime, civil wrong or serious misdeed of public importance".[104] In a later case, Gummow J characterised the English defence as "not so much a rule of law as an invitation to judicial idiosyncrasy by deciding each case on an ad hoc basis as to whether, on the facts overall, it is better to respect or override the obligation of confidence".[105]

Some Australian judges, on the other hand, have appeared willing to adopt the broader English defence. Thus, in an Australian *Spycatcher* appeal, Kirby P accepted the existence of a public interest defence that required the courts to balance the public interest in the open discussion of matters such as those contained in the *Spycatcher* book with the equitable duty of confidence.[106] Also, in *Esso Australia Resources Ltd v Plowman*,[107] the High Court held that the exception would apply where the public had a legitimate interest in knowing material that was otherwise confidential. The court confirmed that, in relation to information held by the government, there was an onus on the government to establish that non-disclosure would be in the public interest.[108] The court was not, however, required to determine the boundaries of the exception so that its nature and scope under Australian law remains unclear.[109]

[102] (1987) 8 NSWLR 341, 382.

[103] *Corrs Pavey Whiting & Byrne v Collector of Customs (Vic)* (1987) 74 ALR 428.

[104] *Corrs Pavey Whiting & Byrne v Collector of Customs (Vic)* (1987) 74 ALR 428, 450.

[105] *Smith Kline & French Laboratories (Australia) Ltd v Secretary, Department of Community Services and Health* (1990) 17 IPR 545, 583.

[106] *Attorney-General (UK) v Heinemann Publishers Australia* (1987) 75 ALR 353, 434.

[107] (1995) 128 ALR 391.

[108] *Ibid*, at 402.

[109] *Ibid*, per Mason CJ; at 416 per Toohey J. It may be that the future development of the "public interest" defence in Australia will be influenced by the constitutional implication of freedom of political communication explained at page xx above. In *Commonwealth v John Fairfax Publications Pty Ltd* (Unreported, Supreme Court of NSW, 26 June 1995) Bryson J held that the implied freedom should be taken into account in determining whether to vary an order to restrict access to evidence protected as confidential information, but that it was not conclusive of the matter.

An additional area of uncertainty concerns the availability of an interlocutory injunction to restrain publication where there is a likelihood of the "public interest" defence being satisfied. The English cases appear to establish that, in deciding whether to award an interlocutory injunction to restrain publication, the courts will take into account any public interest in disclosure.[110] Given the more flexible attitude of Australian courts to the award of injunctions in defamation actions, however, it appears unlikely that rules limiting the discretion to award injunctions in actions for breach of confidence will be accepted in Australia.

Defamation

Defamation law protects individual reputation and, in so doing, restricts or penalises the communication of some information, thereby constituting the most significant legal restraint on publication by the media under Australian law.[111] The substantive principles of Australian defamation law attempt, however imperfectly, to balance the protection of individual reputation and freedom of expression. Insofar as defamation law protects reputation, it incidentally protects aspects of personal privacy. In the absence of express legal protection of privacy, the extent to which defamation law has been relied upon to protect privacy interests has influenced the development of defamation law, arguably undermining its coherency.

Australian defamation laws bear the marks of the complex history of English defamation law, but are even more complex. As Australia is a federation, there is no single defamation law, but separate laws in each of the States and Territories. In each jurisdiction, defamation is a combination of common law and statute law, but in differing degrees.[112]

---

[110] See especially *Lion Laboratories Ltd v Evans* [1985] 1 QB 526 at 538–39 *per* Stephenson LJ. See also *Woodward v Hutchins* [1977] 1 WLR 760; *The Church of Scientology of California v Kaufman* [1973] RPC 627; *Francome v Mirror Group Newspapers Ltd* [1984] 2 All ER 408; *Lion Laboratories Ltd v Evans* [1985] 1 QB 526.

[111] The historical distinction between "libel" and "slander" continues to have some significance under Australian defamation laws but, as it is of little significance for the media, is not dealt with in this chapter.

[112] In Victoria, South Australia, Western Australia, the Australian Capital Territory and the Northern Territory, the common law is the main influence on defamation law. In Queensland and Tasmania, defamation is largely codified by statute. In NSW, the law is not codified, but the common law is significantly modified by legislation.

The disclosure of private facts will amount to defamation if the disclosed material is defamatory and it sufficiently relates to the plaintiff. It is difficult to define what is defamatory with any precision and Australian courts continue to be influenced by tests developed by English courts.[113] The current test commonly applied in Australia requires an imputation to be "such as is likely to cause ordinary decent folk in the community, taken in general, to think less of" the plaintiff.[114] Defamatory material is not, however, confined to material that disparages a plaintiff, but extends to material that will cause a person to be "shunned or avoided", or displayed in a ridiculous light, regardless of personal responsibility.[115] For example, it has been held to be defamatory to allege that a person has been raped,[116] or is suffering from a disease, such as hepatitis B.[117] Moreover, in *Ettingshausen v Australian Consolidated Press Ltd*,[118] it was held that a prominent footballer was defamed by publication of a naked photograph, not because it was disparaging, but because it would subject him to ridicule. The extension of defamation to material where there is no imputation of moral responsibility would appear to be directed more at protecting against publication of private material than protecting reputation.[119]

The extent to which defamation may protect privacy is limited by the defences to an action for defamation, especially the defence of justification. At common law, the defence of justification permits publication if the defendant can establish the substantial truth of a defamatory imputation.[120] The defence of justification undermines the extent to which actions for defamation can be used to protect privacy, as a person concerned with the disclosure of private matters will

---

[113] See the tests established in *Parmiter v Coupland* (1840) 6 M & W 105 at 108; 151 ER 340, 342 *per* Parke B; *Sim v Stretch* (1936) 52 TLR 669, 671 *per* Lord Atkin; and *Youssoupoff v Metro-Goldwyn-Mayer* (1934) 50 TLR 581, 587 *per* Slessor LJ.

[114] *Gardiner v John Fairfax & Sons Pty Ltd* (1942) 42 SR (NSW) 171, 172 *per* Jordan CJ; *Boyd v Mirror Newspapers Ltd* [1980] 2 NSWLR 449, 452 *per* Hunt J.

[115] *Boyd v Mirror Newspapers Ltd* [1980] 2 NSWLR 449, 452 . See also *Berkoff v Burchill* [1996] 4 All ER 1008.

[116] *Youssoupoff v Metro-Goldwyn-Mayer* (1934) 50 TLR 581.

[117] *Henry v TVW Enterprises Ltd* (1990) 3 WAR 474.

[118] (1991) 23 NSWLR 443.

[119] See, for example, Walker, n 10 above, 88, 137; Walker (1994) 19 *MULR* 729, 735.

[120] See, for example, *Sutherland v Stopes* [1925] AC 47; *Howden v "Truth" and "Sportsman" Ltd* (1937) 58 CLR 416.

wish to prevent true disclosures just as much, and perhaps more, than the publication of false material.[121]

The common law defence has been modified by legislation in the some jurisdictions. In Queensland, Tasmania and the Australian Capital Territory, in addition to establishing truth, a defendant must show that the material was published for the "public benefit".[122] In NSW, apart from establishing truth, a defendant must prove either that the material relates to a matter of "public interest" or is published under qualified privilege.[123] The addition of a "public benefit" test provides greater protection against the exposure of private matters than the common law defence, and was evidently introduced to fulfil this function.[124] Moreover, in determining whether there is a "public benefit", the courts balance the public interest in disclosure against a plaintiff's interests in retaining privacy. Thus, in *Cohen v Mirror Newspapers Ltd,* the court stated that:

> Public benefit requires a weighing of the right to privacy against the public interest of free discussion of matters of public concern.[125]

There are few reported cases on what amounts to a "public benefit" or "public interest".[126] It appears, however, that there is no public benefit in the disclosure of the private activities of a public figure, unless the activities are relevant to his or her capacity to perform public duties. For example, in *Mutch v Sleeman*,[127] it was held that a newspaper could not rely on the public benefit to defend the publication of details of a politician's divorce, including allegations of wife-beating. Similarly, there was held to be no public interest in the

---

[121] See, for example, ALRC (1979) para 123. The practical and evidential difficulties of proving truth may be substantial, amounting to "a powerful brake on public debate and the flow of information by underscoring the wisdom of caution and self-censorship": Fleming (1998) n 62 above, 611.

[122] Defamation Act 1889 (Qld) s 15; Defamation Act 1957 (Tas) s 15; Defamation Act 1901 (NSW) s 6 (as applied to the ACT).

[123] Defamation Act 1974 (NSW) s 15.

[124] Fleming contends that the "public benefit" test was originally introduced in New South Wales to "assist the social integration of former convicts": Fleming (1998) n 121 above, 614.

[125] [1971] 1 NSWLR 623, 628 *per* Jacobs and Manning JJA.

[126] There would appear to be no "discernible difference" between "public benefit" and "public interest": see *Allworth v John Fairfax Group Pty Ltd* (1993) 113 FLR 254 at 263 *per* Higgins J.

[127] (1928) 29 SR (NSW) 125.

disclosure of allegations of adultery made against a prominent cricketer, who was involved in the administration of a player's code of
conduct.[128] The court rejected the argument that the plaintiff's private behaviour was relevant to his public position. At the same time,
the court pointed out that a private matter can become a matter of
public interest if the plaintiff brings it into the public domain, for
example, by claiming to have high standards of private morality.[129]
Furthermore, there is unlikely to be a public benefit in preventing
disclosure of private material that has previously been publicised.[130]

> In NSW, in addition to truth and public interest, the defence of justifi-
> cation may be established if the material is true and published under
> qualified privilege. The most general statement of the defence is that it
> will protect the publication of material in the performance of a duty or
> interest of the publisher, provided the person to whom it is commun-
> icated has a corresponding interest in receiving the material.[131] Although
> the media have argued that their public function means that they have a
> legitimate interest in receiving and publishing information, the courts
> have rejected the argument.[132] The NSW defence has therefore been
> confined mainly to certain personal communications, such as commun-
> ications between an employer and employee, or parent and child, and
> not to disclosures to the public at large.

In the Code States, the common law defence is replaced by a statutory defence which sets out a list of circumstances, including publication "for the public good", which are protected by qualified
privilege.[133] The Code defences allow the media much greater lati-
tude in publishing material than the common law defence.
Differences between Australian defamation laws may well mean that
publication of private facts is unlawful in some jurisdictions, but
permitted in others.[134]

It was explained above, that the High Court in *Lange* held that the
constitutional implication of freedom of speech required a modifica-

---

[128] *Chappell v TCN Channel Nine Pty Ltd* (1988) 14 NSWLR 153.
[129] (1988) 14 NSWLR 153, 167.
[130] *Cohen v Mirror Newspapers Ltd* [1971] 1 NSWLR 623.
[131] *Adam v Ward* [1917] AC 309, 334 *per* Lord Atkinson.
[132] See *Morosi v Mirror Newspapers Ltd* [1977] 2 NSWLR 749.
[133] Defamation Act 1889 (Qld) ss 16, 17; Defamation Act 1957 (Tas) ss 16, 19.
[134] See, for example, *Morosi v Mirror Newspapers Ltd* [1977] 2 NSWLR 749.

tion of the defence of qualified privilege in relation to communications concerning political or government matters. Under the "*Lange* defence", political communications are protected by qualified privilege if a publication is reasonable, and not actuated by malice, in the sense that a publication must not be made otherwise than for communicating government or political information or ideas.

Australian courts rarely grant interlocutory injunctions in defamation actions. Thus, in *National Mutual Life Association of Australasia Ltd v GTV Corporation Pty Ltd*, the court stated that:

> the very great importance which our society and our law have always accorded to what is called free speech, means that equity exercises great care in granting injunctive relief and does so only where it is very clear that it should be granted.[135]

These considerations led the English courts to adopt rigid "rules", including that an injunction would be granted only if a jury's finding that material was not defamatory would be set aside as unreasonable.[136] An application of these rules is the principle that, if a defendant pleads justification, an interlocutory injunction will not be awarded unless there is no prospect of the defence succeeding.[137] The English rules have been applied in a number of Australian cases.[138]

In *Chappell v TCN Channel Nine Pty Ltd*,[139] however, it was held that inflexible rules could not replace the court's discretion to award an injunction. Nevertheless, it remains the case that the discretion to grant an interlocutory injunction will usually not be exercised, especially if justification is pleaded, unless the plaintiff can establish irreparable harm such that damages would be an inadequate remedy. Moreover, an interlocutory injunction will not be awarded "if its effect is to restrain the public discussion of matters of public interest or concern".[140]

---

[135] [1989] VR 747 at 764.

[136] *William Coulson and Sons v James Coulson and Co* (1887) 3 TLR 846.

[137] *Bonnard v Perryman* [1891] 2 ch 269, 284 *per* Coleridge CJ.

[138] *Edelsten v John Fairfax & Sons Ltd* [1978] 1 NSWLR 685; *Lennox v Krantz* (1978) 19 SASR 272; *Shiel v Transmedia Productions Pty Ltd* [1987] 1 Qd R 199.

[139] (1988) 14 NSWLR 153. See also *Jakudo Pty Ltd v South Australian Telecasters Ltd* (1997) 69 SASR 440, 443 *per* Doyle CJ.

[140] *Chappell v TCN Channel Nine Pty Ltd* (1988) 14 NSWLR 153, 171 *per* Hunt J.

Data Protection Laws

Legislative protection of information privacy has been introduced in Australia in two main stages: in 1988 to regulate personal information held by the federal government and federal government agencies and, more recently, to regulate personal information held by the private sector. In addition to federal laws, some States and Territories have introduced data protection laws.[141]

Privacy Act 1988 (Cth)

The Privacy Act 1988 (Cth) introduced rules that apply to the handling of personal information by the federal government and federal government agencies. The rules apply only to the protection of personal information and not to other infringements of privacy.[142] The legislation defines "personal information" to mean:

> information or an opinion . . . , whether true or not, and whether recorded in a material form or not, about an individual whose identity is apparent, or can reasonably be ascertained, from the information or opinion.[143]

The rules establish standards for the collection, storage, use and disclosure of personal information, which are contained in eleven principles, known as the Information Privacy Principles (IPPs).[144] The IPPS are subject to a number of important exceptions.

The legislation established the office of a federal Privacy Commissioner,[145] which has a number of statutory functions in relation to the protection of personal information, including investigating complaints concerning breaches of data protection standards.[146] In performing these functions, the Commissioner is required to have regard to a number of matters, including:

> the protection of important human rights and social interests that compete with privacy, including the general desirability of a free flow of

---

[141] To date, data protection legislation has been introduced into two states: New South Wales in 1998 and Victoria in 2000.

[142] Privacy Act 1988 (Cth) s 13.

[143] Privacy Act 1988 (Cth) s 6(1) (definition of "personal information").

[144] Privacy Act 1988 (Cth) s 14. The IPPs were based on the 1980 OECD *Data Privacy Guidelines:* see OECD (1980) above.

[145] Privacy Act 1988 (Cth) s 19.

[146] Privacy Act 1988 (Cth) s 27.

information and the recognition of the right of government and business to achieve their objectives in an efficient way.[147]

Privacy Amendment (Private Sector) Act 2000 (Cth)

Federal legislation was introduced in 2000 to extend data protection laws to the private sector. The legislation applies to all Australian businesses with an annual turnover of A$3 million and to some small businesses.[148] It will come into effect from December 2001, but will not apply to most small businesses covered by the law until December 2002.

The legislation establishes a co-regulatory regime with base line standards contained in ten principles, known as the National Privacy Principles (NPPs).[149] In general, the standards ensure that individuals have the ability to know why a private organisation is collecting personal information, what information is held concerning them, how the information will be used and who the information will be disclosed to. The NPPs also establish qualified rights of access to personal information held by the private sector, and to correct inaccurate information.[150]

The legislation is designed to encourage the private sector to build on the minimum standards set out in the NPPs, by developing privacy codes of conduct. There are a number of exceptions to the private sector privacy rules. For the purposes of this chapter, the most important is the exception relating to the activities of media organisations.

The Media Exemption

The legislation attempts to balance protection of personal information and the public interest in freedom of expression by exempting certain acts and practices of media organisations.[151] Three conditions

---

[147] Privacy Act 1988 (Cth) s 29(a).

[148] Specifically, health service providers, businesses that collect or disclose personal information, and small businesses that choose to opt-in to the regulatory scheme: Privacy Act 1988 (Cth) ss 6C–6E.

[149] Privacy Act 1988 (Cth) Schd 3.

[150] NPP 6.

[151] The Second Reading Speech stated that: "In developing the bill the government has sought to achieve a balance between the public interest in allowing a free flow of information to the public through the media and the individual's right to privacy": Hon Daryl Williams, Attorney-General, House of Representatives, *Official Hansard*, 12 April 2000, 15752.

must be satisfied for the exemption to apply: the organisation must be a media organisation; the relevant act or practice must be undertaken in the course of journalism; and the organisation must be publicly committed to observe published standards dealing with privacy in the media.[152] A "media organisation" is defined to mean an organisation whose activities include the collection and dissemination of news, current affairs, information or documentaries for the purpose of making the material publicly available.[153] The exemption applies only to acts and practices in the course of "journalism", a term deliberately not defined.[154] The third condition, a requirement to comply with standards dealing with media privacy, was included to ensure that minimum standards apply to journalists, while avoiding supervision by the Privacy Commissioner. As explained below, most Australian media organisations and journalist groups are covered by codes of conduct, which include privacy provisions.

Media Codes of Conduct

The rules governing media content in Australia are established mainly through codes of conduct developed by the media under co-regulatory or self-regulatory regimes. Separate regimes apply to broadcasting and the press.[155] In addition to industry codes, a code of ethics has been established by the trade union responsible for journalists.[156]

---

[152] Privacy Act 1988 (Cth) s 7B(4).

[153] Privacy Act 1988 (Cth) s 6 (definition of "media organisation").

[154] See Privacy Amendment (Private Sector) Bill 2000 (Cth), *Supplementary Explanatory Memorandum,* Amendment 2.

[155] The Internet Industry Association (IAA) has produced a draft *Privacy Code of Conduct* that is designed to apply to the Internet industry, including Internet Service Providers (ISPs) and content hosts: Internet Industry Association, *Internet Industry Privacy Code of Practice* (Draft Version 1.0), 28 December 2000, available at http://www.iia.net.au/. The IIA intends to submit the privacy code to the Privacy Commissioner for approval under the federal private sector privacy law.

[156] See the *Code of Ethics* (1984) of the Australian Journalists Association (AJA) section of the Media, Entertainment and Arts Alliance (MEAA) which applies to the practices of journalists. The way in which the Code deals with privacy was criticised in a review conducted by an MEAA Ethics Review Committee in 1996: *Ethics in Journalism* (Melbourne University Press, Carlton, 1997). The MEAA *Code of Ethics* is not dealt with in this chapter.

Broadcasting Codes of Practice

Broadcasting in Australia is regulated under the Broadcasting Services Act 1992 (Cth), which establishes a co-regulatory scheme for broadcasting content, with the main rules being set by codes of practice developed by sections of the industry in consultation with the Australian Broadcasting Authority (ABA).

All sections of the industry, including commercial broadcasters, community broadcasters and subscription broadcasters have developed codes. The legislation provides for complaints relating to breaches of a code to be handled, in the first instance, by the broadcaster.[157] If the response is inadequate, a complaint may be made to the ABA, which must investigate it.[158] But the ABA has limited power to impose sanctions. If it is satisfied that a code is not operating to provide appropriate safeguards, it may impose a legally binding standard.[159] Where the problem is not widespread, the ABA may impose a binding licence condition on individual licensees, requiring compliance with a code.[160]

The codes developed by the commercial and national broadcasters include provisions dealing with privacy intrusions by news and current affairs programs, which generally attempt to balance personal privacy and the public interest in disclosure. For example, the section of the commercial television code dealing with news and current affairs programs is stated as being intended, in part, to ensure that such programs "take account of personal privacy and of cultural differences in the community".[161] In particular, the code provides that, in broadcasting news and current affairs material, licensees must:

---

[157] Broadcasting Services Act 1992 (Cth) s 148.

[158] *Ibid.*

[159] Broadcasting Services Act 1992 (Cth) s 125. The list does not expressly include matters relating to individual privacy, but does include "promoting accuracy and fairness in news and current affairs programs": s 123(2)(d).

[160] Broadcasting Services Act 1992 (Cth) ss 44, 88, 100, 119. An extraordinary provision of the legislation provides that a code or standard may be amended by a federal House of Parliament: s 128.

[161] Federation of Australian Commercial Television Stations (FACTS), *Commercial Television Industry Code of Practice*, April 1999, clause 4.1.3.

not use material relating to a person's personal or private affairs, or which invades a person's privacy, other than where there is an identifiable public interest reason for the material to be broadcast.[162]

Other provisions of the television code deal with the use of sensitivity in broadcasting images or interviews with the bereaved, and survivors or witnesses of traumatic events; the identification of murder or accident victims before families are notified; and reports of suicide or attempted suicide.[163]

A comparatively small proportion of complaints to the ABA concern invasions of privacy.[164] In its *Annual Report,* the ABA records upholding three complaints concerning breaches of the privacy rules in the commercial television code in 1999–2000. For example, it found that there was no identifiable public interest in a report that revealed the identity of a homeless 12-year-old girl alleged to be involved with prostitution and drugs.[165]

Australian Press Council

Complaints concerning the press are dealt with under a self-regulatory scheme administered by an industry body, known as the Australian Press Council (APC).[166] The APC is able to accept complaints about the press from those not affected by material, as well as those who are affected.[167]

In 1996, the Council adopted a Statement of Principles, which it applies to complaints.[168] Principle 3, which deals with individual privacy, states that:

---

[162] Clause 4.3.5. For similar provision in national broadcasting code see Australian Broadcasting Corporation, *ABC Code of Practice 1998,* clause 2.5.

[163] Clauses 4.3.6, 4.3.8, 4.3.9.

[164] See Chadwick and Mullaly, n 4 above, 60; Australian Broadcasting Authority, *Annual Report 1999–2000.*

[165] Australian Broadcasting Authority, *Annual Report 1999–2000,* 129, finding breach of clause 4.3.5.

[166] The adequacy of the self-regulatory scheme was questioned in a 1992 Parliamentary report: House of Representatives Select Committee on the Print Media, *News & Fair Facts: The Australian Print Media Industry Report* (Canberra, 1992), paras 8.115–8.117.

[167] This feature distinguishes the Australian scheme from press council schemes in other jurisdictions.

[168] Australian Press Council, *Statement of Principles,* October 1996.

Readers of publications are entitled to have news and comment presented to them honestly and fairly, and with respect for the privacy and sensibilities of individuals. However, the right to privacy should not prevent publication of matters of public record or obvious or significant public interest. Rumour and unconfirmed reports, if published at all, should be identified as such.

The procedures for dealing with complaints are informal, with an emphasis on speedy resolution. If, for example, a complaint cannot be mediated, it may be referred to the Council's Complaints Committee, which will hold an informal hearing, before issuing an adjudication. The powers of the Council are limited to ordering publication of its ruling; it cannot, for example, direct the press to make an apology.

In adjudications concerning breaches of privacy, the Council has held that mere "public curiousity" does not amount to a matter of public interest.[169] In the past, the Council has upheld complaints concerning matters such as the unauthorised publication of a photograph of a woman who had recently given birth to quadruplets,[170] and the publication of a photograph of the body of an accident victim known to the local community.[171] Moreover, the publication of identifying photographs of a woman who had attempted suicide was held to infringe her right to privacy as, although the events were a matter of public interest, the identity of the woman was not.[172] On the other hand, a Council adjudication found that privacy was not infringed by the publication of an intercepted car-phone conversation between politicians, as the conversation was a matter of public interest.[173]

The extent to which privacy can be adequately protected by a regime in which the main sanction is publicity has been questioned. Lucas, for example, has argued that those who are concerned to preserve their privacy may not wish to risk further publicity by complaining to the Press Council.[174]

---

[169] Australian Press Council, *Adjudications Nos* 102, 916.

[170] Australian Press Council, *Adjudication No* 9.

[171] Australian Press Council, *Adjudication No* 926.

[172] Australian Press Council, *Adjudication No* 887.

[173] Australian Press Council, *Adjudication No* 336.

[174] Ric Lucas, "The Press Council Guarding the Fourth Estate" (1986) 11 *Legal Service Bulletin* 15 at 17.

FREEDOM OF EXPRESSION, PRIVACY AND THE MEDIA

This section of the chapter examines the relationship between free-dom of expression and privacy under Australian law. The relation-ship is especially complex, largely because of the unique legal form in which these interests are recognised in Australia.

Although freedom of expression is constitutionally protected, the protection is partial, applying only to political speech. Moreover, as the implied constitutional freedom is a relatively recent innovation, there remain areas of uncertainty concerning the nature and scope of protection, and the test for infringement. Apart from data protection laws, privacy in Australia is protected mainly by laws, including com-mon law actions that are designed to protect other interests. This indirect form of protection is ill-suited to balancing the public inter-est in freedom of expression and the protection of individual privacy. Furthermore, there is a tendency for the coherency of areas of the law, such as defamation and breach of confidence, to be undermined, as courts and legislatures strain existing principles to protect privacy interests.

Constitutional Protection of Free Speech

The constitutional implication of freedom of political speech pro-vides the general legal framework for Australian media law. The implied freedom prevails over laws that protect privacy to the extent to which such laws infringe the constitutional implication. As explained above, the High Court in *Lange* established a two-stage test for determining whether there is an infringement of the implied freedom and this is now the main legal mechanism for balancing freedom of expression and privacy in relation to political speech.

To amount to an infringement, the first limb of the *Lange* test requires a law to "effectively burden freedom of communication about government or political matters either in its terms, operation or effect".[175] Prior to *Lange*, two decisions considered whether restrictions on the publication of information obtained from the interception of telecommunications were consistent with the implied

[175] (1997) 189 CLR 520 at 567.

freedom. It was explained above that the *Interception Act* prohibits unlawful dealing with intercepted information.[176] In *John Fairfax Publications Pty Ltd v Doe*,[177] it was held that the prohibition was not inconsistent with the implied freedom, as it was not a law concerning "political communications".[178] Similarly, in *Kizon v Palmer*[179] it was held that there was no infringement, as the prohibition does not deal with "such matters as elections, political discourse, public affairs or the holding of public office".[180]

Despite these decisions, it would appear that, in some circumstances, the prohibition on dealing with intercepted information could burden political communications in either its operation or effect, thereby satisfying the first limb of *Lange*. As Walker maintains, however, it is unlikely that the provision would fail the second limb of *Lange,* which asks whether a law is "reasonably appropriate and adapted" to serve a legitimate end compatible with the constitutional system of representative government.[181] It would seem likely that the prohibition would be held to be reasonably adapted and appropriate to serve the legitimate end of protecting against the disclosure of intercepted communications.

As this example illustrates, although the constitutional freedom prevails over laws that protect privacy, it would be rare for such a law to be inconsistent with the implied freedom. This is because most laws that protect privacy, even incidentally, are likely to serve a legitimate end of government.

To date, the only law relating to privacy held to infringe the implied freedom is Australian defamation law. As explained above, in *Lange* the High Court re-fashioned defamation law by introducing a new form of qualified privilege to apply to political communications. The *Lange* defence may have some effect on the extent to which defamation can be used to restrain the disclosure of private material in communications to which the defence applies. Another law that may possibly infringe the implied freedom is the "public interest" defence to actions for breach of confidence. As explained above, the

---

176 Telecommunications (Interception) Act 1979 (Cth) s 63.
177 (1995) 130 ALR 488.
178 *Ibid,* 495–96 *per* Gleeson CJ and, 513–14 *per* Kirby P.
179 (1997) 72 FCR 409.
180 *Ibid,* 443 *per* Lindgren J.
181 Walker, (2000) n 10 above, 866.

"extended" public interest defence accepted in *Lion Laboratories*,[182] has not been unreservedly adopted in Australia. It may well be that the implied freedom would require a clarification and expansion of the current Australian approach to the "public interest" test in relation to political communications.[183]

Common Law Protection of Free Speech and Privacy

Australian common law protects freedom of speech and privacy in a number of ways. First, it is a principle of statutory interpretation that legislation will be construed as consistent with fundamental rights and freedoms, including freedom of expression and privacy, wherever possible. Secondly, in the absence of a right to privacy, common law actions—including trespass, nuisance and defamation—incidentally protect individual privacy. In relation to some common law actions, the importance of freedom of expression has been recognised in the development of defences to laws incidentally protecting privacy. For example, the defence of justification to actions for defamation is a means of balancing the protection of reputation and freedom of communication. Thirdly, the courts are reluctant to award interlocutory injunctions restraining the publication of material, especially in defamation actions, largely because of a desire not to unduly inhibit freedom of speech.

Australian common law therefore recognises the public interest in both freedom of expression and privacy and, in the event of tension between the two, establishes some balance. In setting this balance, however, Australian courts have tended to attach greater weight to the protection of private legal interests than to the public interest in freedom of expression. In particular, Australian common law has generally refused to attribute any special significance to the role of the media in relation to the public disclosure of information. The approach of the Australian courts is perhaps best captured by com-

---

[182] [1985] 1 QB 526.

[183] At the same time, it should be acknowledged that, under Australian law, government information seems to be protected by an action for breach of confidence only if it is not in the public interest to disclose the information: *Commonwealth v John Fairfax & Sons Ltd* (1980) 147 CLR 39. The special rules applying to government information obviously must be taken into account in determining whether there is an inconsistency between the implied freedom and the action for breach of confidence.

ments of the High Court in *John Fairfax & Sons Ltd v Cojuangco*,[184] in which it was held that the media were not entitled to a general immunity to refuse to disclose sources. In that case, the High Court stated that:

> Information is more readily supplied to journalists when they undertake to preserve confidentiality in relation to their sources of information. It stands to reason that the free flow of information would be reinforced, to some extent at least, if the courts were to confer absolute protection on that confidentiality. But this would set such a high value on a free press and on freedom of information as to leave the individual without an effective remedy in respect of defamatory imputations published in the media.[185]

In general, in private actions, Australian courts have given less weight to the public interest in freedom of expression than English courts. For example, Australian courts have adopted a more conservative view of the public interest defence to actions for breach of confidence than English courts, generally attributing less importance to the public interest in disclosure than to the protection of confidentiality.[186] Similarly, Australian courts have apparently rejected the application of inflexible rules governing the availability of interlocutory injunctions in actions for defamation.[187] The Australian courts apply the two-stage *American Cyanamid* test, which requires the plaintiff to establish that there is a serious question to be tried, then the court to consider the balance of convenience.[188] In considering the latter, the courts acknowledge the importance of freedom of speech, but the public interest in disclosure is clearly not the only consideration. Thus,

---

[184] (1988) 165 CLR 346.

[185] *Ibid*, 354.

[186] Even Kirby P, who appeared to accept the broad English public interest test in the Australian *Spycatcher* decision, stated that: "the public interest in disclosure . . . may sometimes, even if rarely, outweigh the public interest in confidentiality and secrecy": *Attorney-General (UK) v Heinemann Publishers Australia Pty Ltd* (1987) 75 ALR 353, 434.

[187] *Chappell v TCN Channel Nine Pty Ltd* (1988) 14 NSWLR 153.

[188] *American Cyanamid Co v Ethicon Ltd* [1975] AC 396; *The Australian Coarse Grain Pool Pty Ltd v The Barley Marketing Boad of Queensland* (1982) 57 ALJR 425. The Australian approach to interlocutory injunctions may be usefully contrasted with the English approach, as explained in The Australian approach to interlocutory injunctions may be usefully contrasted with the English approach, as explained in *Holley v Smyth* [1998] 1 All ER 853.

in *Chappell v TCN Channel Nine Pty Ltd*,[189] an interlocutory injunction was awarded to prevent a current affairs program from broadcasting allegations of adultery concerning a prominent former cricketer.[190] The court concluded that the potential injury to the plaintiff outweighed other considerations, including any public interest in the allegations. In reaching this conclusion, Hunt J emphasised the importance of protecting public figures against media intrusions in the following terms:

> The Australian media is, in general, reasonably responsive to the need to permit public figures some degree of privacy in relation to their private behaviour. Such a need arises because, if every public figure is to become "fair game" in relation to his private behaviour which is unrelated to his capacity to perform his public duties, the community will suffer grievously from the unwillingness of suitable people to enter public life.[191]

The balance between freedom of speech and secrecy under Australian common law is, however, quite different where the information concerns the operation of government, not the personal affairs of an individual. For example, an action by a government to restrain publication of material in breach of confidence can be maintained only if the government successfully establishes a public interest in retaining confidentiality. As explained by Mason J in *Commonwealth v John Fairfax & Sons Ltd*,[192] in relation to government information, the public interest in disclosure will usually outweigh any interest in confidentiality:

> The court will not prevent the publication of information which merely throws light on the past workings of government, even if it be not public property, so long as it does not prejudice the community in other respects. Then disclosure will itself serve the public interest in keeping the community informed and in promoting discussion of public affairs.[193]

---

[190] See page 180 above.

[189] (1988) 14 NSWLR 153.
[190] See page 180 above.
[191] (1988) 14 NSWLR 153, 172.
[192] (1980) 147 CLR 39.
[193] *Ibid*, 52.

Legislative Protection of Free Speech and Privacy

Despite the lack of an overall constitutional or legislative framework, the public interest in freedom of speech and in the protection of privacy are often taken into account in legislative reform, especially in legislation imposing restrictions on publication. For example, a 1984 amendment exempting statements by broadcasters and publishers from a legislative prohibition on misleading or deceptive statements was introduced to protect the media and freedom of expression.[194] And as explained above, in some jurisdictions, the common law defence of justification to actions for defamation has been modified by the statutory addition of a "public benefit" or "public interest" requirement. It is clear that this extended defence has been introduced, and retained, more to protect privacy interests than individual reputation. Also, as discussed above, the new private sector data protection law attempts to balance freedom of speech and privacy by means of an exemption for media organisations.

Although freedom of expression and privacy are often taken into account in drafting legislation, legislative protection of both is partial, and legislative resolution of tensions between the principles relatively ad hoc. For example, legislative protection of privacy obviously depends upon the interest falling within an established legislative scheme, such as the data protection, telecommunications interception or listening devices legislation. There are, moreover, important differences between State and Territory laws protecting privacy, including inconsistencies between State and Territory defamation laws, and between listening and surveillance devices legislation.

In sum, apart from the influence of the constitutional implication of free speech, legislative protection of freedom of expression in Australia does not follow any consistent principle. The relevant legislation generally does not expressly take account of the role of the media. The legislative resolution of conflicts between free speech and privacy is often implicit, such as the limitation in State surveillance devices laws on the use of optical surveillance devices to "private activities". In some circumstances, however, there is express legislative

---

[194] Trade Practices Act 1974 (Cth) s 65A; see Mark Armstrong, David Lindsay and Ray Watterson, *Media Law in Australia,* 3rd edn (Oxford University Press, Melbourne, 1995).

acknowledgement of the importance of freedom of expression. The media exemption to the private sector data protection law is a good example of an express exception designed to limit privacy protection in the interests of freedom of expression. The piecemeal common law and legislative approach to the protection of privacy necessarily means that the resolution of tensions between freedom of expression and privacy under Australian law is achieved mainly on a case by case basis.

Freedom of Expression, Privacy and Media Codes of Conduct

Unlike most other areas of Australian law, media codes of conduct established under co-regulatory and self-regulatory schemes, deal directly with media intrusions into privacy and, in general, address conflicts with freedom of expression by prohibiting invasions of privacy unless there is a public interest in the publication of material.

There are benefits and disadvantages with these media schemes. A positive feature is that they provide complainants with a relatively inexpensive, accessible and informal means of dealing with invasions of privacy. Moreover, the standards established by the media codes may have an educative influence on media practitioners. On the other hand, as explained above, the schemes provide complainants with little in the way of remedies. Also there are underlying problems with the schemes., Thus, a complaint which receives publicity may repeat, or exacerbate, the original invasion of privacy; and complaints are only dealt with after there has been invasion of privacy, as there is no mechanism to forestall the publication of private material. These features may significantly inhibit use of the media schemes as a means of privacy protection.

Another problem is that the sectoral approach to broadcasting regulation in Australia has resulted in the proliferation of different statements in different industry codes as to what amounts to an invasion of privacy.[195] Moreover, there appear to be inconsistencies in the interpretation of the privacy provisions even within specific codes of practice.[196] There is little practical guidance as to what will amount

---

[195] The codes do not attempt to define privacy. The meaning of "privacy" under the New Zealand broadcasting law has been considered in *TV3 Network Services Ltd v Broadcasting Standards Authority* [1995] 2 NZLR 720.

[196] See Chadwick and Mullaly, n 4 above, 59, dealing with inconsistencies in Press Council adjudications.

to an unacceptable invasion of privacy, or when there is likely to be a public interest in disclosure. This is unlikely to promote an understanding within the media of the circumstances in which individual privacy should prevail over freedom of communication. Furthermore, the informality of the media schemes means that there is little consistent precedent to rely upon in interpreting the relevant provisions.

Nevertheless, of the mechanisms established under the Australian legal system, the media codes provide the clearest, most direct statements of the desirability of protecting against media intrusions, and the need to balance freedom of expression and individual privacy in doing so. Whether the relatively inconsistent and vague principles contained in the media codes are an adequate means for balancing the fundamental interests at stake must, however, be questioned. This is especially so in the absence of an overall framework of analysis at other levels of the Australian legal system.

CONCLUSION

As Australian law does not recognise a legal right to freedom of expression or rights to privacy, these rights are protected by a patchwork of laws and legal principles. There is no general legal statement of the balance to be struck between them. In the event of a conflict, there is no express, binding statement of which should prevail, nor of the principles to be applied in resolving tensions.

Australian laws, instead, establish a series of relatively ad hoc balances between the public interest in freedom of expression and the protection of privacy. From a comparative perspective, there are advantages and disadvantages with this approach which, to a considerable extent, mirror the comparative merits of a common law approach to resolving tensions between fundamental rights and freedoms. This is unsurprising as, in the absence of a bill of rights, the Australian common law has a much more important continuing role in protecting free speech and privacy than in comparable common law jurisdictions.

The main advantage of the common law approach is that it allows for the flexible application of legal principles, with results closely tailored to the facts of individual cases. Australian courts have been anxious to retain this flexibility, for example, in rejecting artificial rules constraining the ability to award injunctions in defamation actions. On the other hand, Australian courts have been more conservative than English courts in developing common law principles in relation to freedom of speech or privacy. Thus, Australian courts have not welcomed the wider "public interest" defence to actions for breach of confidence, and have generally given less importance to the public interest in free speech than English courts. The flexibility of the common law has therefore been leavened by a greater sense of fidelity to established common law rules than that shown by English courts. In relation to the media, the flexibility of the common law has been supplemented by the flexible co-regulatory and self-regulatory media codes of conduct. The media codes are probably the most important feature of the Australian approach to media regulation. The codes have the advantages of accessibility and informality, but are unlikely to provide those subject to a serious invasion of privacy with adequate remedies, and seem to have limited ability to alter the practices of media organisations.

Another advantage of the Australian approach is the high value and considerable protection given to freedom of communication in relation to political and government information. Furthermore, under Australian common law, greater weight is placed on the public interest in the disclosure of government information than is placed on the disclosure of personal information. It is arguable that, in practice, Australian courts have established an acceptable balance whereby, under the common law, personal privacy tends to prevail over the interest in freedom of expression, whereas in relation to government information, free speech is accorded greater importance than competing interests.

The main weakness of the Australian approach is the obverse of its main advantage: the benefits of flexibility must be matched against the dangers of inconsistency. First, the legal system accords only partial legal protection to both freedom of expression and privacy. Although the constitutional implication of freedom of communication provides some overall consistency, this protection is limited by the extent that it must be related to the constitutional system of representative government. Thus, non-political speech falls outside the constitutional umbrella. Australian privacy law is even less systematic: a plaintiff must fit within established forms of action that were not designed to protect privacy. This has resulted in the distortion of common law principles in areas such as defamation and breach of confidence, as the courts have strained to protect individual privacy. Moreover, although the courts have been willing to stretch the common law to protect privacy, they are understandably reluctant to re-make established balances for fear of usurping the role of the legislature.

Secondly, there are real concerns as to whether common law processes are suited to adequately balancing competing claims of freedom of expression and privacy. The common law develops incrementally, being closely tied to the facts of individual cases and its response to recurring conflicts is generally piecemeal, not systematic and analytical. For example, quite different considerations appear to have been taken into account in determining whether to award interlocutory injunctions against the media in defamation actions as opposed to actions in trespass. Moreover, in general, the common law has not developed specific rules to take into account the central and continuing role of the media in both facilitating freedom of communication and in threatening personal privacy. Overall, the preference for judicial discretion over objective standards means that there is always a danger of the courts applying a relatively subjective assessment of a combination of considerations in the place of rigorous analysis of fundamental principles.

The Australian legal system—together with social norms and media practices—has, in general, provided pragmatic and workable means for the protection of freedom of speech and privacy. Nevertheless, the generally conservative approach taken by Australian courts to the development of the common law suggests that, in the future, the courts may be slow in adapting the law to changing technologies and social values. The main problems with the current approach are, first, that it may not adequately protect freedom of expression and privacy and secondly, that there is little in the way of principled guidance to determine the outcome of conflicts between the two fundamental interests. This suggests that the introduction of a bill of rights would result in better protection of freedom of expression and privacy, and more consistency in the legal resolution of tensions between the two social values. It is likely that a bill of rights would also provide the basis for the development of clearer principles relating to the central social role of media organisations. There is little doubt that the failure to assimilate the central social and political importance of the electronic media was a major failing of the common law in the last half of the twentieth century. Nevertheless, the conservative Australian attitude to constitutional reform and the absence of a strong history of public debate concerning fundamental rights and freedoms, suggests that it is unlikely that an overarching bill of rights will be introduced in the foreseeable future. The Australian legal approach to freedom of expression and privacy is therefore likely to continue along its own unique path, relying principally upon the common law with ad hoc legislative patches.